The Gun Ringer

Geoff Allen

Jack Vitnell riding the Feature Horse,
Brunette Downs Race Meeting, 1962.

The Gun Ringer

Outback Legends of Jack Vitnell from Queensland to the Kimberley

Geoff Allen

First published in 1998 by Central Queensland University Press

Second published in 2013 by Boolarong Press, Salisbury, Brisbane, Australia.

National Library of Australia Cataloguing-in-Publication entry

Author:	Allen, Geoff.
Title:	The gun ringer / Geoff Allen.
ISBN:	9781922109217 (pbk.)
	9781922109248 (ebook)
Subjects:	Vitnell, Jack, 1929-1970.
	Stockmen--Biography.
	Stockmen--Australia--Biography.
Dewey Number:	636.213092

Typeset in 12 on 14.4 point Minion by Jane Dorrington

Typeset by Carlin Yarrow

in Times New Roman and Gaze Normal

Printed and bound by Watson Ferguson & Company, Salisbury, Brisbane, Australia.

Although Jack Vitnell was a real, historical figure, he was also larger than life and inspired many campfire yarns and legends, *Gun Ringer* is at times fiction constructed from a mixture of memories and yarns. A few of the characters are fictional and do not refer to any human being, alive or dead.

Contents

1	The Boy Who Rode Outlaws	1
2	The Road to Connmara	12
3	On to the Territory	21
4	An Old Poddydodger	29
5	Riding with Smokey	37
6	The Underworld Retreat	51
7	The Underworld Dogger	66
8	And Rusty Rode the Wagon	76
9	Just a Lend of Lulu	85
10	Borroloola	92
11	A Saddling Lesson	98
12	Brunette	105
13	Gordon Creek	114
14	The Dashwood Yard	121
15	Death in the Men's Quarters	128
16	Midnight Valley	137
17	Cattle Duffer's Son	149
18	The Kimberley Kid	163
19	The Mongrel From Mungindi	171
20	Halls Creek	182
21	Elgie Cliffs	190
22	Droving to Wyndham	200
23	The Last Camp	209
24	The Kid Returns	221
25	Kununurra	232

Preface

Jack Vitnell ripped through the country up north like a cyclone. Some said he created as much havoc. He was utterly fearless, and in his youth, arguably the best rough rider, bull thrower, roper, whip cracker, camp drafter, bare knuckle man and boozer in all the country. If ever a man had an urge for new experiences and fresh excitement it was Jack. You never knew when he was going to roll his swag and answer its call.

To write Jack's life as it happened, would be like trying to follow the streaks of lightning in a thunder storm. Accordingly, some incidents that take place in this book actually occurred elsewhere. But this book is not meant to be a scholarly history. It is an attempt to restore the mood, the excitement and the many yarns provoked by that living legend, gun ringer, Jack Vitnell. The characters are mostly true to life and many appear under their correct names. Sometimes names have been changed. Some characters are inventions but are attached to events which were much related around the campfires of the Territory and the Kimberley. The Kimberley Kid is the only person in the book able to steady Jack a little, and as that was a task beyond any one mortal, the Kid is a composite of several. The late Don McLachlan is one, but I hasten to add, Don never had any dust ups with the Law over stolen horses.

Some may disagree with how I have presented Jack in this book. Jack was many things to many people. Probably depending whether you knew him in town or out in the scrub. Or whether you were a manager and belatedly found out your head stockman had shot through to ride a feature horse at a race meeting a hundred mile away. Or whether you discovered that the horses Jack had broken-in and been paid for, hadn't been shod or mouthed properly. Jack's idea of breaking-in was rather primitive. He could ride anything and expected the same from others.

'They're ringers, aren't they?' He would run a horse in the yard in the morning, ride it outside in the afternoon and next day send it out to the stock camp. In between times he threw it, tacked a set of shoes on, dropped a couple of hobble chains in its mouth and tied them back to the saddle for a few hours mouthing. 'Those ringers have strong wrists. It'll soon settle down.'

But to the ringers who rode with him out in the stock camps and daily saw him in action, he was, 'The Best of us All'.

My thanks to those who provided information on Jack's life; the Vitnell Family, Eric Burgess, an old school mate of Jack's still living in Kurri Kurri and Jack's staunchest mate, the late Bill Yeomans, of Cloncurry. I would also like to thank Professor David Myers and Holly Smith for their helpful advice which, I am sure, has made *The Gun Ringer* a better book.

Bill Yeomans retired in 1989 and went in search of Jack Vitnell's last resting place. He located it at Kununurra, East Kimberley, and had a grave and headstone erected. Unable to determine the date of Jack's death, Bill had 1964 inscribed. Jack actually died on the twenty-second of January, 1970. Jack was born the 21st of November, 1929.

Geoff Allen
'Balgowlah, 1997

THE ARTS OFFICE

Dedication

To all who took a turn on watch,
I dedicate these tales and rhymes,
Who ever plodded back and forth,
And knew the lonely droving times,
To all who shared an old greatcoat,
As cattle huddled close at night,
Forced a song through shivering lips,
Just beyond the fire's light.

Who swung upon a skittish horse,
And took a buster on the stone,
Rode a barren water course,
Camped amongst bush blacks alone,
Threw a cleanskin by the tail,
Knew a scrub bull's snorting breath,
Waited months for sight of mail,
Saw a best mate lie in death.

Rose at three to fan a hat,
Coaxing fire from the coals,
Heaped hot ashes on the tins,
In Bedourie oven holes,
Boiled up drums of black sweet tea,
Took the last turn riding watch,
And when the flour bags got soaked,
Pulled the belt another notch.

And if somewhere you see a face,
A name or two that takes you back,
That helps you see those far off parts,
Where you battled on the track,
I hope the memories that they bring,
Make you glad you spent that time,
Living hard and camping rough,
In those days we called our prime.

1.

The Boy Who Rode Outlaws

McConville owned a buck-jump show,
That travelled far and wide,
He had an outlaw Swanee,
Man was yet to ride,
He pitched tent at Kurri Kurri,
And passed the word about,
No Hunter Valley stockman,
Would ride his outlaw out.

Mr Hollingsworth, the teacher of this small bush community twenty miles from Maitland, New South Wales, lived in a tiny brick cottage in the school grounds. The school grounds comprised about two acres of lightly timbered country and had been fenced around to hold the students' ponies. But of the children attending this year, only the three Enrights rode. They lived six miles away, over the mountain to the south. They arrived each morning clinging to the reins and mane of an old sleepy draft mare. Most of the other children owned ponies but unless it was raining hard, they walked. There wasn't much feed up in the school paddock. Besides, their struggling parents had work at home for even a child's pony.

The school itself consisted of a large brick classroom, small office and flagged veranda. It had been designed to hold forty children but had not seen that many for years. Currently, thirteen attended, ranging in age from eight to fourteen. Mr Hollingsworth was a kindly, elderly man who worried about his charges and wondered about their future in this land of small dairy farms and grubby coal mines.

About three-quarters of a mile from the school, along the main road to Maitland, stood a small timber post office boldly proclaiming Buchanan. Next to it was a yellow weatherboard general store and opposite, a small brick butcher's shop. This was the town. Before this war year of 1940, it had been considerably larger, but now the mine and racecourse, hotels and other buildings were just a memory.

Back then, before the land was cut up into farm lots and settled, people came to Buchanan to work at the mine or attend the monthly horse races. It was never called Buchanan by the local predominantly Irish settlers. Because of all the fist fights the name became Donnybrook. It had been a tradition amongst certain of the wild young bloods to walk amongst the crowd, dragging their coats behind on the ground. That was an open challenge to fight. Anyone wanting to take up a challenge had only to step on a trailing coat... A wild place in its day, this sleepy hamlet of Buchanan.

Mr Hollingsworth sighed as he called the roll this morning and hoped the lessons he had prepared would prove interesting enough to hold the class' attention. It was summer and already the day was hot.

'Murray!'

'Sir!'

'Smith!'

'Sir!'

'Sullivan!'

'Present, Mister Hollingsworth.'

He looked up and smiled. Sullivan was a beautiful girl. Almost a woman now, and taller by far, than any of the boys. Would she go on to high school in Kurri or would she leave this year and stay at home? Times were so hard, parents sometimes resented the hours their children spent at school. There was so much to be done on their farms...

'Vitnell!'

'Not present, Sir!'

Nunky Holmes couldn't get it out quick enough. He looked around grinning. The class sniggered. Mr Hollingsworth flushed. Dreaming again! He hadn't meant to call that name. Young Jacky Vitnell hadn't sat in class for months. It was a regular embarrassment. There was nothing he could do about it. Everyone had tried. Jack just wouldn't come to school.

'But he goes to school, Mr Hollingsworth! I watch him every morning.'

'Yes, Mrs Vitnell,' he would say gently, 'I know. But he doesn't come in.'

Mr Hollingsworth had watched it so many times. The Vitnell farm was only a small paddock away from the school. Every morning at 8.30 sharp if he looked out the south window of his house, Mr Hollingsworth would see a young lad of eleven trudging through the grass towards him. Then as the boy reached the split-rail school yard fence and climbed over he would turn and wave. And four hundred yards away, at her kitchen window, Mrs Vitnell would wave back. Jack had gone to school!

If Mr Hollingsworth then walked the thirty paces to the school and looked out its north window, he might just be in time to see young Jack disappearing over the fence on the other side of the school grounds.

Many times, before he gave up, Mr Hollingsworth had scampered out of his house at first sight of Jack leaving home and waited by the bushes near the front door.

'Ah there! Vitnell!' he used to call out in welcome. 'Ready for school so early!'

'Yes sir! Got to get something first though. Be back in a jiff.'

Mr Hollingsworth never found out what the something was, for Jack never fetched it back. Didn't come back, in fact, until school was over. If Mr Hollingsworth chose to look out the north window, just as the children were filing out of school in the afternoon, he would see a small boy running up from the creek to join the children as they reached the front gate. Then if he kept watching, he would see young Jack waving to his mother at the kitchen window. Jack was coming home from school!

Once he had caned him. Only once. It was like striking a store dummy. There was absolutely no response. Jack thrust his arms out, opened his hands and swish went the wild peach stick. Three times on each hand. There was no flinching, no sign of pain, nothing. The hands remained out so Mr Hollingsworth struck them again, six more times. Again no response but the clear grey eyes never left his face.

'Sit down, Vitnell. Sit down.' He didn't know what else to say. Jack turned and marched straight out the door. Mr Hollingsworth didn't ever remember feeling so bad. It was a month before he looked out the window again.

'What do you do all day, Jack?' his best mate Nunky asked him once.

'Go to Leggett's farm! They got horses there. Wild horses. Leggett gets 'em over in Maitland, at the sale-yards. We ride 'em. If they don't buck I grab 'em there.' He made a lunge at Nunky's crotch. Jack's boyhood nickname of Knacky Jacky was born.

'Don't he tell you to go to school?'

'Sometimes. But he don't care. He never went to school much. I can read and write anyway. I don't want the rest of it, I'll never use it.' He gazed with distaste at the neat dairy farms dotted amongst the green hills. 'Geez, I hate this place. I'm going droving soon, up to the *real* cattle country.'

Grandad knew he didn't go to school.

'What you learn in school today, Jacky?'

'Nothing. Never went. They got a new stallion over at Leggett's, Pop. Want to come over an' watch me ride him?'

Leggett's farm occupied the hill opposite the school, and was about two miles distant. To reach it, Jack crossed over the little creek at the bottom of the school hill and walked up to The Rocks. This was a band of rock that divided Leggett's into top paddocks and bottom paddocks. Most of the land was below The Rocks. Perched on the very edge of The Rocks were the cow and horse yards. Back from them, towards the road that led in from the hamlet of Heddon Greta, were the house, piggery, vegetable garden and small orchard.

The Rocks cliff-face was only about forty foot high and was not entirely vertical, but the steep slope provided an effective barrier to stock. The bottom paddocks ran a mile and a half from the foot of The Rocks down to the creek. There was no need to fence the paddocks at The Rocks end. In places, The Rocks was only about six foot high, but young Jack Vitnell scorned to walk along to a low section. He scaled The Rocks where the horse yards were perched, at the highest part.

Leggett's farm was worked by old Charlie Leggett and his good-natured nephew, Alf. They soon became aware that their farm was the first stop for young Jacky Vitnell when he left home for a morning's activity.

As Jack arrived one morning, Alf was saddling a skittish brown mare. Jack was about thirteen at the time. He stood at the yard rails watching, then suddenly yelled out, 'You're scared of that mare, Alfie.'

Alf looked up guiltily, aware that he was nervous about mounting the mare.

'Would you like to come and ride her then?' he called with a grin. 'I wouldn't like to stop you having your fun. But don't take her cheap, and don't take her outside. She's a bolter, I reckon.'

Jack was through the rails in a flash and quickly on the brown.

'Hell!' he complained as she walked sedately off. 'Hasn't even got a pig-root in her. Open the gate Alfie, I'm going to see if she's got any go in her.'

It was not long since Jack's Grandad had told him the story of Adam Lindsay Gordon's famous leap over a high paling fence. On the other side of the paling fence was a ten foot wide ledge. Below the ledge was a three hundred foot drop.

There was no similar situation around Buchanan, but since hearing the tale, Jack had been eyeing off The Rocks. If he could gallop a horse over the forty foot rock wall, well, that would be almost as good as Gordon's leap. It would have to do, anyway, until he could get down to that place in South Australia where Grandad said Gordon had made his leap. If the fence had fallen down after all this time, all the better. He would build a higher fence ...

Alf Leggett, against his better judgement, opened the gate. Jack spurred the brown across the yard, out the gate and set her straight for the cliff-edge. The mare had no idea she was facing a steep drop. She was over and slithering down the almost sheer cliff-face before she had time to jib. Jack leaned back in the saddle reefing at the reins. It was only his strong hands and the mare's ability to handle the rough that kept them upright. Neither Alf nor Jack was aware that the mare had cut her teeth brumby running in the ranges before becoming broken-winded and sold.

When Jack reached the bottom, he rode along to a low part of the Rocks, jumped off the mare and pulled her up the sloping rock-face. Then he rode nonchalantly back to the yard and an admiring Alf Leggett.

Jack's father never heard about the episode or knew that his son didn't attend school. He was a miner and lived several miles away, close to the pits, in the town of Kurri Kurri. Jack rode over and spent weekends there. The house had a big yard and down the back his Dad had built stables and a round-yard. Jack's father was also a good horse-breaker and blacksmith and people from all over the district brought him horses.

But it wasn't as much fun as Leggett's. Jack Vitnell Senior would not allow his son to make the horses buck. He never learnt why his son was known as Knacky Jacky.

'If a horse is handled properly from the start it won't buck. If I ride a colt for the first time and it bucks that means I haven't done my job properly.'

But from time to time he did have horses that bucked and both he and Jack rode them. Young Jack wished they would buck all day. He couldn't get enough of bucking horses. But at least there were always Brandon's bullocks.

On the far side of the school from the Vitnell farm was the butcher's paddock and yards. There was a crush, holding yard, forcing yard and killing pen. The paddock was well grassed and watered and able to support twenty or so big bullocks. Ben Brandon, the butcher lived behind his shop a mile away. He only killed a couple of times a week so the cattle were mostly left alone.

Afternoons when school was over, Jack and his young mates — Jack's Gang — would race their ponies up and down a straight stretch of the Maitland road, opposite the old racecourse. Though there were several older boys in Jack's gang none of them questioned his leadership and none were anxious to fight him. He was too tough, too hard. Bigger boys who had knocked him down found he bounced straight back up, fists flying. It just wasn't worth tangling with him. The fights just went on and on. Besides, he was well known for his habit of picking up a rock when getting up again, to allow him to punch harder ...

'Hey!' he called one afternoon, about the time he rode the mare over the cliff, 'I got something better for us to do than race up and down the road pretending to be jockeys. Follow me.' And he led them up to the butcher's paddock.

'We going to muster 'em. Then we going to ride 'em.'

The boys looked at each other. They knew the cattle were for slaughter and should be kept quiet, but Jack was already opening the gate. They kicked up their ponies and followed. The bullocks were big fat sleepy Shorthorns and no trouble to muster. The gang soon had them yarded.

'What we going to do now, Jack?' Nunky asked.

'This!' Jack answered and ran towards a surprised bullock and sprang on its back. The boys were astonished. The beast snorted in fear and gave a huge bound. Jack held his legs tight against the bullock's shoulders as it bucked across the yard. It didn't buck high or give any twists and spins but with its loose rolling skin it was a challenge nonetheless.

Being heavy and unused to such activity the bullock soon stopped its cavorting and Jack slid off. Then he was on another. The lads watched in awe. Now they understood what their leader had been doing instead of attending school.

It wasn't long before Ben the butcher noticed bruising on his prime beef. One evening he took a ride up towards his holding paddock. As Ben Brandon passed the school he could hear yells and laughter ahead. He slipped off his horse and walked on quietly by foot. Peeping from behind a tree at the brow of the hill he was amazed to see a fully fledged rodeo in action in his holding yard, and using his prime beef cattle for buckjumpers.

Young Jack Vitnell was standing in the centre of the yard holding one end of a long greenhide head-rope. The other end was looped around the flanks of a big, powerful bullock. Ben Brandon distinctly remembered paying top price for the animal at the last Maitland sales. On its back, sitting proudly with right arm outstretched, and mimicking a professional rough-rider, was Mick Maguire, the fourteen year old son of his best customer.

The tighter young Jack pulled the rope, the higher and wilder the bullock bucked. When the inevitable happened, and young Maguire fell off, Jack Vitnell rushed at the snorting animal and fought it with his hat. Then he leapt upon its back and raked it with a rusted pair of jockey spurs.

Ben was a solid, thoughtful fellow. Although his first reaction had been to charge down the hill fists flailing, he restrained himself and stole quietly away. Every one of those boys belonged to a family who bought his meat or had Ben kill and dress their own stock. It would not do for him to take retribution upon the errant sons of his customers. Ben would let the boys' fathers do that.

For the next couple of days he rode around the farms and contacted each one. The fathers were shocked at their sons' activities and decided to lay a trap. At the bottom of the hill from the butcher's paddock ran a creek and the hill up the other side of the creek was covered in timber and scrub. Here one evening the fathers waited on horseback, stockwhips ready. Ben Brandon closed his shop and took the Maitland road toward his paddock.

As soon as the butcher appeared, the boys left the cattle and raced for their ponies tied to a clump of trees in the paddock. Ben took the long way around the yard to give them plenty of time to open the paddock's bottom gate leading towards the creek. The boys galloped down the hill towards the safety of the timbered hill the other side of the creek. Soon Ben Brandon heard yells and the cracking of stockwhips. He rode off home. There would be no more bruised beef.

For a week afterwards the bullock riders didn't ride their ponies up and down the road after school. Their skinny rumps were too sore from the beatings handed out by their fathers. But the ring-leader still rode. Grandfather had taken Jack down to a shed a hundred yards from the house. He wore a heavy leather belt. But whether he used it or not no-one up at the house ever knew. No sound came from the shed.

Jack didn't pretend any more he was heading off to school. He spent his days riding horses or bulls on Leggett's farm or on any other farm where he heard a rough horse might be available for riding. The local farmers had never seen anything like young Jacky Vitnell. He was fearless and would climb on any beast offered. A way of making money in those hard early war years was horse dealing. They would attend the local sales and buy any unwanted horse going cheaply. That usually meant the horse was a rogue and needed re-handling. If they could do this successfully they could later re-sell the animal at a good profit.

A young lad keen to take the buck out of these animals was a very welcome visitor to their farms. And he was such a pleasant young lad. If there was nothing for him to ride he would help at whatever job was on. By the time he was fourteen he was an old hand at straining sagging fence lines, cutting fence posts, mortising yard posts and rails, making and swinging gates — all the endless tasks required around a farm. But he showed no interest in machinery or milking. He would work only with horses or timber.

He was a good looking boy with strong, regular features and already displaying great strength of body and mind. He was very sure of his own ability and never thought a task might be beyond him. When he was shown a rogue horse pacing up and down eager for battle Jack never wondered if he could ride him. He wondered how well the horse would buck and whether he was worth climbing on.

One morning he arrived at Leggett's to find old Charlie in a furious temper. He was just back from the Maitland horse sales and someone had got the better of him in a deal. The horse Charlie had bought was standing now in centre yard, a savage looking black, with ears laid back, showing the whites of its eyes. It had just put Charlie and Alf over the fence. They couldn't get near it.

Jack walked into a stable and took down a stock-whip from a peg. He opened the gate to the yard and walked in with the horse. He stood still as it charged, then quickly swung the whip and tore a piece of flesh from its nose. The horse skidded to a stop and wheeled away. Jack followed, slicing at its rump with the whip until it trotted into the forcing yard. Now he turned to the Leggetts. He was fourteen years and ten months and it was their farm but he took control.

'Give me a hand, will you? We'll run him along the crush and get a halter on him. Then I'll take him for a ride and find out how good he is!'

Jack lowered himself down from the crush top rails onto the horse's back. He would ride it bareback. He grabbed the end of the rope halter as the horse commenced to rear and plunge.

'Get the gate open!' he called and with a tremendous bound the outlaw took off.

It would have been difficult enough to ride the brute in a saddle. Bareback it seemed impossible. It bolted, bucking as it went, straight out along the paddock. Then it propped, wheeled around and rose high in the air. Next it crashed down, spinning in circles trying to shake the rider. Jack sat, right hand held out for balance, legs gripped tightly at the horse's shoulders. Twice the watchers thought he was gone, off sideways, but the strength of his legs pulled him back. When the horse stopped bucking, Jack reached his hand down and kept the sport going for a while. Then he rode it back to the yard.

'Fetch me the collar rope, Charlie. I'll bag him down a bit and then he's all yours.'

Charlie watched the proceedings with admiration. 'No doubt about you, Jacky. Reckon you're about ready to take on Swanee.'

Jack spun around.

'Swanee? Is McConville back in town?'

'Next week, Jack, so I hear. And that big feature horse of his is still looking for a rider.'

Thorpe McConville's Wild West and Buckjump Show had been coming to Kurri Kurri for years. Thorpe usually stayed in town a week and yarned with the locals at the three big pubs. He knew many by name and they regarded him as a friend.

'What you got for us this year, Thorpe?' they would ask. 'Any good buckjumpers? We got some good riders here, you know.'

'I know,' Thorpe would answer, 'But none good enough to stick on Swanee. He ain't been rode yet.'

Thorpe had hawked the big chestnut around for six years as his Ten-Pound horse. Ten pound was offered to any rider who could stop on for ten seconds.

Thorpe could count a very slow ten seconds had he a mind to, but he never had to count slowly when Swanee was in action. He had thrown every rider who had tried.

If there were no takers amongst the crowd, the riders with the show would ride him, but only for a few bucks. Thorpe made sure they slid off after that. If they rode him right out that would ruin his mystique. Thorpe's riders were mostly Australian or ex -Australian Champions. Each of them could have ridden Swanee had Thorpe allowed. Once a champion rider learns the way a horse bucks, he will ride it.

The secret in having an unrideable horse was never to let anyone from the audience have a second chance. Thorpe had a good memory for faces.

This night in Kurri there were no takers. Thorpe didn't like that happening. It was best when some popular local champion tried and was thrown. That helped spread the word and keep up the horse's reputation. He led Swanee around the ring. It looked harmless enough.

'What's wrong with all you Kurri guns?' Thorpe sung out from centre ring. 'Are you scared of a little old chestnut pony? Ain't there any one of you game to try?'

Jack was in the crowd with Grandpop. Grandpop had never missed one of Thorpe's shows and he and Jack had travelled in earlier by sulky. Now they waited like everyone else for someone to take up the challenge. There was total silence in the tent.

Finally Grandpop said in a loud voice, 'Looks like it's got to be a fourteen year old kid.'

He nudged Jack.

'Go down and ride him boy!'

Jack had entertained no real thoughts of riding. He had come to watch, certain that one of the district's well known riders would accept the challenge of making the wild ride. Now he stood up, heart thumping with excitement and walked down the steps to the ring. There was a titter of laughter as he jumped over the low fence. He was just a lad. Was it a joke? Part of the show?

Thorpe looked at the youngster with interest. Was this the lad he had heard of during the week. Who rode buckjumpers bareback? He would find riding a champion horse was different to climbing on some farmer's idea of a buckjumper.

'Sure you want to try him, lad? He bucks bad, you know.'

Jack made a grab for the reins. 'I'll taste him.'

Thorpe held on to the reins and retreated in mock horror.

'Hey! Easy lad! Not that way!'

The crowd laughed.

'He'd have you on the deck before you got set. We're going to give you every chance,' and he led the way over to the chute. 'What's your name?'

Two of his men now took over while Thorpe called out the rules to the crowd.

'Ladies and gentlemen we have a rider. Jack Vitnell from Kurri Kurri. Give him a big hand, will you?'

There was lots of applause and calls of, 'Good on you Jacky!' Jack looked around in surprise. It had never crossed his mind that he was a noted district horseman.

'When he comes out that gate,' Thorpe continued, 'He's got to stay on Swanee's back for ten seconds. If he can do that he gets the ten pound. If not, he gets a busted head. That's his problem. The show takes no responsibility.' He called across the ring where Jack was already astride the horse. 'You still want to ride him lad?'

'Get this gate open!' Jack yelled.

Old Leggett jumped to his feet and shouted down to Thorpe, 'I'll have ten with you, McConville, he rides him!'

No-one knew if Thorpe heard. He was busy climbing out of the ring as Swanee charged out the chute and exploded.

Jack had never ridden such a horse. The sheer force of its bucking shocked him. He was lost for a moment and only the power in his legs held him on those first wild seconds. And determination. Jack had no doubts he would ride him. It was a slippery poley saddle, with knee pads two inches deep that favoured the horse. Jack lost an iron at the first buck, then felt the other swing free. It didn't matter. He would ride this Swanee bareback later if they wished.

He was battling to maintain his balance as the outlaw bucked high and rolled sideways. Jack twisted at the hips to keep upright. The animal squealed in rage, crashed to the ground and commenced to spin. Spin didn't worry Jack. It was what happened when the horse came out of it that mattered! Swanee went straight up in the air. Jack lay against its neck. When it came down Jack was lying back, head close to its rump. He could handle this. Old Leggett saw a hand reach down out of habit towards the chestnut's flank.

'Bloody Knacky Jacky!' he muttered admiringly.

Every champion horse has a king buck. Swanee had only needed to display his a few times. It took a lot of doing and he only produced it when he had to. As he came down from a high climb, he would suck back underneath the rider. That left the man sitting in mid-air for an instant, before he fell to the dirt. It was the most difficult movement of all for a rider to counter. Tonight he had to use it again.

As the horse was coming down, some instinct told Jack this was going to be it. He had heard enough talk about Swanee to know what it was about to do. He gripped harder with his legs and threw his body backwards. The horse shrilled in anger as it straightened up. The rider was still aboard. Thorpe looked at his watch. Twenty-three seconds.

'Get him off!' he yelled to his chute men. 'He's rode him. He won't come off. Stop that horse bucking!'

The pick-up man thundered across on his horse and crashed it alongside Swanee. It was still desperately trying to dislodge its rider. Jack made no attempt to leave the horse. The pick-up man reached across and grabbed Jack under the shoulders.

'Get off him, mate. You've rode him. Don't break his spirit!'

Jack allowed himself to be hauled off and dropped to the ground. It was only then he realised the whole crowd was standing cheering.

'I've done it.' He grinned. 'Rode their best. Look-out now! Just you look-out now, here I come!'

Even Thorpe was grinning. He'd just lost his champion horse. He could never feature it again. But what a ride! What a rider! He didn't often allow himself to think that. The riders coming into the show were the enemy. He never wanted them to win. But this lad! He was something special. He walked across and grabbed Jack's arm.

'Great ride, lad, here's your money.'

Thorpe held the ten pound note up to the crowd.

'Ol' Thorpe don't like giving this stuff away but tonight I'm proud to. I've travelled this country for twenty year and been to a lot of places. Seen a lot of riders. And a lot of horses. Swanee's as good a horse as I've ever had but tonight he was beat fair and square. By this young lad from Kurri Kurri. I'm proud of him and I hope you're all proud of him. Give him another hand.'

Jack was so excited he could scarcely stand still. All he wanted to do was race up the steps and show the money to Grandpop but Thorpe still held him by the arm.

'— and this lad,' Thorpe was finishing up by saying, 'can ask me for a job any day, when he's left school.'

That brought a great hoot of laughter from around the tent.

Thorpe wondered what he had said that had made the crowd laugh so heartily.

2.

The Road to Connmara

Queensland way they call it,
He's riding Queensland style,
They sit upon the top rail,
And say it with a smile,
That stockman with his hand out,
That fellow spurring high,
You can bet he comes from Queensland,
That ringer in full cry.

Jack was soon bored with the Buck Jump Show. There was not enough action. It was all right at show time but there were a lot of flat times between. At first it had been fun to rig the huge marquee with the men. There were seven of them now working for Thorpe. All top riders. There wasn't one Jack hadn't heard spoken of back in Kurri. Each one had won a State or Australian Buckjump Championship title.

After each show the marquee and smaller tents would have to come down and be folded, packed and loaded onto the old Dodge truck. As well as other chores, the rows of seats, timber chute and ring fence had to be disassembled.

It wasn't the work. Jack thrived on hard work. The packing up, unpacking and setting up again became monotonous. But even more boring for Jack was the horse-tailing. When the Show reached a town, each man had to take a turn tailing the horses on the Common until the advertised show days. It was all too quiet for Jack. He needed plenty of action every day.

The best part of the Show for Jack was not riding exhibitions on the outlaws — which he could have done blindfolded — but the Deadly Medley. Thorpe never used the two feature bucking bullocks, Ferdinand and Slippery Sam for the Medley. He always borrowed four or five big steers from a nearby farm or station in return for having his men handle any bad horse the owner might have.

During the show, the steers would be let out of the chute, one after the other, with surcingles girthed about their flanks to make them buck. Aboard would be Thorpe's roughriders. The audience loved the Deadly Medley. Out the steers would charge, bucking in all directions. The winner was the rider who stayed on the longest. No-one won more times than Jack.

At least, travelling with Thorpe was a way of getting out of Kurri. But Jack was used to roaming the farms seeking rogue horses to ride, chasing any bull he passed and jumping on its back.

'I must have been a wild kid,' he thought one day. He had his fifteenth birthday travelling through St. George.

'Old enough to leave school,' he thought wryly.

Soon after Jack had ridden Swanee, Thorpe had sold it to a rival buckjump show. It was no use to him now. The other show could change its name and bill it as an unrideable horse if they wished. Thorpe could not.

Slippery Sam had to step in as the feature ride for a while. He was a big Zebu with a good 'twister'. Not too many had sat him. Thorpe's other horses were all top buckjumpers but had no king buck like Swanee. But Thorpe knew of a place. He left the show one morning in Warwick and drove off to a horse stud with one of his men. When they drove back Thorpe had a new feature horse. Spitfire. It could climb like a fighter plane. Jack was not allowed near it.

'You ruined my last feature horse,' Thorpe told him, only half joking. 'You're not getting on this one!'

The difference between Jack and the other riders was Jack's determination. He would not be beaten. He had to win every time. That was his attitude to everything and he had the confidence and ability to go with it.

Things would have been a lot more boring for Jack if it hadn't been for Spider O'Brien's Boxing Troupe. In many of the towns where they stopped, it was local show week. The travelling showmen all knew these annual events, particularly in the bigger towns and a crowd of showmen would arrive together.

Mostly Thorpe's Wild West Show and Spider's Boxing Troupe set up alongside one another. Jack had always been a good scrapper, now he learnt to box. All his spare time was spent next door at the boxing tent, with the pugs. They were mostly ex-champions or contenders who for various reasons had been squeezed out of the big time and now thought themselves lucky to have a job in the only trade they knew.

The men had a lot of free time once the tents were set up. The boss showman's major task then was keeping them sober. One evening Jack was in the tent he shared with three others, waiting for the show to start, when Thorpe came in.

'Spider wants a loan of you. Don't have to go if you don't want to.'

'A loan of me!'

'Butcher and Jimmy Dunn are drunk. Choked down. He's got no welter for the night. Wants you to help him out.'

Jack had always been small for his age but he was now an average man's height and weighed eleven stone. Thorpe had watched him sparring and occasionally seen him fight. He was lightning fast and hit like a heavyweight. Spider's men treated him with respect.

'I can do it,' Jack said. 'But where does that leave us?'

'Set. We'll cover. I owe Spider one.'

There was no talk of money. Money was of no interest to Jack. He wasn't like an average boy, wanting this and that. He didn't care where he slept, what he ate, but he did like good clothes. R M Williams stuff. That's where his money had gone so far. All Jack wanted was excitement and, more than anything, a challenge.

He stood up on Spider's outside board.

'Can I hit the big drum?' he asked.

Mickey Molloy, star bill for the night, smiled. 'You can belt it silly, Jack.' He thrust his chin at the crowd of faces gazing at them. 'Don't worry about them mugs. You'll set 'em on their arse. Any that wants a fight!'

Jack had a wild night. There didn't seem to be any welters in the crowd. They were either middles or heavies. Jack tried them all. He had to. Spider had only told Thorpe half the story. Four of his troupe had passed out on wine.

Jack had eight fights that night. He let none go the three round distance. He had been taught a good combination. Walk straight in and bang them hard on the face. Then rip a couple to the belly then two more good hits to the head. It was a combination that would serve him well in the future when he hit the rough cattle towns of the north.

Spider slipped him ten bob later. 'You done well, boy. Anytime you want a change...'

One night after the show as Jack headed for his tent, Mickey Malloy caught him up. His battered face was creased into a grin. 'There's someone wants to meet you, Jack.'

'Who would that be?'

'You'll find out.'

Mickey led the way to the back of the Midway Show tent. Two girls stepped out of the shadows. One was a singer with the show, a pretty but cheap looking redhead, the other Jack knew as Niagara Falls, the lady in Spider's ticket box. She was known all over the country by that nickname because her large shapely breasts were always threatening to spill over the top of the low cut blouse she habitually wore. The straining top button that so many men had envied, was bawdily referred to as The Man in the Barrel.

Mickey and the redhead quickly disappeared into the night and Jack was left standing awkwardly in front of Niagara Falls, wondering what was going on. But not for long.

'Hello, Jack,' she whispered, stepping forward and grabbing his hand, 'It's about time we met. You know me don't you, I'm Dora.'

Before Jack could answer Dora pushed against him and kissed him on the mouth. She was considerably older than Jack and not very attractive but the softness of her body and perfumed hair gave him an instant reaction. Embarrassed, he tried to back away but Dora held him tight. 'This way, Jack,' she whispered in an urgent voice.

He let himself be led into the darkness between two marquees where a rug lay on the ground. Dora pulled him down and knelt before him. She looked into his eyes and slowly unbuttoned her blouse. Jack was nervous and tried not to look, but suddenly Dora placed her hands under her heavy breasts and held them up to his face. This was too much for young Jack and he nuzzled her eagerly.

'Hurry up,' she gasped after a few seconds, 'Get your pants off.'

There were no more preliminaries. Dora wriggled out of her panties, lay back on the ground and pulled Jack on top.

'So this is the way they do it,' Jack marvelled. 'Lift their knees up!'

He had occasionally looked at the prim full frontal nudes in men's magazines and wondered how you actually got it in. He knew it wasn't from behind like stock on the farm. Now he was in himself and understood everything. Suddenly he stopped, embarrassed again, and looked out at the night.

'What is it?' Dora whispered, immediately frightened. 'Is someone coming?'

'No,' Jack groaned. He leaned forward and mumbled into her ear.

'Oh, no!' She held him tighter and giggled. 'You young quick trigger! Come on then.'

After it was over, all Jack wanted was to get up and get away, but Dora still clung to him. Finally the slamming of a nearby caravan door made her loosen her hold and sit up.

'Just you wait, my young horny buck,' she threatened in a low voice. 'I'll soon wear you down to where I want you!'

But there were to be no more meetings. The next day Mickey Malloy took Jack aside and gave him a conspiratorial grin. 'How was Spider's missus? Hot as she looks?'

Jack looked at him blankly. 'What do you mean?'

'Last night. Didn't you know Niagara Falls is Spider's wife?'

Jack was shocked. 'Oh, you lousy bastard. Why didn't you tell me? Spider's always done the right thing by me and now I've done his missus.'

'I wouldn't worry about it Jack,' Mickey soothed. 'Spider's into anything he can lay his hands on. Someone's got to give it to her, he don't.'

But it did worry Jack and he made sure he kept well away from Spider's tent after show time.

'Next time I have a woman,' he vowed, 'she'll be mine, not someone else's.'

But that was not to be. Jack left his innocence behind in Kurri Kurri. From now on he was amongst men, hard men for the most part, and older. And when those men went to town in search of booze and women he went with them. He soon learnt the knockabout's Golden Rule. *Never drink when you're working and never work when you're drinking.* When you had money you boozed it up in town until it was gone. And if any woman wanted to help you spend it, you let her. And she let you. When the cheque was all cut out, you left town as quickly as you came in, and lit out back to the scrub and earned more.

They left Kurri Kurri in August and by the following March were way up in Western Queensland. They showed at Windorah and headed north.

'What's the next place?' Jack asked.

'Stonehenge.'

It was to be his last town with the Buckjump Show.

The further north they travelled the more restless Jack became. They were now edging into the cattle country. Jack had noticed the many ringers in the audience and the way they vied with each other to take a turn riding the buckjumpers. These were not farm boys or plodding sheep men. They came in with tales of frantic scrub riding and throwing wild bulls. Riding fresh colts and breaking them in. Droving trips from West Australia. The poddy dodgers of the North Kimberley. Fights in the pub at Daly Waters, Katherine, Mt Isa ...

A group of them came round to the showground the day after the show.

'Thought you fellas would be packing up.'

'Can't,' Jack answered. 'We got a broken axle and no spare. Gettin' one up on the train to Longreach, Friday. Where you lot from?'

'Connmara, out the Diamantina.'

'Rough country?'

'Some. Ranges and scrub. Plenty cleanskins out there. Takes some ridin' to get 'em.'

'When you heading back?'

'We're not. Pulled out. Good place to work but we're headin' south for a spell.'

Jack lost interest. The train had arrived in Longreach, now they were waiting on the mailman.

'Won't be out till Saturday afternoon,' Thorpe raged.

On Saturday morning Jack followed a few of the boys up to the hotel. He had started drinking regularly now and was getting a reputation as one who could hold his liquor. He was fifteen and a half.

The bar was empty except for a big brawny looking cattleman. He knew they were the rough riders from the show and nodded as they fronted the bar.

'Have one on me fellas. Harry Johns is the name. I been drinking with the flies all morning.'

He looked at Jack. 'Saw you win that mad medley last night. We could use you on a few of our outlaws out at Connmara.'

'Connmara! You work out there?'

'Mate, I'm supposed to be the boss, but I got no men to boss. Season about to start and three of 'em up and left. I got four men and I need eight.'

'You got five,' Jack said. 'I'm ready to leave town when you are.'

'You'll be back,' was all Thorpe said. 'This show business gets in your blood. Station life won't suit you, Jack. Too quiet.'

'What do you know about working cattle, Jack?' Harry Johns asked him as they drove off next morning.

'Nothing about the way you work 'em out here. But I been amongst 'em all me life. I'll pick it up quick, don't you worry.'

'I'm sure you will, Jack. Sure you will.'

Jack looked out the window at the country. A line of flat topped stony hills showed in the distance. Beyond was the Northern Territory. He was heading there soon and going to ride all over it and throw every scrub bull he could find — out where horses were bred to galloping stone and scrub. And he was never going south again, ever. But for the moment this Connmara would do.

Jack still had a bit to learn. He could ride and break-in and repair yards and fence, but he had never mustered wild cattle or galloped thick scrub.

'Jack,' his new boss said as they neared the homestead, 'I want to have a little fun with the boys. They going to be down the yard now as we drive up, breaking-in some colts to take out the camp next week. I'm going to tell 'em I picked up a young jackaroo in town. I want you to play along with it a bit, then show 'em how you can ride.'

Jack opened the horse-paddock gate and down they drove to the station drafting yard. Three ringers were lunging colts around the big yard. A fourth was holding a saddled horse in the round yard.

'That's Billy King, my head stockman. Looks like he's about to get on that thing for the first time. He's a good man, but getting old. He don't like getting on now and that's a bad mare he's holding. Not bad, she's quiet, but bucks bad first off every season.'

'She looks tight. Want me to try her?'

'You're a new chum, remember? Let's say hello to Billy.'

'A jackaroo!' smiled Bill. 'Well, pleased to meet you, young Jack Vitnell. Where you get him from, boss? In town?'

'Yeah, and he's pretty keen to ride a horse. What about this mare? Can he ride her?'

'This mare! This mare, boss, would kill him! I don't even like getting on this mare. Should find a sandy creek an' take her down there. She gets me every year. Real climber. Good mare but.'

'That old thing,' said Jack, playing along. 'Why that horse don't look like a buckjumper to me. I seen pictures of buckjumpers and they don't look like that.'

'Oh, don't they now! How do buckjumpers look, young shaver?'

'Well, I dunno. But they don't look like that old thing. Anyone could ride that horse.'

'Oh! And could they now. And how would you like to try?'

'You think that wise, Billy?' Harry interrupted, trying to keep from grinning.

'Boy got a silly mouth. Time he found out a few things I reckon. Here! Come and get on her. That is if you can.'

Jack walked across and gingerly took hold of the reins. 'Which foot goes into the stirrup first?' he asked just managing not to laugh.

'Get away!' Billy snorted. 'Give me the reins, boy. Go and sit on the top rail and see what you can learn.'

Then Jack snatched the reins and sprang into the saddle. He didn't bother with the irons. She was a very difficult mare to ride. She was a big animal, very powerfully built. Her first few bucks were always sensational. She would go straight up like a rocket ship blasting off then come straight down. She didn't just drop back. She would plunge down with as much force as when she went up. Then she would go up and down again. After that she would buck, but not as badly.

Jack had already dispensed with the stirrups. Now he lost the reins as she rose up and slammed back to earth. When she went up again, Jack was on his feet, on the ground with his back to her. He was furious. His first ride on his first station and he had come off. Harry Johns had heard about black looks, now he saw one. Jack's face went livid.

He grabbed for the reins and flew on again. This time he didn't lose them and didn't come off. When the mare stopped bucking he grabbed her by the flank and made her go up again. Then he was satisfied.

Everyone had been watching. The horse breakers had left their job and dashed over to the round yard as soon as they saw the mare bucking. Now they stood, with Billy King, gaping in amazement. Even Harry Johns, who knew Jack's ability, was looking at Jack in awe.

Jack was never a great lover of horses. He rode horses as a means to satisfy a wild urge. He never spoke about horses as most ringers did. 'By jings he was a good horse. Best horse I ever rode. By ghost I was sorry when I left that place and that horse.'

Horses were all good. Good for what he wanted out of them and they were there to be used. He never abused a horse but he was hard on them. But later, he was often to speak of that big black mare on Connmara.

Jack was immediately accepted by the ringers on Connmara. Billy King and his chief helper, Don Kirk, had never known a lad like him. A man was measured up north by the way he rode a horse. They had never seen anyone ride like Jack. He was able to make any horse, not only buckjumpers, perform like a champion. No matter what horse he was riding when chasing after cattle he would get to the lead. The other stockmen were proud of him — particularly Don Kirk.

Don had lately been run out of Mt Isa by the police for brawling. He was holing up at Connmara until he built up another stake. Then he was going 'back up the Territory'. He was thirty five and a gun ringer. He rode alongside Jack whilst mustering and was surprised and pleased to learn that the young buckjump rider was also an excellent bushman. Don showed Jack every facet of the ringing trade. When he found out Jack could fight as well, he knew he had found the mate he had been seeking.

The season was over and Harry Johns had paid them off and driven them into town. There was nothing to do but booze at the pub. The bar was crowded with drovers and ringers and inevitably there was a fight.

Jack laughed at the round-house swinging.

A big rough drover walked over and snarled, 'What are you laughing at kid?'

Jack was no longer a boy. He had always been tough and the season in the stockcamp had made him tougher. He was now a solid twelve stone. Get in first, he had been taught.

He smashed a right into the man's face, and ripped two lefts into his belly. He didn't need the rest of the combination. The drover folded. The drover's mate walked over.

'Keep out of it, mug,' Don Kirk drawled.

The drover's mate wheeled and made for Don. Don was six rangy feet tall and thirteen stone of gristle. He lifted the drover a foot high with a powerful uppercut and watched him drop to the floor.

'Never seen it done that way,' grinned Jack. 'I'll have to try it.'

'Not here, Jack. Time we got out of this. Let's scout around for a lift into the railhead and catch a freight up to the real cattle country. You want to go out to the Territory?'

'Of course!'

'Well, it's the wrong time now, cattle season's over, but I got a good mate runs a place Borroloola way. Seven Emu he calls it. He gets out and about early storm time and picks up a lot of cattle when they come in on the green pick. He'll give us a job till the Wet, then we'll give him a hand doing up his saddles till the season starts again. That'll pay for our tucker. After that we can take off where we like. What do you reckon?'

Jack downed his drink. Their swags lay on two iron frame beds outside on the verandah.

'Don, let's roll 'em! We can walk to that train before we get a lift.'

'It's forty mile.'

Jack looked at his high Cuban heeled boots.

'Okay, we'll wait for the mailman. But I hope it don't rain and bog him. I can't hardly wait!'

The Legend was on his way.

Jack Vitnell aged 10, Buchanan Public School
(Kurri Kurri) Jack second from left, Eric Burgess centre.

Eric Burgess pointing to the old Buchanan Race Course
(Donnybrook) where Jack and his gang raced their ponies after school.

Eric Burgess at the spot at The Rocks, Leggett's Farm, where
Jack Vitnell galloped the horse over the cliff as a boy.

Alf Leggett, 1994. "Still mucking about with horses."

3.

On to the Territory

He struck him in the shoulder,
The black squealed in reply,
And shot up heading skywards,
Twisting on the fly,
It rolled and kicked out sideways,
The rider held his grip,
And rode him to a standstill,
One hand on his hip.

Two weeks after leaving Connmara, Don Kirk and Jack stepped off the train at Mt Isa.

'This town's different to most, Jack. It's got plenty ringers about but it's a mining town basically.'

During the journey Jack had gazed out the window at the maze of stony hills that had started to emerge as they steamed into Cloncurry.

'Makes you wonder how they found the mine amongst all these hills, Don.'

'No-one had to go and look for it, it came to them! Horse-tailer found it fetching the horses in one morning. Picked up a piece of rock and knew straight off by the weight it was mineral. That's what started 'em looking. Found the lode half a mile away. If it hadn't been for that ringer camped by the Leichhardt crossing they mightn't have found it for years. We'll be making our camp not far away from the spot.'

They carried their swags down the dusty yellow road towards the mine and the river. There was little weight in their swags. Each contained two blankets rolled up in a cover of canvas. A towel, spare shirt and trousers were stuffed in an empty flour bag. Between them they also had a piece of soap, two toothbrushes but no paste, a Rolls Razor, a tin of Zambuck and needle and thread. Each wore three small handmade leather pouches on his belt containing a knife, tin of wax matches and a watch.

Don selected an old river bloodwood to camp under.

'There's no fear of anyone pinching your swag out here, Jack. That's one good thing about this West. There's an old saying, 'As long as you can live in the country!' That means no matter a fella may be a bit of a rascal or a no-hoper, as long as he's living up here he's okay. Otherwise he would have been run out years ago.'

'How we getting out to this Camooweal, Don?'

'Only way is a lift with a carrier or by horse. We'll take a look up town and see what we can come up with. We got a few quid left but we don't want to get boozing heavy. We going to need that money. It's a long way to Seven Emu. Ringers mostly drink at the Isa but we'll look in on the Argent first. It's got the biggest bar in Australia. That's where the miners drink.'

As they reached the main street the sergeant of police was waiting. He was not a big man but he had the town's respect and had spent many years up north in the rough cattle towns.

'Heard you were back in town, Don Kirk, hope you going to leave our miners alone this time.'

'Hello, Sarge. I won't touch them long as they don't interfere with me. But I get the feeling they don't like us ringers coming in to town. I don't know why. There's plenty of beer for us all. Might be the women, hey?'

'Women! Only women here are the ones out the Three Mile camp. Any white bloke caught out there after dark can taste my missus' cooking for a month!'

'They pretty hard to see in the dark, Sarge. You must have good eyes. This here's Jack Vitnell, my mate. Jack's new up this way and I'm showing him the ropes, so we'll be quiet.'

The Argent Hotel was crowded when they walked in. The bar was enormous and ran around the room in a kidney shape. Jack bought a round. The stools were all occupied by hard looking men talking boisterously. They squatted down against the wall and rolled a smoke. Don bought and was returning with the drinks when he bumped a big fellow's glass of beer. The drink sloshed on the floor.

'Whoa, bullocks!' Don grinned at him. 'Damn bar's too crowded.'

He squatted back down beside Jack. The miner followed him over. He was a surly Yugoslav.

'You! You spill my drink!'

Don placed his glass on the floor and clambered to his feet.

'So what, pal!'

Then he hit him. It was another uppercut. Jack was to learn it was the only punch Don Kirk knew. But it didn't matter. In all the brawls Jack was to see Don engage in, he never needed to swing more than once. The miner must have been a fourteen stoner but Don lifted him a foot off the floor. No-one took any notice. If the miner was drinking with a mate, he didn't choose to buy in. They finished their drinks and left.

'Pity that Sergeant wasn't there, Don. He would have seen for himself you don't go looking for fight!'

'I've learnt the same as you have. There's only one way to handle those situations. Get in first.'

'Hard and fast!' smiled Jack. 'Let's check this Isa pub out.'

Boy Beaumont, an old mate of Don's, was in the bar at the end of a two week bender.

'I'm ready to go home, Don,' he croaked. 'This fella I'm boozing with is really getting on it.'

There was no-one else with him.

'Will you give me a hand to muster me plant and get me going?'

'I'll do better! Me an' me mate Jack here will muster 'em up and come home with you.' He turned to Jack. 'Ol' Boy's not the best. We'll look after him, maybe he'll look after us. It's forty mile over a dry track to his block. We'll get his horses and go with him.'

They were two days and nights getting out there. Boy couldn't sit the saddle for long each day. He had brought his bullocks in to the saleyards, paid his men off and stopped on drinking. They rationed him a few nips of rum and by the third morning he was looking brighter.

'There's the station roof,' Don called. 'You're home old mate!'

'Where you fellas headed?'

'The Territory, Phil Hanlon's place.'

'Seven Emu. I got two of his mules here. You want to take 'em with you? You got any horses?'

Boy set them up with two riding horses each and packs and saddles for the mules.

'Drop 'em back anytime or send 'em home with a drover.'

A few days after leaving Boy they rode into Camooweal, Queensland's most western town. Jack saw a long wide street with a few stores and houses strung along either side. The first building passed was the Top Pub. A big old weatherboard place with wide louvered verandahs. At the far end of town was a similar building, the Bottom Pub. If they had names, they were forgotten. They sprawled by the road as bleached and as dry looking as the bones of the perished cattle on the yellow plains around them.

Don led the way through town and down to the Common. The Common was more of the dry yellow plain and stretched for several miles. It was surrounded on one side by a drooping and broken rusted barb-wire fence that was only good as a rib scratcher for stock. A creek with a muddy water-hole was another boundary.

'This will do,' Don said. 'Here under these coolibahs. There's no shade but we won't be here long. Check out who's in town and go.'

'What's happening yonder?' Jack pointed across the flat towards the back of town.

'Somebody breakin'-in, look like. That's Redwell's Yard. Be a drover for sure. Let's go take a look.'

They reached the yard just as a young ringer was thrown. He had come off a big, sour bay. 'He had him good,' someone told them as they took their place on the top rail. 'Then the damn thing tried to buck over the rails and knocked him off. Lucky he wasn't bad hurt.'

The rider was a little fellow who now climbed slowly up the rails and sat next to Jack.

'Wild ride, hey mate.' Jack grinned.

'He's wild all right. An' bad with it. Ripped me new strides.' Then Don spotted him and thrust his hand out.

'Hello Billy. Still having a go, hey! This here's Jack Vitnell. Billy Yeomans, Jack. Me an' Billy rode together one time. What's Ab going to do now?'

Ab Lewis was handling the bay. It had been broken in previously but had got away with a few riders and become a rogue.

'He's going to choke him!' someone said.

Ab had thrown a rope over its head, taken a few loops around a post and was making it fast. The bay lay back on the rope choking itself by the neck.

'Jings I hate to see that done,' a voice called out.

The bay soon realised the futility in straining on the rope and walked towards the post. Ab lunged at, hitting it on the nose with his hat. It back-peddled and lay back choking again.

'Don't do that, mate!' the same voice called out. 'Get on and run him. That's what he needs. A good gallop around the flat.'

It was a brute of a thing, the bay. Today it had struck, bit and kicked Ab. Then tried to smash its way out of the yard when young Billy Yeomans mounted it. Ab now planned to use some force. He was known as a good-natured fellow but his patience was gone. He looked up at the ringers on the rails circling him. Now one of them was jeering at him.

'You come and gallop him around the flat!' he snarled. 'Never mind sitting hiding up there on the rails. This is where the action is down here in the yard. Anyone who wants to talk galloping around the flat, get down here and show your face!'

The ringers looked around, wondering who had spoken. There was no movement. Whoever it was had decided to shut up. Jack was grinning and just about to jump into the yard and mount the horse when a jockey-sized ringer slid off the rails and climbed down into the yard.

Ab Lewis' dust-reddened eyes opened in surprise. A few of the ringers sniggered. The little chap was no more than five feet tall and weighed around seven stone. He stepped daintily across the dusty yard in his high heeled boots to where Ab stood.

'That's Johnny Harrison, an ex Adelaide jockey,' Don suddenly whispered to Jack. 'He can ride. Seen him in action before. Let's try and get a bet on. A fiver he rides him!' he shouted.

Ab gave him a baleful look. 'You're on!' Then he swung on the jockey. 'What do you think you're going to do?'

Johnny Harrison looked calmly at him. 'Shorten these stirrups then take him outside. That's what he needs. A good riding out then a whip around the flat. This yard's too small to take a bend out of a big mongrel like him, I'll ride him in the open.'

'The big yard, you mean?'

'No! Outside on the flat.'

That caused some talk. The round yard was the place to start, so the horse couldn't get into its stride bucking. But the little fellow had seen how the horse had tried to climb the rails with Billy Yeomans aboard. The big yard was the next best place to get on. Space enough to keep off the rails but still confined. Outside it could buck and bolt. It was a brave decision to mount it outside.

'Flash little beggar!' Jack thought admiringly. 'Style! He's got style.'

Soon as Ab led the horse out the gate it started to rear and lunge.

'Give me a shirt, someone. If I don't cover his eyes, he'll never get on him.'

The horse stood trembling with rage as the midget swung into the seat. He was riding very short. The ringers had left the top rails of the round yard and were lined along the rails outside.

'Have your money ready, Don!' Ab called.

The onlookers were about to witness something most had only heard about. From time to time would come stories of horsemen who could stand in the stirrups and let the horse buck underneath them. Most ringers thought it was a myth. They couldn't comprehend how it could be done. Today they would see it.

'Are you set, mate?' Ab called.

'Let him go!'

Ab whipped away the blindfold and stepped back. The horse stood still momentarily, then the rider struck it with his hat. It leapt high in the air, twisting and kicking out sideways. There were eighteen inches of daylight between man and horse.

There came a buzz from the crowd. 'He's standing in the stirrups!'

'Same as last time,' Don said. 'What a little gem!'

Jack had never seen it done. He watched amazed as Johnny Harrison allowed the horse to buck beneath him.

'He's not ridin' it,' someone called. 'He's standin' on it!'

He made it look so easy they argued about it for weeks whether he really rode it or not.

'Course he rode it! Did he come off?'

'He never sat in the saddle!'

But towards the finish, when he knew the big bay was beaten, the rider did sit in the saddle. With one hand on his hip, nonchalantly waiting for the horse to quit.

'Oh, that's flash,' Jack grinned at Don. 'That hand on the hip. That's really flash! I'm going to do that from now on.'

When it stopped bucking, the little jockey took it for a gallop across the Common.

'Don't mind losing five quid to see a ride like that,' Ab said handing the money over to Don Kirk. 'What you fellas doing in town?'

'Heading up to the Gulf. This here's Jack Vitnell, used to ride with Thorpe McConville.'

'That so! My brother's got a horse that will try you. He reckons no-one has rode it yet. He rides it, but it don't buck with him. Look out anyone else who tries! Give our brother Zac a hell of a hiding. Smashed him up against a tree.'

Jack's eyes lit up. Here it was again! A horse that couldn't be ridden.

'Where's your brother?'

'Like as not up at the Top Pub with that big pig-eyed Kruger hung up outside. He brings it in to quieten loud-mouthed ringers. Old Kruger shuts 'em up. They don't have much to say when they know he's outside waiting to be rode!'

'Where's that miniature stockman?' Don asked. It was a name that would stick to the little jockey all his time up north.

Johnny Harrison had slipped off the big bay and was up on the top rail again.

Big Ab grinned up at him. 'You want an offsider's job, mate?'

'No,' said Don, 'He's coming with us. Come on mate, give us a hand to drink this fiver out.'

He started for the Bottom Pub.

'Hey, not that one. The other.'

'But we always drink down the Bottom, Jack.'

'Tomorrow. Let's go take a look at this big Kruger. Come on Miniature, it's my turn now!'

There was no horse tied up outside the hotel. They walked across the wide timber verandah and into the bar. A few ringers sat around on stools sipping beer and yarning. The Miniature Stockman placed a crushed pound note on the bar. Don placed the five on the bar.

'Put yours away, mate. We'll cut this one out first. You been in town long?'

They sat talking until late afternoon of horses and places they had been.

Suddenly the bat-wing doors crashed open and Don saw the huge frame of Ab Lewis' brother, Elmore. He looked around, blinking in the darkness for a few seconds then headed over. He nodded curtly at Don and stopped in front of Jack.

'They tell me you can ride.'

Jack grinned up at the sneering face. 'I'm generally there at the finish.'

'I got a horse will try you out, if you're game!'

Jack looked him straight in the eye. 'I think I might be game enough to get on him. Where's he at?'

Elmore turned to Don Kirk. 'You want to risk the rest of that bet you won?'

'Hey!' Jack swung around and faced Elmore. 'You're dealing with me, mate!' He spat out the word mate. 'Don't turn your back and leave me standing with the flies! Go and get your broken-down, knock-kneed ladies' hack and hang him up outside and when I've finished me drink, I'll ride him into the dirt for you.'

Big Elmore straightened his six foot four frame. The slightest suggestion of a smile curved his lips.

'We'll be outside waiting... mate!'

The whole bar followed Jack outside. Kruger was hung up to a wire fence that ran beside the pub. Another horse stood next to it belonging to a local ringer, Siddy Biondi. Elmore unhooked Kruger, led it away from the fence and called out to Jack.

'I'll hold him for you mate, otherwise you'll never get on him.'

Jack gave a grin and swaggered across to the horse. 'Oh, I think I'll manage to get on him okay.'

He took the reins from Elmore, cherishing the moment. This was the stuff! An unrideable horse and a crowd. He slipped one split rein under the horse's neck and over its wither, held both reins loosely and contemplated his boots.

'He'll never mount it,' someone muttered. 'That's no way to get on a buckjumper.'

Suddenly Jack sprang into the saddle. He didn't bother with the stirrups, but sunk his spurs straight into the animal's shoulders. Kruger did not submit easily. When it had tried everything and Jack was still hanging, it threw itself on the ground. Jack stepped off an instant before the animal rolled into Siddy Biondi's horse. Biondi's horse took fright, pulled away from the fence, a wire snapped and soon both horses were entangled. Suddenly a voice called out, 'It threw him!'

Jack was furious. He had weathered the horse's worst bucks in champion fashion, now after he had stepped off, someone was saying he'd been thrown. In a rage, he threw himself on the horse and started to spur it. 'Get up, you mongrel, get up!'

Kruger struggled to rise but was trapped by the wire. It threshed around on the ground, kicking. The Miniature Stockman jumped down from the pub verandah and ran across the yard. He placed his skinny arms around Jack.

'Leave him, mate, leave him. He can't get up. You've rode him at his best, you don't need to prove any more.'

Jack allowed Miniature to pull him from the horse. He looked at the men lining the verandah and rocked on his heels like a boxer ready to pounce.

'Any of you want to say I didn't ride him?'

No-one answered. They could see what this young ringer was all about — a proper rip-snorter. Jack turned and helped Elmore untangle the wire from the two horses' legs and get them to their feet. Kruger stood — sullen, beaten.

Jack gave Elmore a nudge.

'Thought you had an outlaw, matey. Not this broke down old carthorse.'

Elmore stuck his hand out and grinned. 'There's a few horses around this Territory going to look like cart horses soon I reckon.'

He turned to Kruger.

'You're gettin' a pack-saddle next season!'

'You want to come out to this Seven Emu with us?' Don Kirk asked the Miniature Stockman later. 'Plenty of wild horses and cattle out there to test a man.'

'You can count me in. That's what I come north for!'

4.

An Old Poddy-Dodger

There sitting by a deep clear pool,
A lithesome native belle,
Coyly smiling as they passed,
That naked Jezebel,
Two more heads bobbed in the pool,
Two pairs of laughing eyes,
But little did the drovers know,
They all were Smokey's spies.

Most stockmen take years before they make a name for themselves up North. Jack Vitnell took one day. After he rode the 'unrideable' Kruger to a standstill outside the Camooweal pub, word travelled fast about this new young ringer.

'Didn't even bother with the stirrups! Jumped straight on. Elmore was going to hold it. This Jack fella pushed him out of the way, grabbed the reins and flew on. Then later when the horse tried to roll on him, just stepped off. Cool as you please. Then sprang back on again. Never seen a fella ride like that in me life!'

The following morning Don Kirk, Jack and the Miniature Stockman were packing up, when Billy Yeomans rode up.

'Which way you fellas heading?'

'Seven Emu.'

'You got a job for me up there?'

Don looked up at the young ringer. He was barely twenty and had only been a few years up North but was already known as a good man with cattle. He sat his horse like an old timer.

'We got no job to go to mate. Just going out on spec. I know the way Phil Hanlon works and he'll be out chasing cattle first early storm brings on a green pick. He can always use men. But he runs a rough camp. Tin of jam in the camp if you're lucky and Territory wages. No Queensland Award out there.'

'Rough camps don't worry me. All I'm used to. I want to get away from this town and the boozing. If he gives me a quid a week it's better than sitting down here till next season earning nothing.'

'What do you say, Jack?'

Jack was barely seventeen. 'Be good to have some young company,' he thought. 'And this bloke can ride. May have even rode that bay horse yesterday if it hadn't took the rails.' He nodded to Don Kirk. 'Okay by me. We can always keep riding if this Phil don't like it. There's a heap of places out there I want to see.'

The horses had been on a patch of good feed all night and were standing quietly by, hobbled and waiting to be saddled.

Don glanced up at the sun. 'We might have to keep riding anyway, if we don't take ol' Phil out a bottle of rum. Come on, leave the packs for a while, these horses won't move far. Let's have one for the track.'

Big Elmore Lewis was in the bar. He walked over and shouted a round. 'What are you doing, Miniature?'

'Going out with these blokes.'

'Never mind them fellas, they'll get lost out in the bush. Stop in town for a while, I got a mob of colts to break, I'll cut you half. Then next season you can come out west with me, I got two mobs to bring in from VRD. If you don't want to come back inside you can stop there. They got six stockcamps, always after good men.'

They left town without Johnny Harrison, The Miniature Stockman.

The affable Phil Hanlon was pleased to see them, but pretended to be angry. 'Get off this place, you randy Queenslanders. You're only here to root my studs.'

'Studs!' Don Kirk growled. 'That'll be the day Phil Hanlon when you've got anything worthwhile on the place. You're too mean to buy your blacks rations, let alone dresses.' He grinned. 'We've come out to give you a hand to muster all those Macarthur River cleanskins you sneak in and thieve over the wet.'

Phil grinned back. 'Sounds okay to me. I can do with a bit of free labour.'

'Free labour! Mate, we come dear! We're top hands. Tell you what, but. If we don't get you more cattle than you've seen in your life you owe us nothing!'

Don Kirk knew Phil from old. He would make sure they got something for the wild riding they would need to do to muster his rogue cleanskins.

Phil had an old pensioner, Lester Kerrigan, cooking. There wasn't much to cook. All Lester did was bake bread and boil beef. There was no green feed around yet to bring in cattle and there was a lot of talk to catch up on. So most days found them yarning in the bough-shed adjacent the kitchen.

Phil pointed to Lester. 'Don't you get taking notice of this old rascal. He's an old Kimberley outlaw. Ain't you, Lester? An old poddy dodger from the Underworld.'

'The Underworld!' exclaimed Jack.

'Land of wild blacks and thieving white men, hey, Lester!'

The old chap cackled and spat a stream of tobacco across the dirt floor.

'You bloody old boori,' Phil told him. 'Where's your manners?'

Lester pretended to be hurt. It was an old joke. 'I not a boori, Phil Hanlon! I'm a white man, no matter I look black. I'm most Afghan.' He knew that would cause a smile.

'How that make you a white man, Lester?'

'Them Afghan people been civilised lot longer than you white fellas!'

Jack was much taken with old Lester and encouraged him to talk about his early days.

Phil said, 'Tell him about that lady journalist come up to Wyndham to marry you, Lester.'

Lester snorted. 'She never come up to marry me, she come up for information and I give it to her. I'll tell you about it, Jack ...

I never wanted to talk about my outlaw days. I wanted to forget about them and almost had until I met a journalist by the name of Miss Foster. Miss Foster come up North to write a book. The West Australia Government had asked her to tell the story of the Wyndham Meatworks. The history of it. I know she finished it because later on I saw it for sale in town. About two thirds way into the book she drops about all the stolen cattle that went through the 'Works and how no-one was any the wiser. That wasn't quite right because a lot of people knew what was going on but couldn't do anything about it. Not at that end anyway. They tried to stop it out on the ridges where it started but they may as well have tried stop old Bluey boozing as that.

She refers to an interview she had with a Mister John Colt, which was the name I said to use, and how he told her the way those cattle duffers operated. She done it pretty cleverly too, as the exact words I spoke were there in the book so I can't argue with anything. And I read 'em myself, not like the old days when I had to go to someone else.

But I could have used any old name. The old hands around there would have known it was me. It kind of revived the whole thing and a lot of the old-timers started dropping by to talk. Particularly about the cattle duffing and the outlaws up the Underworld. That's how word got around that I was John Colt and then all kinds of people wanted to talk to me.

I even got a letter from a Professor of Australian History asking me for information about the Underworld and its outlaws. Underworld was a name that fired everyone's imagination, and I should never have used the word because some things, I reckon, are best forgot.

Before Miss Foster left, she said she'd better copyright me. That meant I didn't have to talk with other journalists if they poked by, but tell 'em to contact her.

'Just say you're under copyright to me.'

She was only trying to stop me getting hassled but I never saw any other journalists that I know of. A few strangers come out to my camp at the Seven Mile.

I told them that the bloke they were looking for wasn't there, and that he had caught leprosy and they had him up in Fanny Bay.

That used to get rid of 'em. The letters I sent on to Miss Foster.

I can still see her climbing out of Roy Sergeant's taxi that first afternoon. She was wearing a yellow floral sun frock and an Akubra straight out of the box. When she got up close I saw she could have looked pretty had she wanted. She had nothing on her face but freckles and a wisp of pink lipstick. It was a hot May afternoon but she looked cool enough. She never walked, she marched. Straight over the stone and spinifex staring at me.

'There's a track yonder,' I called, as Roy Sergeant bounced away in his big old American Ford towards the main road.

Then she smiled. It was seeing a tin of peaches opened when you haven't tasted fruit in a year. It was a lovely sight. She was a little girl then, with a big book and a pencil shyly walking up to the teacher, not a woman of forty.

'You're Mister Kerrigan. And I'm Jill Foster. I'm a journalist and I'd like you to tell me some stories about the Meatworks if you will. About when it was built and how many men worked on it and why there are so many graves of construction workers in the old cemetery.'

'Well, you better have a drink of tea because that's all you're going to get. I don't know anything about those things. Except the graves. The workers died of fever. And some of them fell, they had scaffold two hundred foot high. Shipped it all the way from China. Bamboo.'

'There! You've told me things already! Everyone's the same. Think they don't know till they start talking, then they come out with all sorts of interesting things! But in town they told me you were here during the construction and would know a lot.'

'I was in the country, yes, in '15. But if I was in town I was drunk and wouldn't have known what was goin' on up at the Landing. That's all we come to town for them days.'

I thought that would shock her and might make her lose interest in me. I didn't want to talk to any journalist.

But she only laughed.

'The Landing. What was that?'

'Where the boats pulled in to load the cattle. That's where they built the 'Works. Cattle all went live before that. Fremantle. Manilla. All over. Old MP was always trying for new markets.'

'MP Durack. I've read a lot about him. A wonderful man. Did you meet him?'

'Saw him often enough. Never met him. Kept out of his way. Would have jailed me if he could.'

That was a mistake. She pounced on it right away.

'Jail you? I can't understand that. Whatever for?'

I'll make her go away this time, I thought.

'Burglary. Stole all the young black girls off his head station.'

But that only made her laugh more. 'I'm sure you had a lot of girlfriends in your time Mister Kerrigan. Don't put me off. Were you a cattle duffer?'

Someone had been talking, else she was smart. Both I reckoned. But I was starting to like her. I like direct people. And I like small dainty white women with brown eyes shot with green. There was nothing sexy about her and I liked that too. It was just her an' me talking as though I was with a mate.

So then we had that conversation she put in her book. Me telling her that the Meatworks changed the way we operated up the Underworld. Except I didn't make the mistake then, I just made now. I didn't say *we* operated. I remembered in time and said *they* operated.

During our talk one name slipped out and I asked her not to print it but she said not to worry, she didn't want those kinds of names. She only wanted to know what happened and how it affected the Meatworks. And I thought that was pretty square of her.

It didn't take her long to realise the cattle we sent in didn't affect the Meatworks much. But she asked could she leave what I said in the book as it was going to be a pretty dry old book and what I had to say would add a bit of colour.

If you haven't read the book and are wondering what I told her, I'll tell you. I told her those fellas up the Underworld, the outlaws, only stole horses before the 'Works opened. Which was true. There was mobs of cleanskin cattle running around but we never touched 'em. Too hard to off-load. You needed a special licence to send cattle by ship. And they were all inspected for Redwater, Pleuro and such, an' the brands an' earmarks had to tally. We wasn't prepared to get involved in all that.

With horses it was different. The stations were so short of good horses they would buy most anything. Well, not quite. You couldn't sell 'em the Bull's Head of Victoria or the Wineglass of Newcastle or well known brands like that. You had to doctor them up and come up with something that looked like a genuine brand.

They were short because the Kimberley was rife with a poison that killed off horses in a week. Walkabout it was known as and that's what they did. Walked around in circles until they dropped. No-one knew what caused it and they still don't.

The Meatworks opened during the First War and that's when we started bringing cattle into Wyndham. All we had to have was a registered brand and they were easy come by. Best of all, the cattle were under the hammer and cut up the day after we delivered 'em.

So we concentrated on cattle for a few years as there were thousands runnin' wild up in the Underworld. That was the name for the unexplored rough country north west of Wyndham. It's still a wild place and not long since the last white man, Bob Anderson, was speared.

But I never had any trouble with those people as I rode with Smokey, the king of the outlaws all those years and he knew how to handle 'em.

He was half-caste too, but a lot blacker than me as his father had been Afghan. He was the most easy man to get on with that I ever met. Always smiling and ready for a joke. He wasn't a big man. But he would knuckle quick if he had to. Most of all he was a marvellous horseman, not only great on a rough horse but great with bad horses. He specialised in taming outlaw horses and I never knew one to beat him. Or a man. He always had to win.

I rode with Smokey from age fourteen to near forty so knew him well. Smokey's name was the one I dropped to Miss Foster when she told me not to mention names but she got rather interested in what I had to say about him.

Anyway ... Miss Foster.

Miss Foster and I finished up good friends by the time Roy Sergeant drove up to take her back to town.

'Goodness!' she said, when she saw the taxi, 'Two hours already and we're still talking. Can I come back out again tomorrow?'

The next morning we talked about the early drovers. She put all their names down and they went in the book, then she got back to the subject of old MP wanting to jail me. I couldn't see any harm in telling her. Not after all these years an' everyone else dead.

'It was because me an' Smokey took a mob of cattle off his men when they were on the road.'

'Mr Kerrigan, I didn't know you had roads up here then.'

'Neither we did. On the road with cattle, that's what I mean. See the ranges yonder? That's the Cockburns. Beyond is the Underworld. Old MP used to take a short cut that way when he was bringing over the range cattle into Wyndham. He did a lot of droving for those stations this side of the Leopolds. They were always short of horses but he had plenty.

'At the particular time, there were two mobs of bullocks travelling together, one day apart. Drovers didn't like that Underworld country. It was a spooky place to be camped with cattle and they would often rush. Mostly cattle will go back the way they come, so the drover coming along behind has the chance of picking 'em up next day.

'And that's what happened this time. Reggie — I'll call him that — who had the lead mob, lost his bullocks in a rush and, ah, Ben, who was coming along behind picked 'em up next morning. But only half. The rest went bush. It was decided to box the two mobs and Ben would continue in to Wyndham and Reg and two of his men would get after the runaways.

'This Reggie fella was a pretty smart stockman. He never found his own mob but he run into another mob of bullocks feedin' about. Quiet bullocks, branded of course, that had got away from some other drover. That never bothered Reggie, he took 'em just the same. They was about equal in number to the ones he'd lost and he reckoned with a bit of luck no-one at the 'Works would spring the different brand.

'Only problem for Reggie was, me and Smokey were watching. And Smokey had been so long up in that Underworld country, he thought any cattle not in charge of a drover belonged to him! It was no use telling him different, so when he said we were going to get 'em back, I just tagged along.

'A little further on was a big billabong full of lilies with bulbs just right for pluckin'. Camped beside it was a big mob of bush blacks.

'Me an' Smokey knew them well. We knew all the people up in the Underworld. There was none we were related to but we were on good terms with all of them. That's why we never had to keep nit for police patrols. We knew soon as they placed a foot in the Underworld. None of those blacks ever went short of stick-tobacco or flour neither — long as we had some.

'We rode up to the camp and Smokey explained to the old men — the boss ones — there was a mob of cattle poking along and would soon be waterin' at the lily hole. Then he pointed to three young women wearing big smiles and nothing else. All those people got around naked.

'When you see these cattle,' Smokey told them, 'I want everyone to go bush bar these girls. They can keep on diving for lily roots.'

Then he passed around a few tobacco sticks.

'Come on,' he says to me. 'We going to keep out of sight too.' And off we rode into the scrub.

'It wasn't long before we saw the cattle. The drovers let 'em come up to the water to drink, then they saw the girls splashin' around.

'You can imagine what happened next. They tied their horses up and decided to take a swim too. The cattle could wait! With bellies full of water they wouldn't wander far and could be rounded up again in no time. The girls giggled and watched the drovers climbing into the water then swam coyly away out of sight around a bend. The drovers swum after them and that was the last they saw of their cattle. And their horses. Me and Smokey took the lot.

'Them three fellas had to hoof it into Wyndham, sixty mile away. Smokey took pity on 'em and left them a bag of flour from out of their own packs. Stockmen don't do much walking and high-heeled boots don't help. They were pretty much wore out by the time they got to town five days later. Then they had to explain how they lost their horses as well as the cattle.

'Of course the story got out and the whole countryside was laughing at them. Old MP was so mad he come into Wyndham and demanded more be done to clean out the outlaws from the Underworld. But the troopers had no hope, it was all so rough and wild. And big. Someone told me that country's bigger than Europe and in those days it was empty of cattle stations. Even today, there's only three.'

'What did you do with the cattle, Mr Kerrigan?'

'Sold 'em. That's why Smokey wanted that mob so bad. They were branded BCX. He had a registered brand, 88X.'

Miss Foster looked puzzled. 'What did that mean?'

'Easy to over brand, see?'

I traced out the first brand in the dirt. Then I drew the second brand over it. She watched me then she took the stick and done the same. Then she looked up and smiled.

'Mr Kerrigan, I think I understand now why Mr Durack wanted to jail you!'

5

Riding with Smokey

The Underworld the place was called,
North of the Leopold Ranges,
An eerie and forsaken place,
Hidden from roving strangers,
Over the granite mountain peaks,
Beyond long lines of hills,
And only the outlaw bands and blacks
Knew its tangled rills.

Jack rolled into his swag that night thinking about the Kimberley outlaws. He did not go along with all that horse thieving stuff. Cattle, yes. If stations were too lax to brand their cleanskins they deserved to lose them to someone who would. And they did not really belong to anyone until that brand was burnt on. But horses ... they were a man's life blood, his horses. And a station's.

He was up early and in the kitchen for a pannikin of tea as the first wash of dawn paled the east. Lester was pleased to see him. Not many young blokes were interested in the old days. He took down a huge camp-oven from a shelf and tipped out a cart-wheel of brownie. He cut a thick wedge and pushed it across the table where Jack was squatting rolling a smoke.

'This'll hold you together till breakfast. Still no early storms about. You fellas be here another day or two yet, I reckon.'

'How come you got mixed up with all that outlaw mob, Lester? That your country over there?'

'I was born on Greenvale, Jack. That's on the edge of that Underworld country I was telling you about. Born and reared in the blacks' camp till I was twelve. I never set out to be an outlaw. You want me to tell about it?'

'I became an outlaw by chance ...

The Underworld. That may seem a funny name to call a place up in North West Australia and I don't know who named it. But that's all we ever called it, the unexplored rough country further on from over the range.

Over the range was north of the Leopold Ranges. The King Leopolds. A big rocky wall that runs across West Kimberley from Derby on the coast to where the Fitzroy River heads two hundred miles east. Most of the cattle stations were south of the Leopolds, but a few pioneers had struggled over them and formed stations to the north. These places were said to be over the range and it was a rough isolated place.

Bush blacks still ran wild, living off the land and the white man's cattle so the stations mostly clung close to the foothills of the Range. Further north the country was called the Underworld. There was nothing up there except more wild blacks — and outlaws.

They weren't real outlaws like you read about in books. And they weren't bushrangers bailing people up like Ben Hall. It was a local word for cattle and horse thieves, but no-one ever used the word thief. People always said poddy-dodgers or cattle duffers. And if you were one and operated from up the Underworld, they called you an outlaw.

Cattle duffing is ages old. Back a thousand years I reckon cattlemen were branding unmarked stock as their own. I know that because of a poem old Billy Madden read me once about a big scuffle over cattle up on the Scottish border. Bill reckoned all them Scotchies ever did was drink whisky, fight the Hinglish and steal each other's cattle.

When I was about fourteen I became a joey for the biggest cattle duffer of all — Smokey. That meant I was one of his lookout men. If Smokey had another name I never heard it. For a long time I wasn't sure Smokey really was an outlaw, but I'd heard plenty of stories. None of my people ran with the outlaws, they were all honest and would only take things occasionally if they really needed them. And then it was only from amongst themselves. But when you live in a blacks' camp there's nothing much to make off with anyway. They would never steal from a white man. Unless, of course, he was a stranger. Then they might.

I was eleven when I went out with the stockcamp first time and when we came back to the station the end of that year, Alf Moses made me camp up the homestead. Alf owned Greenvale and said he was going to make a white man of me. That was good but it was also bad. It cut me off from my people. But he said if I didn't keep away from them he'd send me off to Derby and let the missionaries have me.

Alf Moses knew my white father. All the old people did, but I never saw him. He was a drover come out from Queensland to take back bullocks. He did that year after year. Then he got drowned in a flooded river crossing. That was about the time I was born. When he was at Greenvale he always camped with my mother. My black father didn't mind. That's the way things were done those days.

Smokey was also a half-caste, but he was a lot blacker than me. He looked different too. The shape of his face and nose was more like a white man's than a black's. Later he told me his father had been an Afghan. He could read and write and count good because he was brought up on a mission. He wasn't in the Greenvale stockcamp the first few years I was, he rode for a few places. But when he did turn up I felt I already knew him, I had heard so much about him. I found out afterwards that Alf Moses gave him a job so he wouldn't steal Greenvale stock. All those outlaws were like that. Never stole off a place that gave them a job during the Dry.

You might think they didn't need a job being outlaws and that they made plenty of money. If they did no-one ever saw much of it. There were so many to share it with. And they were always gambling. Amongst themselves mostly, but sometimes with the Chinese in town. Come to think of it, I reckon those old Chinese store-keepers in Wyndham got most of their money.

I was to learn they only went horse duffing for the excitement of it and because they liked being around horses. All they talked about was horses. They swapped them and gambled them, stole them and sold them. No-one hardly ever stole branded cattle. They weren't worth galloping after. There were mobs of cleanskins running wild which you could brand without bothering to chase branded stock. Branded cattle were hard to sell. But horses! Anybody would buy horses. They had to because so many died each year in the Kimberley from an unknown disease.

Walkabout it was known as because that's how it affected them. They walked till they dropped. It must have sent them blind too, because they would walk through or try to walk through everything. Trees, bushes, fences, anthills, they just kept going, stumbling along till they fell and died. No-one knew what caused it and there was no cure. It wasn't everywhere. Some parts were clean. Stations that didn't have it might have 500 horses. Those that did were lucky to own forty. It was a terrible curse but a great thing for the outlaws. There was a ready market for all they could sell. Year after year.

Anyway, that year Smokey joined the stockcamp, it had been a good season. Plenty of branders and three big mobs of bullocks turned off. Apart from me and Smokey and the boss, there were about twenty full bloods. And the two Jacks, white mates of Smokey's. Rowdy Jack who hardly said anything and Silent Jack who was always talking. They were both little fellas, but long in the legs like all good stockmen. It's a big help if you own a pair of long legs to wrap around a horse that's trying to turn itself inside-out while you're on it. They were about the same age as Smokey and had ridden with him a while I reckon.

I was fourteen that season and as good a rider as any in that camp — until Smokey come along. I never knew anyone could ride a horse like him. No matter what horse he was on he always managed to hit the lead. He had the knack of turning a hack into a champion. I never learnt how he did that. Later on I became as good a buckjump rider but I could never get the best out of a horse like Smokey could. It was just a gift he had.

I took to Smokey straight off and mostly we rode together. He was always laughing and ready to joke about things that happened during the day and was never sour in the morning like the others. Those stockboys had never seen anybody quite like Smokey either. The way he could handle horses and wild cattle and men! He would knuckle up quick, old Smoke, if anyone gave him cheek! He was always showing and explaining things to me and I learnt a lot from him but he wasn't head stockman.

We had a grumpy white boss, Arthur Betts, skinny as a reed. I thought he was about 60 tho' Smokey told me he was only same age as he was, 40. But he looked old and got around like he was old. He never joined in with all the laughter now we had Smokey and the two Jacks with us. He was a Queenslander and I thought, knew everything there was to know about stock.

He never told us what to do but he was boss just the same. Every man knew what had to be done. Only on the bullock muster Arthur might give a few orders like setting the watches. And he always took the boss' watch, the last one in the morning, the daylight watch, as that was the one when cattle were most likely to jump.

We mustered cattle from before sunrise to dark and then had to watch 'em at night. We made 'em into a big circle on dark and then every man in the camp took a turn riding them 'til daylight. Otherwise they would just take off back where they come from. Sometimes they still took off, if they got a fright from a dingo sneaking by and we had to gallop and bring them back. But mostly they just slept or lay chewing their cud and we rode around singing to keep awake and let them know there was a guard.

I was pretty ashamed about my singing. I only knew Annie Laurie and corroborees till Smokey come along. I couldn't sing corroborees now I was going to be a white man so I used to sing Annie Laurie for the whole of my two hour watch. Old Billy Madden taught it to me when he come out to Greenvale saddling. But Smokey changed that. He'd sing during the day riding behind the cattle and make me learn. The Hash Grove was his favourite and A Fine Whole Hinglish Gentleman and one about poachers getting about of a shiny night. Poachers were cattle duffers, Smokey reckoned.

Arthur also took first turn cutting out bullocks for the drovers. We would hold them in a mob and then the top hands would ride in on their best horses, their cutting horses, and shoulder out the fat cattle to go with the drover. And sometimes those bullocks wouldn't want to leave their mates in the mob and then there would be a good deal of yelling and galloping to get 'em out.

Before Smokey come along I had never got a turn cutting out but very first day he took me in with him. He didn't have to show me what to do, I had watched it so often. I only needed the chance and I was as good as any of 'em. Arthur didn't mind. It was just he'd never thought to give me a go I suppose.

Me and the two Jacks and Smokey ate at Arthur's fire, all being classed as white, and the black stockboys ate at their fire a good step away. But Arthur never had much to say. Not that he thought he was any better, it was just his way. I used to call him uncle sometimes, just to get him going as he was married to an Auntie of mine down the black's camp.

'Don't you call me huncle!' he'd snort. 'I hain't married to that Lilly.'

But of course he was, far as we were concerned. He had his own hut at the station and when we were in, from November to March, Auntie Lilly stopped with him. Other times she lived down the camp with the people.

All the time we rode together that season Smokey never mentioned about outlaws. Neither did the two Jacks or anyone. But a strange thing happened when we reached Eagle Peak. That was one of our cattle camps and the name of a steep hill close by. Straight across from Eagle Peak was the Rocky Range. The station was about twenty mile on. We never mustered past the Rocky Range. It was impossible to cross. Huge cliffs of granite hundreds of foot high run for miles. It was Greenvale's western boundary and beyond it was the Underworld.

Eagle Peak was a big muster, a full week. It was very scrubby and took hard riding to get the cattle and dang me, just as we needed them, Smokey and Rowdy disappeared! And no-one said anything. Not Arthur Betts, Silent Jack or any of the blacks. We just carried on as though they had never been with us. Then when we had finished and branded everything, we just sat around spelling.

Somehow I sensed we were waiting on Smokey and Rowdy. I got nothing out of Arthur or Silent so I sidled up alongside Big Saturday, who was kind of boss over the other black stockboys.

'Where them fella?'

'Where what fella?'

'Rowdy and Smokey.'

Saturday rolled his eyes and looked around nervously.

'Might be all gone somewhere,' he hedged.

'Which way?' I pressed.

'Might be that way,' he mumbled, indicating the looming Rocky Range with puckered lips and a thrust of his jaw.

'That way?' I was perplexed. 'But there's no track that way. It's all munjon country!'

'Might be Smokey know all them munjon fella and they can't hurt him,' and that's all I could get out of him.

Munjon country, the aboriginal name for wild bush black country, that's what the Rocky Range was, and beyond it, the Underworld. Outlaw country. What was Smokey doing up there if he wasn't an outlaw? It seemed the stories were true. It didn't worry me that much. I felt a bit disappointed I suppose and wished he'd told me about it and that he'd be away a while.

A few days more and Smokey and Rowdy rode in to camp like they'd never been away. They swung off at the fire and said good-day to Arthur and Silent, but I wouldn't look at them. I was so cross I just turned my head and pretended to be busy boiling the billy.

I heard Smokey yell out his nickname for me.

'Hey Colt! Look what I brought you!' And dang me if he wasn't holding out a pair of Boulia spurs! Everybody in the country wanted to own a pair of Boulia spurs. But not many did own them. They weren't easy to come by in West Australia. I took them and couldn't help grinning.

'Where —' I began.

'No questions, Colt.' He smiled. 'Just let's say I got them from a wandering munjon.'

'Did you see some wild blacks then?'

'Heaps of tracks, Colt,' and that's all he would say.

Two days later we were back in at the station, finished for the season. We yarded the horses, pulled off their shoes and bushed them. They could wander the run for four months now and get fat for next season's muster. We stacked away all the gear in the saddle shed and carried our swags up to the men's quarters, a stone and antbed building with a wide stone flagged verandah. Then we trooped into the kitchen for a feed.

Later that evening, Smokey and the two Jacks went to see Alf Moses and get paid off. They were pretty happy when they came back to the Quarters and I think Alf must have shouted them a rum.

They walked straight past where I was squatting in the dark and I heard Smokey say, 'Time to muster the moonlight mob when we leave here tomorrow. They'll bring ten quid each over the range.'

Then he saw me and stopped. I never looked up but kept tap, tapping a stick against my boot, but I was thinking plenty. A moonlight mob! A stolen mob! So it was true, Smokey was one of the Underworld outlaws. I wished I was anywhere but where I was.

'Colt!' he was saying. 'What are you doing sitting out here like a crow on a post? Ain't you going up for your pay?'

'I got a job for the Wet doin' up the gear. Thought you knew. And in the meantime he's sending me out dogging. On my own.' I hoped it didn't show that I had overheard.

'Good for you, Colt.' Smokey was smiling down at me but his eyes watched mine closely. The two Jacks stood by looking a bit guilty then one of them said, 'Well, how about a game of cards before we turn in?'

Next morning they packed up. I stood around watching. Rowdy ran their mounts up from the horse paddock. Every ringer had his own horses. Smokey and the Jacks had two apiece and two pack mules between them. They saddled the mules and led them up to the store to load up. They wouldn't need to carry much. Tea and sugar. Four fifty's of flour. With all the bush tucker around that would last them a couple of months or more.

They were ready to leave by smoko. Smokey walked across to where I was watching.

'So now you know, Colt.'

'Now I know. And I don't care one way or another. But I wish you'd told me earlier. We spent a lot of time together Smokey and you never said a word. And you're taking a risk aren't you?'

'Don't we do that every day on the stone, galloping around? And Colt, couple of times I was going to tell you but I dunno, just kept putting it off I suppose. But I'm glad you found out because now I need you.'

'Need me?'

'Yes. We got some news from Alf Moses last night. There's going to be a patrol out this Wet looking for Major. He's still not caught and the police are stopping bush till they catch him.'

'So where do I come in?'

'Colt,' and here he came up close and looked me straight in the eye, 'You don't have to do anything you don't want to. But what I would like you to do is act joey for me till we get these horses through the Rocky Range.'

'Through the Range!'

'There's a gap. A little gully leads to it. It cuts right through the Rocky opposite Eagle Peak. There's one or two steep pinches but nothing a mob of horses couldn't get over, taken slowly. That's where me and Rowdy went. We followed it through and it takes us right where we want to go. The munjons told me about it ages ago and it's true. It's so well hidden you would never know there was a gully till you was upon it.'

Right where he wanted to go! His hideout no doubt. There would be yards to brand stock and a rough hut. I suppose they had gone on there to check it out. I stood wondering how to answer, but his next words made my mind up.

'There's an unbranded creamy filly running with the mob we're lifting. Neatest little thing you ever seen. Go like the wind, I reckon. When you see me next season, I'll be riding her. But she'll be yours. And wearing your brand.'

'My brand?'

'Sure. The first two letters of your name. That's how everyone starts.'

I didn't even own a donkey. A creamy filly!

'How you going to brand her?'

'Same as always. Piece of bent wire in the fire. You can bend a piece up now before we go. You know how to spell your name?'

'Almost. But I can do the first two letters easy. And okay, I'll joey but I can't wait around the Rocky Range for ever. I got the whole run to trap.'

'No-one's asking you to. Only at next full moon. That's when we lift the mob and two days later we'll be passing Eagle Peak on our way to slip through the range. But we're going to have more than eighty horses and I don't want to blunder on any police patrol. We'd have to gallop off and leave them. If there's any great risk I'd rather go in the old way but we can save two weeks travelling by going through that gap.'

'What do you want me to do?'

'If you see the patrol, drop a match in the spinifex. Top of Eagle Peak. No need to set the whole hill on fire. Pick out a big clump that will burn an hour. We'll be watching and go the old way in. But anyway, it's only an off chance. There's a hundred thousand square mile ol' Major could be holed up in.'

'Okay,' I grinned. 'See you full moon!'

'I hope not,' he answered soberly. 'Because that will mean trouble. Maybe for both of us. You understand that?'

'I'm in,' I replied. 'Can't get into trouble for burning off a patch of spinifex.'

'Well Colt, if anything does happen and you need help, I'll tell you how to find me.' But he paused for a few seconds as though he was making his mind up. And I almost said to him, 'Don't tell me, I don't want to know.' But of course I did want to know so I didn't say it.

Then he looked hard at me and said very quietly, 'I know I can trust you, Colt.' And I can tell you I was pretty proud when he said that.

'Ride down to the river that's between the Range and the Peak. It's dry this time of year. Follow it downstream and keep up on the far bank. You'll see a little bit of a gully running in that looks like nothing at all. But that's it. The bank's covered with big boulders but you can thread a way through and across to the mouth of the gully.

'Follow it along till it narrows to nothing. To just a crack that peters out into the wall of the cliff face. Except it doesn't. That crack goes right through for a mile or more. You can just squeeze a horse through it. It winds around and comes out onto a slope of rock that you can follow way up to the gap that leads over the Rocky.

'Now you got a long way to ride. A good ten mile till you come to a big sandy river. When you reach it, pull your saddle off and make a camp. Don't cross that river! Someone will come and fetch you.'

'Come and fetch me!'

'A munjon! Painted up, spears and all. But don't worry, he'll be mine.' Then he grinned. 'They all are up there! How do you think I've kept going for so long without being caught?' And then he threw back his head and laughed. 'Every munjon bush black son of a gun in the Underworld joeys for old Smokey! And gets tobacco from him!'

'What about Major?'

'Don't worry about Major, Colt. He'll be nowhere near where you are. But those damn troopers won't know that. They'll be riding all over.'

A thought struck me. 'Where is Major?'

Smokey grinned. 'How should I know? But I know where he was last week. I traded him some tobacco for a pair of Boulia spurs he had pinched.'

I stood looking after them as they rode off across the red ground that surrounded the homestead and down to where the edge of the timber hid them. Away off in the distance I could see the jagged peaks of the Rocky Range. That's where I'd be heading soon. Eagle Peak was that way.

Then I walked up to the office to see Alf Moses. He was a white haired kindly old gentleman and had taken Greenvale up years before. We never saw him out on the run these days, he left all the cattle work to Arthur Betts. He was always in the little stone hut he called his office.

'Lost your mates,' he said, eyeing me carefully. I wasn't sure if he thought it was a good thing or a bad thing. But he must have known how quiet it was before, with only Arthur in the camp.

'Yes, it was good having them along. When do you want me to head off dogging?'

He looked at me shrewdly for a moment. 'You don't have to go at all if you don't want to. You can make a start on the saddles right away. I just thought you might like a spell out in the bush on your own.'

'Yes, I'd like that,' I said, trying not to sound too eager. 'I'll pack up later today and head out in the morning.' Then out of devilment I added, 'Do you think I'll see Major? If I do, I may capture him.'

'Major! What makes you talk about Major? You leave Major alone if you see him. He's never hurt anyone bar that stockman who run off with his woman. Now they're hounding him, calling him a murderer and we're going to have those damn troopers about the place for a fortnight.'

'Troopers! What troopers?'

'From the Fitzroy. Be here in two weeks. Going to make Greenvale their base for a week or so while they hunt around for Major. Just come through on the wireless.'

That was nice! I would need to warn Smokey after all. Too late to do anything about it now. They would be well on the way to where they planned to steal the horses. It was two weeks to full moon. They would arrive back on Greenvale territory just in time to run into the patrol.

Next morning I ran three horses up to the yard. I loaded one up with stores, kept one as a spare and rigged my saddle on the other. Then I rode up to the office.

'See you in two months when the tucker cuts out!' and I was off.

I was in no hurry to reach Eagle Peak. I just poked along camping here and there setting my traps during the day and checking them next morning. Dingoes are cunning. Sometimes I would be an hour or more planting one trap. Then next day I would go back and see tracks where a dingo had been trotting along only to veer off right where my trap was hidden. He'd seen something strange or caught my man smell.

It was lonely with only the horses for company. Sometimes I'd wake up at night to the sound of cattle passing and think for a moment it was horsemen. It's never quiet in the bush at night. There's always an old owl flapping past or a dingo howling or a bull calling out for its mate. Or cattle filing by on their way to water. Daytime's the quietest. You could sit on top of a hill and overlook a hundred mile of country and see nothing but maybe a big old eagle circling. And all you would hear was the chirping of a few finches nearby.

It's different in the stockcamp at night. Your mates around and the sounds of the black stockboys corroborring. And somebody waking you up in the middle of the night in time for your two hour stint around the cattle. Then talking with the man on watch for a while till he heads in for a warm by the fire and his swag.

Every night, wherever I camped, I sat around my fire and looked at the moon getting bigger and bigger. Then one night it was full. No-one can ever mistake full moon. Maybe it looks full but then next night, wham! There she is proper. Big and round and glowing full to burst. By this time I was back camped at Eagle Peak.

There had been no sign of any troopers or Major. It seemed like I was the only human on earth. I rode up to the top of the Peak and looked towards the station far out of sight. There was nothing but scrub, a few flat top hills and the gleam of limestone ridges. No tell-tale cloud of dust along the track. If the troopers had arrived they weren't headed this way yet.

I turned around and there was the Rocky Range, a huge wall in front of me. This was no flat-topped range of rock with sides gently sloping down to a base. This was granite. Sheer cliffs and peaks of it, black and brooding. I ran my eyes along, searching for the gully that led a way through and over but could see no sign of it. A green line of timber showed the dry river Smokey would be travelling along.

Time for the signal. Alf would see it at the station. But no matter, there were always fires about. I chose a big clump of spinifex, flicked in a match and watched the orange flames race through it. If Smokey was anywhere near he'd see the smoke.

Next morning I rode back up to the Peak and did the same. I stayed up on the hill most of that day searching for signs of horses coming, either along the river or from Greenvale, but all was still.

That night was the second night after full moon and Smokey was due. I couldn't sleep. I kept my campfire burning and sat around listening and wondering where he was and if he'd seen the signal. Daylight found me on top of the hill again sending up another smoke. I sat there a while with my back against a tree facing the station track and must have fallen asleep because next thing I knew I was being shaken awake and there was Smokey!

'Well Colt,' he grinned, 'What a fine lookout you are! I could have been Major and run you through with a spear. Or a trooper and slipped the manacles on you. What's wrong, why the smoke?'

I felt pretty foolish being caught out like that but I quickly told him about the troopers based at Greenvale and likely to be heading this way at any time.

'Well, we've dodged 'em,' he grinned. 'We were just turning into the gully when we spotted your smoke. We done thirty mile last night. Holed up yesterday and travelled all night. The two Jacks will have 'em well into the Range by now. We picked the mob up earlier than expected. Rode right onto them. Thought I'd better slip across and see what was doing.'

We sat and yarned a while. I wanted to know all about the horses.

'What you going to do with them first, Smokey?'

'Brand 'em. Change the brands. Then we'll draft off the colts and break them in. There's a heap of colts. Then later when the Wet sets in, we'll take 'em down the Fitzroy and sell 'em. We only travel in the Wet. Can't get caught that way. No rain, plenty tracks. Plenty rain, no tracks.'

'What about the tracks you left coming in here last night?'

'I got that covered, Colt. Soon as I leave here the troopers are going to have Major's track to follow. Going the opposite way to us. Only it won't be ol' Major. It'll be one of my munjons.' He waved his hand at the Rocky Range.

'You cover things pretty well, don't you Smokey.'

'Colt, you got to! It's you or them.'

Suddenly I wanted to go off with him. I didn't want to carry on dogging by myself. Or go back to the station working on the saddles for the Wet. There would be nobody around except me and Arthur and the cook. And Alf Moses trying to make a white man out of me. All my people would be off walkabout somewhere, having a good time.

Smokey was standing up, stretching, ready to mount his horse. I looked back across the miles of scrub towards the station and then over at the peaks of the Rocky Range. The gateway to adventure.

'Smokey, I'm coming with you!'

He looked around and the hint of a smile flickered on his face. Then it was gone and he gazed sternly at me a few moments before he answered.

'Don't do that, Colt. You don't know what you're letting yourself in for.'

'Yes I do! And I'm going with you today. Now. I'm not going back to the station. Ever. Not even next year with you, if you go back. I'll find somewhere else to ride. I've had enough of Greenvale.'

'What are you going to do with their horses? You can't take 'em with you.'

'I can take one and send him back later. The others can go bush. They'll get them when they muster next year. I don't want the saddles and packs. I'll ride bareback. Or sit on my swag.'

'Colt that's no way to act. Don't let old Alf Moses down. Go back and do his saddles. Tell him you don't like the dogging if you want, but don't walk out on him. And think about things. I'd like you along but I wouldn't want to start anyone down that track. But you know where to find us. We won't be shifting camp for a while. Don't think being an outlaw's all fun times. It gets mighty lonesome up there in the Underworld and sometimes you don't sleep too well at night, wondering if there's any damn troopers sneaking up on you.

'And you remember this. Once you ride with me, you're branded. For ever. And you can't turn back. Wherever you go, people will look at you and nudge and say, 'He's one of them Underworld horse duffers. An outlaw. Rides with ol' Smokey and them. Don't trust him too far, he'll shake your horse soon as look at you.'

'I never heard anyone say that about you.'

'Colt, you ain't travelled, that's all. You'll hear it all right, from here to Queensland.' Then he added a little bitterly. 'If they kept to the truth it wouldn't matter.'

So I did it. Went back and told Alf I didn't like trapping dingoes and that I wanted to go walkabout a spell but first I would do up his saddles. I counter-lined every saddle on the place in three weeks. It should have taken two months. I toiled at it day and night, I was so eager to get going. Then I told Alf I was ready to head off and asked would he give me a horse of my own. He told me to pick out three and to take a pack saddle and set of bags. And to load up with tucker.

The police had never even turned up. There was a white man murdered at one of the stations over the range and they rode up there instead. All the time I was mustering my horses and packing up I was waiting for Alf Moses to ask me where I intended to go. All sorts of answers were running around in my head. But I needn't have worried. He never asked. The morning I walked up to the office to say goodbye I was so excited I hoped it didn't show.

He looked at me a moment. 'How many horses did Smokey get this time?'

I nearly fell down in shock. My mouth dropped open and I stared at him.

'I saw your smoke — Colt.' He'd never called me that before. 'Wasn't hard to work out why you sent it up. Why do you think I sent you out dogging in the first place? I'm one of Smokey's joeys too!'

I grabbed at his table for support. I couldn't believe what I was hearing.

Then Alf said, 'It's not too bad a thing he's doing. Those Territory stations got too many horses anyway. They could never use 'em. He's only shifting them from one place where they don't need 'em to one where they do.'

He came across the table then and put his hand out.

'Off you go, Colt and good luck. Remember,' and now he smiled, 'there's always a job at Greenvale for you doing up the gear — or mustering.'

I didn't say one word. I was so stunned. I just walked away and climbed on my horse. Alf Moses knew all the time! One of Smokey's lookouts! There was a lot to learn.

I rode straight for the Rocky Range, head whirling.

Next day I was back at Eagle Peak cutting around for Smokey's tracks. They led me across the river and amongst the boulders on the far side bank. Then they turned in towards the cliffs and there was the gully mouth. It was small all right. I would never have believed it led anywhere, but as I reached the end of it I saw the crack in the cliff face. It was narrow with just space for a horse to pass like Smokey said, and took me right into the heart of the range. It was dark and spooky but high above I could see blue sky.

Suddenly I came out into a big open space with high rocky cliffs all about. I was in the centre of the range. The tracks led straight on towards a gap in the distance. I looked back at the slit in the cliff-face. I could turn the horses about, ride through, and go back to Greenvale or on to Halls Creek or Wyndham. Anywhere. I didn't have to become an outlaw. I could go horse-breaking, droving, maybe even take a trip into Queensland.

I sat there for a while thinking about things. I didn't have much to weigh up. I wouldn't be letting anyone down. Alf Moses and Arthur Betts worked in with

Smokey and hadn't tried to stop me. The only one who had tried was Smokey himself and I knew he really wanted me to join him.

I told you I became an outlaw by chance. One chance was meeting up with Smokey. But if someone like Alf Moses had chanced to speak out and tell me I was looking to do a foolish thing I may have listened. Maybe not. Probably not.

I sat there. And all I could think of was the exciting times ahead riding with Smokey. My mount had dropped its head and joined the other two picking at the corn tops of some straggly spinifex. Now it cocked an ear back wondering which way we were going.

'Come on, old horse,' I said suddenly, pulling up the reins. 'Let's get after Smokey's tracks.'

Buchanan School photo of Jack Vitnell (left) at age 10.
With Jim and Mavis Watson.

Sixteen year old Don McLachlan training for a bout at Brisbane Stadium.

A Kimberley "double header" bronco panel.

The Mongrel from Mungindi (Jeff Tribe) on a newly broken colt.

6.

The Underworld Retreat

They're combing the ranges, scrubs and the hills,
Troopers and trackers with keen bushcraft skills,
Searching for Smokey that daredevil thief,
Smokey the Outlaw, cattle duffer in chief,
And all the wild riders who roam the far north,
Are ready to ride as Smokey sets forth,
Eager to plunder big stations of stock,
Just a small token from every large block.

Jack was in the kitchen sipping a pannikin of sweet black tea. It was not yet daylight and Lester was busy pounding away at a batch of bread.

'What made you leave that Kimberley country, Lester, and come over here to die?'

The old man looked up and grinned. 'I left Wyndham to meet a woman. She wrote to me after that book of Miss Foster's come out. Claiming to be my daughter. She wasn't after money or anything, she knew I was just an old pensioner. Just wanted to meet me. After we'd wrote a few times I agreed to take the boat up to Darwin where she was living. She was a fine looking woman about fifty, a coloured woman of course, but a good deal lighter than me. Anyway from things she told me I could see she wasn't my daughter and I was all set to head back to Wyndham when I run into Phil Hanlon. When I found out he was the owner of Seven Emu, I asked him could I pay the place a visit. I'd known this place years before when me an' Smokey delivered a mob of cattle here. I been here ever since.'

'I thought all those Kimberley cattle went into Wyndham for killing those days, Lester.'

'Most of them did but Alf Moses, the owner of Greenvale, where me an' Smokey worked most seasons, had a brother Amos who had this Seven Emu station. Amos wrote a letter to Alf asking if he had any cattle that wasn't fat enough to go into the works at Wyndham. If he had some, Amos said, why not send 'em across and he would fatten 'em. Then when Amos sold 'em, he and Alf would go halves.

'So we mustered up a good mob of stags, shelly old pikers, anything at all we thought would make the journey. Nine hundred in all. Smokey knew all that country so Alf put him in charge and seven of us took 'em across. We picked up a few on the way too. Delivered a thousand and seventy! That Smokey! He never could resist a cleanskin.'

'Reckon you blokes picked up more than cleanskins,' Jack grinned.

'Come to think of it, Jack,' the old half-caste chuckled, 'we did run across a few bullocks some other drover had lost one time.'

'What else brought you back to Seven Emu, Lester?'

'What you mean, Jack?'

'Well, you could have had a yarn to Phil in Darwin about the place and gone back home to Wyndham. You didn't have to come all the way to Seven Emu. You got family this way, Lester?'

The old man looked at him strangely. 'How you figure that out Jack, or has someone been talking?'

'No-one's told me anything, old timer. Just a thought I had. You don't have to tell me. No business of mine.'

'I have got relations here, Jack. Some I never knew about till I came back. They not here now. Out walkin' about. You'll meet them after the Wet I reckon. You want to hear the rest of that story of when I joined Smokey? Lester launched into his next story ...

Everything looked different to Greenvale now I was the other side of the Rocky. Strange looking palms grew amongst the trees and littered the ground with piles of dead fronds that crackled under the horses feet. Spear grass grew in huge clumps and hid a mess of small orange boulders. It was a rough ride. My mount slid from rock to rock. A dangerous place to gallop. Smokey would need to be on better country than this to hold stock.

By mid afternoon I was riding down a slope towards a line of green timber to the river Smokey had told me about. Then the tracks cut out. There had been a storm since he had come along.

'*Don't cross that river*!' Smokey had said.

'Someone will come and get you — a munjon bush black, one of mine.'

The munjons were the natives who refused to come into the stations and work for the whites. They still lived in the bush the old free way and were the only people, apart from the outlaws, who inhabited the Underworld. The country was too isolated and poorly grassed to attract settlers.

It was a dry river with big drifts of grey sand and bars of dark rock. I rode along to a small rock-hole and watered my three horses. It was black water stained from the leaves of huge overhanging figs. I looked across at the forbidden far side — a tangle of trees and scrub.

All was silent. Creepy silent. With not even the call or sight of a bird.

In my mind I could see black faces hiding, with ochre painted bodies, spears ready, should I cross.

'If you're ever up amongst them, don't let them into your camp! They'll pretend to be friends then stick you with a spear and feast on your kidney fat!'

That's how everyone spoke of the munjons. I hadn't thought to bring a rifle. Back on Greenvale it had all seemed so simple. One of the munjons who worked in with Smokey would be waiting to guide me on to his hideout. But I didn't realise it was going to be such an eerie place.

I rode back up the bank to a clearing amongst the trees and pulled off the saddles and packs. Then I saw the remains of a fire. Smokey and the two Jacks had camped here. It was late afternoon now and as I was on good grass I hobbled and belled the horses and let them feed about. Next I pulled a billy out of the packs and headed back down the creek. Then I saw something that got my heart skipping. This morning's boot tracks in the sand leading down from the far bank.

Bush blacks didn't wear boots. Someone else was here. Who? Was it someone waiting for me? Smokey? One of the Jacks? It could be. But unlikely. They should be miles away, up at the hide-out with the stolen horses. I puzzled over it as I climbed back up the bank and started a fire.

When it was blazing I poured flour and water into a tin dish and mixed up a johnny-cake. Then I raked out some coals and threw on the johnny-cake and a few slices of cooked salt beef.

All the while I ate I kept thinking about the boot tracks and what to do if no-one came for me in a day or two. Maybe I would need to press on and cross the river after all. There would be no tracks to follow but that didn't matter. This time of year the storms were patchy and only extended a few miles. I would soon cut Smokey's tracks again. But the thought of going on alone scared me somewhat.

The sun was nearly gone so I hunted around for more firewood. I walked across to an old dead tree and broke off a large branch, carried it to the fire, then turned back for more. But someone was standing between me and the dead tree — a black, wearing only a pair of trousers. He was holding a scrub turkey in one hand and now he raised it up in a kind of peace gesture and walked towards me. I was nervous but not frightened.

Soon as he got close, I saw he was barefoot. So he was another one walking around! But he didn't seem to be a bush black. He wore no paint and carried no weapons. He looked more like a stockman who had shed his clothes to go walkabout.

He smiled, and I saw a bright pink tongue and white teeth.

'What you doing riding about my country? Where you come from?' he asked.

If he was the guide Smokey said would take me on to the hideout he would know who I was. And whoever he was, this fellow had spent a lot of time with the whites. He spoke English too well to be one of the munjons.

I pointed a good way west of where Greenvale was located and said, 'There. Over the range,' and named a station I had heard spoken about many times. 'Mount Hart. We finished stock work, I'm just riding about a spell looking at new country.'

I wasn't about to tell him I had come through the secret gap of the Rocky Range. Not without knowing for sure who he was. If he was a local black he would know it anyway.

He watched me closely as I spoke and said, 'You got white father, hey? What name they give you, boy?'

He could see I was only half black. To him I would be more white than black for my father had been white. My mother was nothing, it was my father who counted.

'Everybody call me Colt. What name you? This your country?'

'My country, all right,' he answered but looking away and not meeting my eyes. 'Yenga my name.'

Suddenly he held out the turkey.

'You can cook him?'

'I can cook him all right! And I don't need cudea camp-oven!'

Cudea was the Kimberley name for a white man. I picked up a few small round rocks and placed them in the fire. While they were heating I made the oven, a sheet of paperbark for the lid and a hole in the sandy ground for the base.

Yenga burnt the feathers off, roughly plucked it and handed it over. I took my knife, sliced it open and placed the entrails on a small piece of the bark. We'd roast a few pieces while waiting for it to cook. Then I tossed a shovelful of coals down the hole. Every bagman carries a damper shovel.

Yenga placed the turkey on top of the coals and I juggled one of the hot stones between two sticks, carried it across to the hole and poked it inside the turkey.

Then I saw a bullet hole. The bird had been shot. So Yenga had a rifle. Was he also the owner of the boots? It looked that way. I placed the rest of the hot stones on top of the turkey and covered the hole with the sheet of bark. Yenga spread sand around the edges to keep in the heat.

'Many turkey around here?' I asked.

'Plenty. Runnin' everywhere!'

'How you kill 'em?'

'Stick. You can sneak up easy and throw a stick.'

So! He was up to something alright, this Yenga. I would need to watch out. He didn't want me to know he had a rifle.

Time for me to ask a few questions.

'Why you walking about yourself? Where your camp?'

'My mob all back there.' He waved a hand towards the other side of the river. 'I just been walkabout today and going back when I see you. Maybe I camp here tonight, talk with you.'

Just looking about? Someone had seen me coming and sent Yenga to sound me out. Cattle duffers? Was there another gang up here? Bound to be but somehow I didn't think that was it. Yenga's eyes were everywhere. Now he was over by my saddles inspecting them.

'You got good saddle here, boy,' he called. 'Who belong this brand?'

All saddles are stamped with the station brand. When I left Greenvale Alf Moses had given me saddle gear as well as horses instead of wages. But I had nothing to say they were mine. No Bill of Sale. The Greenvale brand was AM7. And that was on the saddles. I didn't know Mount Hart's brand but I was stuck with the lie.

'Mount Hart. They don't belong to me. They just lend them for my walkabout.'

'Ah,' he said knowingly. 'Just for lend. He lend you horse too?'

So he had checked my horses. He had been busy.

Did he think I was a policeman? Hardly. Troopers didn't travel alone.

'How come you speak the cudea language so good, Yenga? You work for them one time?'

'I worked for them. Lot of places but always come back here. Blackfella got to speak English. Too many different language. He can't understand them all. But everyone know the cudea language.'

'How many tribes living up here?'

'Four today. Two gone Mission. Cudea bugger everything now. Soon everybody on mission or station. Not me. Me stopping here meself.'

Meself! So he was on his own. That much had slipped out. He belonged to no tribe around here. A sudden thought struck me. Was he Major? The renegade black wanted for murdering a white stockman? That would explain why he checked me out. But I wasn't scared. Alf Moses had told me Major had good reason to kill the stockman. He had taken Major's woman.

White men taking black women happened all the time. Mostly the people just put up with it. The whites owned the land. The only land the people could roam now was no good cattle country. Like this up here.

It was time to take out the turkey. It didn't last long. I hadn't eaten fresh meat since leaving Greenvale a week ago and I reckon Yenga had been missing out too. There's nothing like bush tucker cooked blackfellow style. The sun was well gone by now and we were squatted by the fire.

'I'll tell him about the boot tracks down the river bed,' I thought, 'and see what he has to say.'

'Boot tracks? Ah! You good tracker, hey! Might be they belong to that Major, he around here somewhere and wear boots. You hear about him?'

He was Major, all right! Playing games with me.

'We heard he murdered a white man and the police are after him. But my boss knows him and says he's okay. You know him too?'

Yenga smiled. 'I know he in big trouble. No good killing cudea over woman. Cudea been taking black woman since they come into the country. Nobody going to stop it. More better get another woman or steal her back. No good get rifle! You know what best?' And here Yenga laughed. 'Lend her! That way you keep the woman, get good job from boss and smoke plenty tobacco!'

'You think policeman catch him, Yenga?'

That made him laugh again. 'Sure of it!'

But then he looked serious. 'He not like most blackfella. That Major never give in to cudea. He hate them for take his country. He stopped bush long time until all his people went in. Then he follow to station and ask for job. That white man, the one he shot, was pleased. Now all the bush blacks had come in to the station and there would be no more cattle spearing.

'Major's wife came in with him. Proper smart looking woman. The cudea give her job in the kitchen. One day he said to Major, 'You got to give me that girl.'

He thought Major was just a simple bush black.

'What girl?'

'That girl you got.'

'That Lucy! She my wife! What you talking about? Get your own woman!'

'Just for lend then,' says that cudea. 'We proper good mates, you and me. I'll give you plenty tobacco.'

'I got plenty tobacco now,' Major tell him. 'From work for you. You my boss, not mate.'

'But that man never give up. He wanted Major's wife bad. He offer him good clothes, not the rubbish stuff they give the people.'

'I don't want that white man clothes,' Major tell him. 'I live before you in this country. Long time before. We got no clothes then. And no flour. But still we live good life in bush.'

'That made that cudea proper cranky.

'Me boss, you know. This all my land all my bullock. Everything belongs to me now. You mine too. And the girl. You got to do what I say or policeman take you away.'

'This not your land,' Major tell him. 'This land belong my people before you ever come here! You on our land!'

'Then that white man went to house and got rifle.'

'I boss, don't worry. I can shoot you now and policeman won't say anything. He know I'm boss.'

'So Major walked off to blacks' camp and the white man took Lucy into the house and kept her there all day. That night he sent her back down the camp with two stick of tobacco. That happened for two week. Major never chew that tobacco. Nobody did. Major throw it in the fire. And all the time did his work like everything all right. Then one day Lucy tell that white boss, 'Major say I can stop tonight.'

'That the night he shoot him. Before bed Lucy take rifle and leave it outside. Middle of the night Major come up from camp and take it. Then he sit down longside tree and wait. Daylight out come that man to make combo. While he standing there Major shoot him. Then he get that girl and go.

'The people all frightened now and one of them go for policeman, Turkey Creek. When that policeman get back all the people gone bush. They never wait around. Too frightened. Policeman follow that Major track but never catch him.'

'Where that girl now, Yenga? He still got her bush with him?' I nearly said, Have you got her with you?

'He got her planted up here somewhere. Woman can't travel fast like man. She stopping with bush mob. He go see her sometimes. Anyway, boy, sleep time now. Maybe you see Major one day soon.'

If he wasn't Major he knew all about him. I'd see what happened tomorrow. I unrolled my swag close to the fire and lay on top. It was a warm night. Yenga still sat cross-legged by the fire.

'You got blanket?' I asked.

'I got fire. All I want.'

I watched him until I dozed off. The fire woke me around midnight, crackling and hissing. Yenga was throwing on more timber. A cool wind blew now and he huddled close to the fire gazing into the flames.

'You want blanket now?' I called.

If he heard, he gave no sign, so intent was he on the fire. The flames reflected redly on his body. Then I saw his lips were moving. He was talking to his father or his father's father or that one's father. I lay and watched him till I fell asleep again. Then grey dawn was creeping and in the distance the horse bells tingled. Yenga was nowhere to be seen. I pulled on my boots and spurs and strode off to fetch the horses.

As I ran them back to camp I saw a black stockman standing by the fire watching. Where did he spring from? Then as I got closer I saw it was Yenga.

'So! You got clothes! And boots,' I said pointedly.

He grinned. 'Down the creek. Hid them there yesterday. Wasn't sure who you were when you rode up.'

Now I was certain he was Major. But I would prove it before admitting I was waiting to join Smokey and the other outlaws. I would show him the Boulia spurs Smokey had given me. The ones he had got from Major for tobacco. I unstrapped them and held them out.

'What you think of these?' I grinned.

Yenga turned them over in his hands, spun the rowels and handed them back.

'They look okay. Never see that kind before. Where you get 'em?'

He wasn't playing games. He hadn't seen them before. So he wasn't Major.

'Who are you?' I suddenly asked.

He laughed. 'You find out directly. Come on, you and me get horse saddled. We take little ride.'

'Maybe I want to stop here!'

Yenga sighed. 'Boy, you gotta come,' and he flicked his eyes across to my gear. There was a Schneider rifle leaning against my pack bags. 'Don't worry, boy. It's empty,' and he rattled some bullets in his shirt pocket. 'No-one going to hurt you but you got to come see someone. Maybe you just looking around the country, maybe you not. Maybe they your horse, maybe you steal 'em. My boss will know. Come on, we go now.'

I had a spare horse but only one bridle. Yenga walked behind with the rifle. We crossed the river and rode for about two mile and then I saw a low hill. Soon we came up with a plant of horses feeding about, but too far off to read the brands. Then we were climbing the hill and ahead was a camp. A white man was standing watching us approach.

I swung round to Yenga. 'Hey! Man up there look like policeman. We better get out of here!'

Yenga smiled. 'It's okay, boy. Keep going. Soon you going to meet my boss!'

I gazed stupidly at him for a moment. Then it dawned on me. Yenga was a tracker, sent to check the stranger out. Then I got a second shock. As we got close I could see a black man standing chained to a tree. He wasn't a myall, I could tell straight off by his clothes that he was a stockman.

'You want to see Major, boy? There he is now,' Yenga called cheerily, pointing to the tree.

'Maybe you be joining him on the chain into Derby if my boss don't like what you tell him.'

But it wasn't Major. I had never seen Major but I knew it wasn't him. The black chained up to the tree was the man I had come to join. Smokey. Smokey the outlaw!

I wasn't sure what to do. I wanted to call out.

'That's not Major! You got the wrong man!'

But I knew if there was one person the police wanted more than Major it was Smokey. But Smokey showed me what to do. Soon as he saw it was me the tracker had hold of, he looked away. So I did the same and rode on up to the trooper. He was a young fella and didn't know much about the bush. You can always tell.

He questioned me about my saddles and horses, looked at the brands, talked to the trackers, then wrote everything down in his book.

He didn't know Mount Hart any more than I did. If he'd had come from Derby, they wouldn't have missed it by far. I was lucky he hadn't called in. So I just stuck to my story of coming from Mount Hart and having a lend of their horses to take walkabout. Finally he believed me — almost.

'Which way you heading now?'

'Nowhere much. Maybe up there,' and I pointed north.

'No,' he said. 'I don't think that's a good idea. I think you been far enough. Better you come back with us. Then,' he added with a smirk, 'I can have a look at this Mount Hart too. And you can take us in and let me meet your boss.'

Well, that was good. Tagging along would give me a chance to get Smokey loose. We travelled about ten mile that day. It was a small patrol. The trooper and two trackers. The other tracker wouldn't look at me so I never did learn his name. He took the lead, then I followed, hunting along the spare horses, and whistling, to show I was quite happy to be going home.

Behind me rode the trooper and Yenga with Smokey striding along between. He was padlocked to the centre of a long length of chain. One end was fixed to a steel dee ring on the trooper's saddle, the other to Yenga's.

It's awful to see a man in chains, wearing an iron band around his neck. To be put in chains is the most degrading thing. It turns him into a dog. When you walk in an iron collar it cuts your neck unless you glide along in a peculiar gait that keeps the collar from rubbing up and down and chafing. The people call it 'turkey trotting'.

'Look out that policeman don't get you! He'll make you turkey trot!'

It was hard for me to see Smokey in chains and not able to do anything. But any time that day I glanced at him, he was striding along, head up, grinning. The way he always walked. That collar must have been cutting his throat like a knife. No way Smokey would turkey trot!

From what I could make out, we were heading for Mount Hart then Derby. That would take about four weeks. Plenty of time to free Smokey. And that's all I thought of that day. How to go about it.

My first plan was to simply grab the trooper's rifle from his saddle scabbard when we pulled up and force him to unlock the padlock that fastened the two halves of the iron collar together.

But what if he refused? Would I shoot? I knew the old saying never pick up a rifle unless you are prepared to use it. And I knew I wouldn't pull the trigger. That meant we'd both finish up on the chain.

Somehow I would need to get that key. The trooper kept it in a pouch on his belt, together with a set of handcuffs, knife and pocket watch. The belt would be placed with his clothes, close to his swag, when he rolled in for the night. It shouldn't be too hard to sneak up and grab when he was asleep.

Soon as we camped that afternoon, the trooper and Yenga walked Smokey across to a big ironwood. They looped the chain around the tree and fastened it with another padlock. He had about ten foot of loose chain to move around on. Of course I was busting to talk to him and find out how the patrol had captured him and why they had mistaken him for Major. But that would have to wait.

We took the horses, the two trackers and me, nearly a mile from camp to a good patch of feed. When man camps he wants to be close to water. But that location mightn't be a good place for his horses. Horses need to be on good grass at night so they can fill up quick and hold their condition. They do plenty of work during the day, carrying men and packs. It's not good to let them loose in camp forcing them to shuffle off in hobbles looking for grass.

As soon as we got away from the camp, Yenga sidled alongside trying to make friends. But I wouldn't have it. We didn't mind white policemen chasing after cattle spearers and murderers, that was their job. But we had no time for the black trackers who hunted down their own people. Mick, the Oobamurra tracker who had shot dead the black outlaw Pigeon a few years before, belonged to the same tribe as Pigeon.

The people knew why they acted that way. The police uniform and rifle took them into a different world. They were no longer ignorant savages living in the bush or slaves working for the whites for their tucker. Now they were 'all the same white man'. Respected. By white and black. The troopers were nothing without their trackers, unable to find their way back to town let alone track down a cattle spearer.

But we knew the police did not respect them as people. Only as trackers. They were able to follow footprints at the gallop a white man could not even see. We all could. We learnt that from kid time. But that didn't make the trackers into white men, except in their own minds.

Smokey told me one time it wasn't their fault. They didn't know any better. And they weren't much different to a lot of whites.

Once people start getting ahead, Smokey said, they want to forget about a lot of things. They look back where they come from, and all the people still there, and hate 'em. They hate 'em, Smokey said, because really they envy them. Because those people don't have to try and be anything more than they really are.

I didn't understand all that. I wasn't educated like Smokey and had never been off Greenvale before. And I never saw good in people all the time like he did. But I understood what it was like to be reared in a blacks' camp. What you learn there is how to survive. Eyes for eyes. There's no place for all that, 'not doing it to him even though he done it to me', business. Specially when you're battling to fill your belly each day. And keeping one jump ahead of someone trying to pinch your share.

Alf Moses had taught me about acting decent when he pulled me out of the blacks' camp. He read me the Ten Temptations of Man and the Forgiveness Story. And said it was good reading and I should know about it and take notice. But we didn't need to take too much notice of it up North. There was only two of those Temptations we really had to stick by. Not to kill anyone and not to take another man's swag. The others, Alf explained, were only put in for people living down South. That's where the temptations mostly were.

Anyway, that night when everyone was rolled up asleep, I slid out of my swag and sneaked over to Smokey's tree. We were far enough away not to be overheard if we talked softly.

'Good work, Colt,' he whispered as I grabbed his hand. 'You came along at the right time.'

'How come they caught you, Smokey,' I started to say but he cut me short.

'Not now, Colt. Later. First up let's get out of here. You carrying a pair of pincers in your packs?'

'Of course!' Everyone carried a set of shoeing gear. A horse could go lame in no time if it threw a shoe on stony ground.

'Good! That's all I need to get out of this necklace.'

'But you can't cut through chain with pincers unless you make a heap of noise!'

I saw him smile in the darkness. 'No-one's cutting through the chain, Colt. I'm going in this way,' and he pointed to the heavy iron padlock.

I looked at the hole where the key slid in. 'Pincers aren't going to fit in there!'

'Of course they're not. But they'll fit down here.' And he placed a finger where the iron clasp snapped home. 'These things are only good for holding poor naked myalls. One good tap in the right place and they fly open. I nearly did it with the tongue of my belt buckle. So fetch them pincers up tomorrow night and Colt, hobble our horses short so we can find 'em quick. I don't want to chase after 'em all night. I'm a mite tired of all this walking.'

Next evening when we camped, I made sure I was late taking my horses out to hobble. I picked up each of their feet and cleaned out imaginary stones with my pocket knife until I saw Yenga and his mate coming back from hobbling theirs. I didn't want them to see I was short hobbling — by-passing the chain and fastening the two greenhide straps together so the horse could only take very short steps. People only did that when they wanted an early start the next day.

I knew Smokey's horse. It was the same he'd been riding that time at Greenvale when we met up on Eagle Peak. The day I decided to throw in with him. It was nearly dark by the time I finished with the horses and as I got back near the camp I could see the others standing out from the glare of the fire looking for me. They still weren't sure whether I'd try and clear out. When they saw me they turned back to the fire and busied around getting their supper. That made it easy for me to sneak over to my pack bags, grab the pincers and shove them in my swag.

I was itching to get started and hoped everyone would soon turn in. But dang me if that trooper didn't want to talk. And about Mount Hart. So I told him everything he wanted to know. About how many worked there, what the boss was like, how many horses they had, how many whites, the yards, whatever he wanted to know. Except all the time I was describing Greenvale. I don't know if he ever got to Mount Hart, but I did a couple of years later. Me an' Smokey sold some horses there. And it was nothing like Greenvale.

Anyway, eventually he was ready to turn in and it was better that way, because being late, he was soon asleep. The two trackers had been snoring for an hour. I counted up to fifty — which was far as I could get without a good deal of bother — and then I counted it again. Twice. By that time the trooper was snoring too so I slid out of my blankets and over to Smokey.

He shoved one end of the pincers down through the top of the padlock and cracked the other end hard against the tree. Clunk! The lock sprung open.

I had our bridles and we walked to where the horses were feeding, unhobbled our mounts and jumped on. All set to scarper. But Smokey wouldn't leave without our saddles! So back we rode to camp and I had to slip off and sneak in for 'em. And dang me if I didn't wake that Yenga. I was stepping carefully past his swag when two of the stirrups clanged. He sat up, looked straight at me, and lay back and rolled over! I couldn't believe it. He must have been asleep with his eyes open.

We saddled up and I was in a stew to bolt but still Smokey wouldn't leave! He wanted to set all the horses loose. So around we went, in the darkness, and unhobbled each one. We were riding away when I spotted one still hobbled.

'Hey, Smokey,' I called in a low voice. 'We missed that bay. He still got hobbles.'

'Oh, we don't want to be too hard on 'em,' he called back. 'Got to leave 'em one to muster up the others in the morning. It's a long walk into Derby!'

He was always like that, old Smoke. That's why he had so many friends I reckon. Long as he slowed 'em up and gave us time to get well away he was satisfied.

We were five days travelling to the valley where Smokey had his hideout — The Retreat, as it was called by every outlaw in the Underworld. And of course we had plenty of time to talk. First up I wanted to know how he'd got himself mistaken for Major.

'You hear about that white man got speared, Colt? On one of those stations over the range? Well, this patrol come looking for the black that done that. But they blundered on me instead. Close to the river crossing where I told you to wait. I knew you'd follow and headed back to look for you. I was off my horse tacking a shoe back on when they suddenly rode up.'

'But you don't look like a bush black. How they think you were the murderer?'

'Them trackers told the trooper I was Major. They knew I wasn't Major. Me and that Yenga knocked about one time!'

I was stunned. 'Why they do that?'

Smokey laughed. 'Frightened of this Underworld country, that's why. Too many devils. They wanted to go back to Derby. That trooper told 'em he was stopping bush all year till he got the murderer or Major.'

'But that wasn't fair, Smokey. What about you? You could have finished up in jail for ten years.'

He laughed again. 'No, they were going to let me get away. We were talking about how to do it when you come along.'

'But that trooper would have made them follow you again!'

Smokey smiled. 'That's right. And my tracks would have been heading back towards Derby. Colt, that trooper couldn't track a camel through soft sand. They can tell him anything, those trackers, if they want.'

Suddenly he gave a great bellow of laughter. 'That's where our tracks are heading now, Colt. You and me. Straight for Derby. Then they'll lose them. Just out of town!'

Something still puzzled me. 'What's in it for those trackers, Smokey? Why would they do that for you?'

He looked at me pityingly. 'Colt, you're not learning! Didn't I tell you before? You gotta have contacts in this business! Every time I sell a mob of horses down the Fitzroy I leave a few pound notes in a tin with the people. They can't use paper money so it's quite safe. Next visit through, those trackers pick it up. Yenga and his tracker mate chew the best pipe tobacco you can buy in Derby.'

So! Yenga had seen me that night the stirrup irons had clanged. No doubt about this Smokey. He knew how to survive.

We passed heaps of bush blacks on our way and one night camped with a big mob by a waterhole. I could see Smokey was no stranger. They treated him like a brother. Or a rich uncle! They were disappointed he had nothing for them but all we had escaped with were our saddles. I looked at their glistening, naked, painted bodies and iron-tipped, shovel-nosed spears as they corroboreed, glad I was not passing through as a stranger.

I hadn't seen anything but flat sandy country since leaving the patrol, but on the fifth morning we turned east towards some ranges. Soon we left the palms and speargrass and rode amongst a maze of rocky ridges. This was more like it. This was the sort of country I had expected the hideout to be in. The hills got steeper and rougher and by late afternoon we were forced to follow a dry sandy river bed. High cliffs of grey, orange mottled limestone ran along either side. This river cut right through the range.

'You see the hideout?' Smokey suddenly asked.

There was nothing ahead but the bed of the river and the walls of rock either side.

'Which way?'

Smokey laughed. 'Next bend.'

The river suddenly curved sharply and the cliffs fell away. It was the entrance to the outlaws' retreat — a secluded valley in the ranges.

As soon as we passed through the gap there was a loud whoop and a figure came scrambling down one of the steep bluffs and trotted after us.

'My brother,' Smokey said.

He soon caught us, a fine framed black clad only in a hat and pair of moleskins. In one hand he carried a rifle. The other held a long stone-tipped spear.

Smokey chuckled. 'Ready for anything, my brother. He can be stockman or myall. Whatever the business at hand calls for!'

He and Smokey started yabbering away in a lingo I couldn't understand. Then Smokey turned to me.

'He know you. Saw you two months ago when you were camped out dogging at Greenvale.'

The stranger gave a big grin.

'Why you never show yourself?' I asked.

He looked at me a little sheepishly. 'I was keep to the stone. Didn't want to leave track for troopers.'

'Oh!' I said, not knowing what else to say.

'Blackfellow call him Walpamur,' Smokey said. He was trying not to laugh. His black eyes were dancing.

'Good-day, Walpamur,' I smiled, wondering what the joke was. 'And what do the cudea call you?'

'Major.'

'Major!' I repeated, gaping. I turned to Smokey.

'Is this Major? Your brother?'

Now he did laugh. 'You meet him at last, Colt! You'll be seeing plenty of Major, he spends a lot of time with us. Right now he's on watch.'

'For police?'

'No, Colt. We don't bother watch for them. They never come this far. He's up on that hill watching for a smoke from the munjons. If they see strangers they let us know. Then we go look. And sometimes we talk.'

'What do you tell them, Smokey?'

He looked at me and his eyes narrowed a little. 'Colt, that depends on the strangers!' Then he smiled.

'Come on, let's get along to the hut. The two Jacks will be anxious to show you around and get you started on your first drawing lesson.'

'Drawing lesson?'

He chuckled. It was easy to see he was pleased I had come along.

'Yep, drawing. Things like letters and numbers.'

I still looked puzzled. Then it dawned on me.

'You mean with a piece of red hot wire? On hide?'

'Colt, for a moment you had me worried. I thought I'd picked up with one of them sleepy Fitzroy drovers. Your education's about to start, Colt. Soon you going to be so neat with a poddy dodger's running iron you're going to use one to write your name!'

7.

The Underworld Dogger

The first one speared is lost in sand,
The last we know full well,
He was trapping dogs in the Underworld,
When he made his sad farewell,
There's Kimberley East and Kimberley West,
And never a line to show,
But the north was called the Underworld,
Where the poddy dodgers go.

The first rain had come and the heat was stifling. Huge masses of white clouds boiled up in the northern sky each morning. By late afternoon they were grey and shot with lightning streaks. By dark the wind was up. Some nights it rained, thundering down on the iron station roofs. Other nights lightning streaks tore the sky and only thunder boomed.

'Early storm time, Jack,' Lester stated one morning. 'Green pick about soon. You blokes will be off then, ripping in to those big cleanskins.'

'Most places don't work that way, Lester, they let the horses go this time of the year and pay their men off.'

'Big stations with plenty men and cattle do that. They can afford to leave cleanskins running about. We can't. This country ain't flash for cattle. And we ain't flash for men and horses, neither. We muster all season but we don't push it.

Why rip the guts out of your horse plant galloping after the mongrels when you can pick 'em up easy early storm time? That way you make the cattle come to you. Just follow the storms a few days after rain and there's your cleanskins. Feeding on the green pick!'

Jack was tired of hearing about cattle. He decided on a diversion.

'Many other white blokes living up in that Kimberley Underworld country when you were there with Smokey, Lester?'

'Not many. It was too far out for most. Lot of blokes passed through and some of them hid out with stolen horses for a time but mostly it was empty. Except for us and Bob Anderson. Bob lived there a good while dogging.'

'Trapping?'

'And poison. Poisoning's easier but unless you got a carcass to hold them, you lose a lot of dogs wandering off in the scrub. Dog don't leave much of a track except in sand. Trapping takes time but you get the scalps that way. Anyway there's a story about old Bob. He became quite famous for a time.'

It was a while yet to sunrise. They took their pannikins of tea and sat at the long bush-timber table under the bough shed. When Lester told a tale he acted it out. He became a one man play. When Bob Anderson was talking, Jack felt he was at the table with them. When the Walmajari woman spoke, Jack could hear her nasal musical voice. He saw the lily pool and the three munjon blacks and he rode one of the getaway horses ...

'That's quite a story, Lester. Here's Phil and them now, I'll hear anymore later.'

It was hot that night and Jack rolled his swag out on the table under the bough shed to catch any breeze. A mosquito net hung from the rafters and draped over him. He went to sleep thinking of the rest of Lester's story about Bob Anderson and the Walmajari woman ...

The Walmajari woman, Susie, was hungry. There was plenty to eat now she was with the cudea, Anderson. Bread and beef and sweet tea anytime. But today she needed bush tucker. And there was plenty at this billabong, especially her favourite, lily roots.

She walked to where Anderson was busy with a bridle.

'I kin stitch him.'

He looked up, grinning.

'Knife more better.'

'How you put 'em buckle back got no stitchin'?'

He held up the broken rein and showed where he had cut three narrow slits a few inches back from one end. Then he twisted the leather and made three loops.

He placed the ring of the bit over the loops, slipped the other end of the rein through the loops and pulled tight.

'Woday! You bin fix 'em!'

She never ceased to be surprised at these cudea. They could do anything. But they could not live in the bush without their rifle, horse and tucker packs. And they couldn't track goannas. Even aboriginal children could track a goanna.

'Me hungry for lily root. I can get 'em?'

Susie never did anything without asking Anderson.

'You can go. But you watch out for munjon. Plenty round this country and they kill you quick. They got plenty big spear.'

'Okay. Me go little bit, not long way.'

She pulled off her dress and walked through the tall cane grass to the water. It was a large billabong surrounded by paperbark trees, pandanus palms and the other strange palms that grew everywhere in this country. She waded out towards some lilies and was soon in deep water. It was black and cold under the surface and while there were no crocodiles this far from the coast, she was nervous in this strange country and quickly swam back to the reeds.

Further across the water she could see lilies close to the bank. She waded back to firm ground and walked around the billabong towards them. Then she saw a woman half hidden amongst the cane grass. She was kneeling with her head bowed rocking from side to side. Susie had never seen anyone as black. The woman was a young woman about Susie's own age, naked except for a little woven reed narga.

As she walked closer she heard a soft wailing — a song of grief. Then the woman saw her. Susie smiled. The woman jumped to her feet, eyes wide with fright. Susie kept smiling. Soon a smile spread across the black face in front of her.

'Who are you?' the woman asked.

Susie did not understand what was said but pointed to herself saying, 'Me Walmajari. Susie. You savvy Hinglish?'

'Little bit, me Julnajulna.'

The strange sounding name made Susie giggle. That started Julnajulna giggling and soon they were laughing and chatting away in a mixture of English, sign language and their own tongues.

Julnajulna had run away that morning from her husband. He was 'Proper cruel fella. Bin belt me all the time for nothing.' She was not going back, because now he would kill her.

'I got 'em white man,' Susie said proudly. 'A cudea. Proper good man. You can come with us. We got everything, horse, tucker, rifle and plenty tobacco. But he never talk. Proper quiet man. I need 'em mate. Come on, we go now.'

Julnajulna was tempted but frightened. She had never spoken to a cudea. She had seen them once, up at the Mission at Kulumbaru and was very much frightened.

'They can't hurt you,' the Mission people had told her. 'They all the same blackfellow. Make 'em combo, cokka, eat 'em tucker. Like 'em girl too, some of them.'

'Might be he don't want me.'

Susie looked at the girl's slim body and small pointy breasts.

'He want you all right,' she said simply. 'Come on, you my sister now. He can have two wife. I heart-sick for mate.'

Bob Anderson was stunned to see the two women approaching. Susie with the brown skin and fair hair of the desert people and the tall glistening body of the other that stamped her as a coastal black.

'She bin runaway. They going to kill her. She kin come with us?'

Bob cursed. How could Susie be so stupid?

'No. Course not. She belong to someone. The munjon tribe who live around here. We can't take their woman. They kill us. They wild man, not like us.' He swung on the woman. 'What for you come here? Go! Go now! You savvy English!'

Julnajulna cringed at the words and turned away but Susie grabbed her arm.

'No! She can stop!'

She looked at Bob.

'You like her? She pretty. You can have her, I don't care. I starving for company Bob Anderson, I can't stop with you meself any more. I need 'em mate.'

Bob looked at her in surprise. She had never spoken out before in their six years together. It had been a lonely life following him around. Always on their own except the few times a year they rode into Karungie to cash their dingo scalps and fill up the tucker packs. Then he scarcely saw her. She spent all day with the people down at the blacks' camp while he yarned with any white men who happened to be on the station at the time.

He didn't want to lose her. It had taken long enough to find a woman to share his solitary life. No white woman would. Not that there were any in the country to choose from. Before he had taken Susie he had known a great feeling of aloneness. It was only last year he realised it was gone. He knew nothing of love and had taken the woman because she was available.

'A bit like this Julnajulna,' he thought. 'A runaway from a wife basher.'

He was still looking at Susie, staring defiantly at him. Then he turned to the other girl. She was pretty all right. Taller than Susie, with long, lithe legs. Two wives! That was something to think about. Six years was a long time with the one woman.

'All right,' he said suddenly, 'You want her, we take her. But we making big mistake. You want a mate, you got one, I don't need another wife. But I'll have her. Get the horses. Get 'em and pack up. We gotta get out of here quick.'

Bob fought down a sudden fear. He had lived in this desolate North Kimberley Underworld country since running off with Susie and only survived by leaving the munjons alone. He had met up and spoken with them often. Given them tobacco sometimes, occasionally flour. He had never camped with them nor let them get too familiar. Susie would never look at them and kept close, eyes to the ground until they were gone.

He admired them, the way they lived in the old way off the land. But he also knew they were tigers, hard and ruthless. There was nothing soft or loving in their lives. It was all harsh reality. Find food or starve. Kill your enemy before he killed you. An outcast cudea wandering their country poisoning dingoes was of no interest to them. Even one with a black woman — as long as he let them be.

But now he had broken the rules, they must leave. Ride for their lives. These munjon wild men would not let one of their women go easily. They would follow to the boundary of their country to get her back. And he would be blamed for stealing her away. For that they would kill him, he was quite sure, if they caught him.

It was late afternoon when Susie brought the munjon woman back to camp and by dark they were packed up ready to leave.

'We got one chance,' Bob told them. 'We gotta get right out of their country. They won't leave their country. They don't like all that stranger place. Too many devil-devil wandering around.'

Julnajulna's eyes rolled in fear as he spoke of the devil-devil country.

'Don't worry. They can't hurt when you with us. We know all them spirit fella. We bin walking about that country long time. And,' he mused, 'we going to be walking about it for a long time in the future if we get out of this. Never going to be able to come up here again.'

'They can't catch us,' Susie said confidently. 'We got 'em horse.'

'Might be we got horse,' Bob answered, 'But them fella can walk all day and never knock up. We gotta get ahead and keep ahead till we leave all this palm tree country behind.'

He led off, the two women followed, hunting along the pack-horses and spare mounts, eight horses in all. It was flat, heavily timbered country. Their tracks showed deeply in the grey sandy soil.

'No matter it was hard stone,' Bob thought, 'They would track us just the same.'

By midnight they were twenty miles away at a spring near the Drysdale River.

'This will do,' Bob said. 'There's good feed for the horses, we'll camp. But no fire. And short hobble every horse, we got to pack up quick in the morning and be gone by daylight.'

They ate some cooked salt beef and damper then the women rolled into the swag. Bob sat with his back to a tree, rifle in hand, listening to the night sounds until the first smudge of dawn.

'Come on, you fella,' he called to the women. 'Time to get 'em horse.'

They rode at a brisk jig-jog and by mid-morning had reached a line of low hills ten mile further on. They spelled the horses at a rock-hole and while the women cooked some johnny-cakes, Bob clambered up a low rocky hill. He looked back the way they had come, eyes sweeping back and forth trying to pierce the timber. Nothing moved except for an eaglehawk circling high in the sky.

'Maybe no-one there,' he thought. 'Maybe I just can't see 'em. Perhaps they never gone looking for her yet and want her to wander in the bush till she gets frightened and comes home.' He gave a short laugh. 'Maybe they watching me right now, waiting to chuck a spear. We better keep moving.'

That day they covered forty miles, sixty in all since leaving the lily pool.

'No fire again tonight,' he told them as they prepared to camp. 'And hobble the horses short again. You two can sleep in the swag. I'll keep watch for them fella again. If we get another good day's travel tomorrow I reckon we safe. Maybe we even safe here. I don't think anyone following.'

Daylight saw them mounted and by late afternoon another forty miles had been covered. Now they were clear of the strange palm-trees of the Underworld and getting close to the Kimberley cattle country.

The horses were slowing down. They were used to just poking about and were fat and lazy. Now they had travelled a hundred miles in less than three days. There were no signs anyone was following and as they prepared to camp Susie was hopeful of a billy of tea and fresh boiled salt meat.

'We light fire now boil 'em tea and beef?'

'No. More better we wait one more time. Little bit cooked stuff left. You two can have 'em. Tomorrow dinnertime we can cook up proper.'

They were at a big waterhole near the head of the Hahn River. The sun was setting. The horses barely moved as their saddles were stripped and they stood and cropped the grass at hand. The girls flopped by the saddles talking softly. Bob pulled the rifle from its scabbard and walked down to the river bank. He was sure no tribesman would travel this far out of his territory. He sat facing the water, his back against a big old Leichhardt Pine, his rifle against the tree.

Suddenly a black arm reached around the tree-trunk and plunged a spear deep in his gut.

The women sprang to their feet at his awful shriek and saw him staggering towards the river. Three naked tribesmen stood silently watching. Julnajulna screamed and fell to the ground. Susie did not hesitate. She grabbed a bridle and lunged for her horse. The natives took no notice, intent on the white man. She slipped the hobbles, threw on a saddle and galloped off.

Bob Anderson reached the waterhole, rifle in one hand and clutching his spilling entrails with the other. He had wrenched out the spear. He put the rifle on the bank and washed at the oozing blood.

'Take her,' he said, looking up at the three natives. 'Take her and go, I never wanted her.'

Then he fell on the bank in a faint.

Julnajulna's husband stalked to where she lay sobbing on the ground. In one hand he carried a steel tomahawk.

'Get up!' he ordered.

He led her back to the river bank and held out the tomahawk.

'Chop his head off!'

Jack woke with a start. He felt he had not slept all night. He lifted the net and looked out. Daylight was spreading across the scrubby flat. He heard Lester banging around in the kitchen and walked inside.

Lester grinned at him. 'Up late this morning, Jack. Been dreamin' about some young barmaid, I'll bet.'

'I been dreaming about a girl, but she was no barmaid. Were you and Smokey around when Bob Anderson got speared, Lester?'

'No. Smokey had left the country by then. I was down the Fitzroy with another mate, selling a mob of horses. We saw the police tracks on our way back and knew something was up. We called in at Karungie and old Dave Rust give us the news about Bob. That was 1935. He was the last one speared up there. The following season I caught up with a fella called Sammy Lynch who gave me the rest of the story.

'Sammy was head stockman on Mt House and had been out mustering way north on the run at the time Bob was making his getaway. The stockcamp was just about to head back in to the station, finished for the season, when they come across Susie. She was a mess. Dress all ripped and covered in mud. Buggered. Been running for two weeks with the munjons on her tracks. But she knew what to do. She kept to the stony creeks that headed up in the ranges and got away.

'Sammy reckoned the munjons had been close behind Bob most of the way from the lily hole. They could travel fast as a horse, them fellas. After the killing, two of them set out to run Bob's woman down. They were going to kill her too, because she had lived with a white man. That horse of Susie's knocked up quick and dropped dead after a few mile. The police saw where the two blacks ripped the saddle to pieces. They were furious that she had got away.'

'What happened to her afterwards, Lester?'

'I don't remember but I bet somebody snaffled her quick. Me and my mate often camped with her and Bob. By ghost she was a fine woman!'

'And Julnajulna?'

'Them policemen never found her, or her husband — the one that done the spearing. They back-tracked the three blacks to the lily hole but there was no sign of them or their tribe. Later, they found the tribe camped way over on the Carson River. But Julnajulna and her husband weren't with 'em. They were miles away, hidden in the ranges. Them police trackers never found 'em. Too scared to look properly, I reckon. So the police packed up and rode back to Derby. Old Bob never was avenged.'

'You ever come across Julnajulna's boy, Lester? The murderer?'

There was silence for a while as Lester busied himself at the wood stack by the stove. He selected two chunky pieces and poked them into the firebox. Then he answered. It sounded like wind sighing far off in the ranges.

'That's a long story, Jack. He give me a lot of trouble later. I might tell you about it one day.'

He stared at the fresh young face before him.

'Don't never get mixed up with anyone else's woman, Colt. There's plenty out there ain't had a rope tossed over 'em.'

'I've already been down that track, Lester,' Jack replied. 'But once I found out the woman already had a bloke I never went near her again.' He gave a wry smile. 'Don't know that I'd do that now. I've really been feeling the need for someone these last few nights.'

Lester nodded. 'That's because you're gettin' older. Well, you better do something about it. You worried about going with a black woman?'

'I wasn't keen on the idea at first, Lester,' Jack admitted. 'But some of those kitchen girls you got are starting to look pretty good — and getting prettier by the day.'

Lester chuckled. 'I know what you mean. It's either black women or bust up in this country and I ain't seen anyone bust yet! How you holding for tobacco?'

'Oh, plenty. Still got some good Havelock plug me an' Don picked up in Camooweal. You want some?'

Lester shook his head. 'Later, Jack. Bring a plug down to the kitchen tonight after supper. But don't say anything. Tell Phil and them I'm going to show you how to knock up a batch of bread.'

That night when Jack walked down to the kitchen it was empty. But the lantern was still burning and the big dough bucket stood by the fire covered with a cloth. Jack lifted the cloth and saw the dough had nearly risen to the top. Lester can't be far away, he muttered. I'll wait. He sat down on a stool in the cool outside and watched the constellations that showed from time to time amongst the clouds. Suddenly he heard a giggle and a female voice called softly, 'Are you there?'

'I'm here, but Lester's not,' Jack replied. 'Aren't you supposed to be knocking back the bread?'

There was no answer and curious, Jack got up and walked towards the voice. A slim young black girl was standing behind the kitchen, head down gazing at the ground.

'You waiting for Lester too?' Jack asked.

The girl shook her head, too shy to look up.

'No,' she whispered. 'Me wait longa you.'

Jack's heart started to pound. So! Lester had told the girl to wait for him and that was why he had been told to bring the tobacco. He was aware it was the going rate. Money was no use to her, there was nothing on the station to buy. She was given a comb, mirror and two dresses each year — the despised 'hobble dresses' cut so meagerly the women could scarcely walk. Her tobacco was a weekly ration of the evil-smelling and foul-tasting 'nigger-twist' to chew.

He did not hesitate. 'Where will we go?'

For answer she turned and walked off in the darkness. Jack followed until they came to a blanket spread on the ground. The girl quickly pulled her dress over her head and lay down. 'Just like Niagara Falls,' Jack thought. 'But without the tits. No fiddling about, no playing hard to get, no talking. Just a quickie on the deck. Well, if that's the way it is in this country, at least it will keep me from busting!'

Lester was busy rolling out the dough when he got back to the kitchen. The old half-caste looked up as Jack walked in. His eyes twinkled. 'Ah, there you are. Get held up?'

'Held up or held down,' Jack mumbled, embarrassed. 'I don't even know her name. What is it?'

'Elsie. A proper good girl. She's had her eye on you ever since you got here.'

'Huh! Well, now she can dream about me while she's chewing my tobacco down the camp.'

Lester gave Jack a wink. 'Old Tiger will enjoy it too.'

Tiger was the ancient blackfellow who chopped Lester's wood.

'What's Tiger got to do with it?'

'Didn't you know? That's Elsie's boy.'

Jack was disgusted. 'Don't tell me I came after him! I didn't know she had anyone.'

'You're never going to be handed a virgin, Jack. You may as well face it. Any time a girl fronts up, you can bet her boy has sent her along to get tobacco. That's the way of things out here. It's a long standing arrangement that's been going on ever since the white man arrived. Trading's the oldest thing known to man, I reckon.'

'So it may be, Lester, but I think I'll give that sort of trading a miss.'

But within a week Jack was back with more tobacco and as long as he remained on Seven Emu, Elsie was his for an hour any night he wanted. And Elsie walked tall amongst her people, proud she had snared the young gun ringer and jealously shielded him from the other girls.

8.

And Rusty Rode the Wagon ...

She held long reins of a four-in-hand,
Where cattle trails were dusty,
And along the tracks where the stock-routes ran,
They called her Jimmy's Rusty,
And every man in the north had tried,
But she smiled and called them mate,
So tired of that they let her be,
To ride her wagon gate.

They were in the saddle shed working on the gear and arguing about the red-headed woman. Phil said he thought he remembered her, Billy Yeomans told him he only remembered reading about her.

'You're going back too far for me,' Don Kirk told them. 'First World War time I was just crawling.'

Jack looked at Lester. He had baked a brownie with the last of the sultanas and brought it down to the saddle shed with a billy of tea for smoko. It was too wet to sit under the bough shed and there was no space in the kitchen. He sat quietly on a box in a corner, chewing away and squirting tobacco juice onto the dirt floor.

'That old monkey knows something about her,' Jack thought. 'I can tell the way he's looking. He won't say anything here, I'll get in the morning for sure.'

Jack was up before daylight, as usual, and in the kitchen. He could have woken Lester in the middle of the night and demanded a drink of tea, he would have got it. Soon as Lester found out how Jack rode a buckjumper, Jack was his mate, no matter there were years between them.

Jack had always been attracted to colourful characters. He was one himself and needed the stimulation of others. The quiet bloke could sit in his corner. Jack wanted no part of him. He was bursting with life and looked for it in his companions or the stories they knew.

'What you know about that red-headed ringer, Lester? She one of your old girls?'

'I never knew any white ladies, Jack. An' this wasn't my country. She was around these parts. But no matter, we heard about her over in the west. Them Queensland drovers brought all the news. They reckoned she was some girl. Not just a passenger out in the stockcamp trying it for a week or two but working as a ringer full time. And breakin' horses, droving. All her folks were drovers.'

Lester told the story so graphically that Jack was there as she rode along ...

Rusty drove the wagonette. She wasn't pleased about it but it was what her Dad wanted.

'Because I'm a woman!' Rusty would snort.

Much of Rusty's life had been spent travelling in wagons. She had been born in a wagon and later carried in a cradle beneath it. But not this wagon. This wagon was only a pup. Her first memories were of the big heavy horse-drawn wagon when her Dad carted stores out to the stations.

The wagonette she was driving was piled high with everything needed on this droving trip. There were few stores along the way. They carried bags of flour and sugar, a chest of tea and a water drum. As well as blackened iron camp-ovens and billies, there was a battered four gallon beef bucket, plus tins and dishes for making bread. On top of the load sat two big heavy tarpaulins and six rolled-up swags.

Rusty would rather have been with her Dad and the other men, poking the bullocks along. It wasn't so lonely that way. With the wagon, she spent most of each day by herself. Her Dad and his three men left camp at daybreak, soon as the cattle moved off. But she stopped and packed up with Charlie the black horse-tailer.

When everything was aboard and the two shafters rigged, she headed off towards the next night camp ten miles or so further on. If there was plenty of feed for the horses to pick at, Charlie poked along behind. If not, he hunted them along till he found feed and Rusty met him at the night camp later.

Just her and the two horses rumbling along. But at least she was out of the dust and could have a drink from the waterbag any time she wished.

'I can drink too often, Dad,' she would say. 'When I get back ringing again I'll be soft.' Then she would smile. 'I'm supposed to be soft!'

Jim Halloran worried about his daughter. She was twenty six now and still unmarried. Didn't even appear interested in men. Well, not that he knew. Certainly she never spoke about anyone and never wrote any letters or received them. She had been away long enough on her own to find someone, but only ringing and horse-breaking on the stations. Still, there were young men working on all those places. Smart men, starved for women.

'They're my mates!' Rusty would fizz. 'You don't find romance out in the stockcamp!'

He knew she didn't like droving. Too quiet. Too slow. She wanted action. Galloping after scrubbers. Riding rough horses. Breaking-in colts. Roping cleanskins in the branding yard. Even night-watching cattle in the stockcamp was exciting. There were always fresh cattle in the mob that wouldn't camp at night, restlessly roaming about calling out to their mates in the darkness. That would unsettle the whole mob and often there would be a rush with the stockmen galloping after them.

But someday he knew, someone special would come into her life and he hoped he lived to see it. She was a good daughter. She had come back when he needed her ...

Rusty was looking forward to reaching the windmill. Yesterday had been a dry day, a no water day for the bullocks but the horses had been given a drink. Working horses must have water every day and Charlie had taken them to a small soak.

Today he had gone on to a patch of feed close to the night camp, so Rusty would have the mill to herself. She would be able to strip off and soak in the trough and put her clean pants and shirt on and wash the dirty ones.

Someone else was anxious to reach the Twenty-Mile Mill that day. Ben Bright the horse thief.

'You sure we going right way?' he called at last to Mick his half-caste partner.

Ben was a good bushman but he didn't know this country. All he could see was a short stretch of burnt plain that kept disappearing into the heat waves of the mirage. But Mick knew the country. Ben was glad to have sold the horses. He hated this desert country and could never understand why anyone chose to live in it. But it was good for off-loading stock. Not as good as that Kimberley country though. By ghost that was good country. Full of horse poison. He could sell all he could lift over there.

'And I'll go back,' he muttered. 'Probably all blown over by now. That blasted trooper! Stumbling onto me tracks.'

The Mill was on the main stock route leading into Queensland from the west. He and Mick were travelling north, back tracking their own tracks of last week. Ben hoped there was no-one watering at the mill. He didn't want to be seen coming up the south track to the Twenty-Mile Mill. There was no legitimate reason to be using that track. There were no mills or bores. Only a few springs if you knew where to find them, a long dry dangerous track to the stations the other side of the desert. A horse duffer's back route.

They still had two stolen horses. Even stations desperately short would not buy well known brands. He shouldn't have taken them but Ben could never resist a good horse that crossed his path. In particular Ben didn't want to meet any drovers. Drovers were good fellows but they spoke to a lot of people. He didn't want a drover to see him using that track. Once on the main stock route he and Mick could be just another pair of travelling bagmen.

Suddenly a windmill head, blades spinning, shimmered through the heat haze. Mick was right on target.

'Might be someone there, Ben. Look like a wagon and horses.'

Ben cursed. A drover. No matter. They would bluff it out. He would say they had been down south mustering and were now heading home to the Gulf for a spell. The horses sighted the mill and got a jog on, Ben rode up to the lead with Mick to steady them. It was a drover's wagon all right. Piled high with bags, boxes and swags. There was no sign of the horse plant. They must have watered and gone on to the night camp. Drovers never camped close to where they watered but always went on a few miles to let the cattle top up with grass. The cattle would be along later, this would be the cook filling up with water.

'Fella splashing around in the trough, Ben. Proper white looking.'

'Hold up, Mick! That's a woman! We better hang on a minute. She's spotted us and getting out.'

Rusty was soaking, half asleep, in the long, narrow cattle trough when she heard a jingling and a thudding of hooves. She grabbed a towel as a line of horses trotted up and sunk their noses into the water alongside her. Then she saw the two men riding towards her. They looked at her for an instant before turning away.

She quickly slipped her clean pants and shirt on and called to them.

'Hey! It's okay. I'm dressed. You can come over.'

Rusty wasn't greatly fussed. She was used to living with men. After a time they treated her as one of themselves. The two strangers rode slowly over to the trough. Rusty's heart gave a little jump. The brawny one was about her age and good-looking. He smiled and lifted his hat. She saw black curly hair.

'How far back are the cattle?'

'We never come that way,' Ben answered. 'We been down south mustering. Now we're heading back north.'

Rusty looked at the dozen horses still nuzzling at the water.

'You got a good plant of horses for bagmen.' Two of the horses wore the Wineglass brand of Newcastle Waters cattle station. She grinned. 'You pick up some strangers?'

'Yeah, well, couple I guess.' Ben removed his hat and wiped away some sweat. 'We run across them a good way back. We going to drop them off on our way back.'

'Thought you were ridin' north?'

Ben fiddled with his hat. Newcastle Waters was west. This was some smart girl. And pretty. He hadn't seen too many red-headed women. Dark-haired ones seemed to drift mostly across Ben's path.

'Yeah, well, we not really decided. Where you lot headed into?'

'Morestone. Out of Camooweal. We come all the way from Sturt Creek, West Australia. You heard of Jim Halloran? He's my father. I'm Rusty.'

'Never met him, heard of him. Didn't old Jim losè his missus last season?'

'Yeah, Mum died over the Wet, that's why I'm with him. I was ringin' out at Rocklands when I got the news. So now I'm his cook.'

'Ringin'!' said Ben, astonished. 'Ringin'!'

'I been ringing more than I been droving. Almost. Except when I been breakin'-in.'

'Breakin'-in!'

Ben sat open-mouthed.

'So what! I been up in this country all my life. Breaking-in a horse is nothing anyway. I'd rather be doing that than droving. I never wanted to come back droving.'

The talk came easily between them and Mick rode off where the horses were busy cropping green feed around the mill.

'May as well be on me own,' he mused. 'They only got eyes for each other! We should be on our way now, don't want to be around when that father of hers lobs here with the cattle. Shouldn't have hung on to those Newcastle horses, neither. She picked 'em straight off. That Wineglass brand stands out like a tin dunny. An' everyone knows Newcastle Waters don't sell their brand.'

Later that same afternoon Jim Halloran rode into the mill to check on the water, his thirsty bullocks close behind. He could see where his own horses had watered earlier and also Rusty's wagon wheel tracks. She would be long gone, at the night camp, helping Charlie hobble the horses and preparing their supper. Then he noticed horse tracks coming in to the mill from the south.

'So they still using that track, eh! Damn horse thieves! Long as people will buy 'em they'll lift 'em. No-one will ever stop it unless they watch all those back tracks. That's today's tracks for sure.'

Old Jim had always run straight. 'They wouldn't put me in charge of their precious bullocks if I wasn't dinkum,' he would say.

He counted a dozen shod horse tracks then cut around the mill to where they led off east. They were mixed in with Rusty's wagon wheel marks. Sometimes the wagon crossed the horse tracks, other places the shod tracks covered the wheel marks. So they were travelling with the wagon. With Rusty.

He wondered if she knew them and that they were most likely on the cross. Well, he would meet them shortly when he got the cattle into camp.

Rusty saw them just before dark, feeding the cattle slowly along so as to arrive right on dusk. Nine hundred lean red bullocks full of water and grass. They would camp better tonight. She could see her father's tall thin frame, sitting straight in the saddle and she climbed on to one of the night-horses and rode out to meet him.

'Dad,' she called happily. 'We got company. Two stockmen I met at the mill at dinnertime. They going to have a feed with us tonight and maybe camp. That okay with you?'

'Well, I don't mind a bit of company, but who are they? You know 'em?'

'No, but they seem okay. Dad,' she hesitated for a moment, 'I like one of them. I know they come up that south track...'

'Got any station brands with 'em?' Jim cut in.

'Not that I saw, Dad,' Rusty heard herself saying. 'Can they ride with us a few days?'

Jim saw them standing by the fire as he rode in. A small thin faced half-caste with the stamp of horseman all over. But it was the sunburnt young white ringer that caught his attention. Here was a man to stand out in any crowd. Close to six feet tall, he had a strong handsome face and carried himself like a man ready for any challenge. He strode across smiling as Jim reined in and dismounted.

'Jim Halloran, eh! Been all around you but never caught up with you before. Ben Bright's my name, from over the west.'

'Heard of you, Ben. You're welcome to a feed and a camp tonight, you and your mate. Which way you headed?'

'Just finished a contract muster job. We might poke along with you a-ways if that's okay?'

'Okay by me.' Rusty was strong enough to straighten this young fellow out had she a mind to. He wouldn't stand in her way.

'There's Rusty heading out on first watch. Why don't you grab a night-horse and keep her company?'

Rusty saw him riding through the gloom.

'Ben, you got to drop those two Newcastle horses if you want to travel with us. I don't want Dad spotting them.'

Two days later they were still with the cattle. Ben rode with Rusty now on the wagon. It was quite clear they had fallen for each other.

'Don't think you need me along any more,' Mick said that night. 'I'll push along.'

Ben didn't argue. 'Sorry it's turned out this way, old mate. Where you heading?'

'West. That Kimberley country you been talking about.'

Ben was pleased Mick was going. He had been a good mate but now he could make a fresh start. In a week or two when they delivered the cattle he and Rusty would get married. They wouldn't dump old Jim, they would keep droving. It was a good way Rusty and he could stay together.

At night the men camped behind the wagon for safety in case the cattle got a sudden fright and rushed towards the camp. As well, the fire was in front of the wagon, towards the cattle and was kept blazing throughout the night. Even stampeding cattle would turn in fear from fire.

But Rusty needed a measure of privacy and camped to one side of the wagon. She had no fear of the cattle rushing. 'Don't you worry,' she would laugh. 'If they did come this way I'd be behind that wagon in one bound!'

The night after Mick left, Ben was waiting by the fire as Rusty rode in from her watch. He had a pannikin of hot tea waiting.

'How they camping tonight?' he asked.

'Quiet. Like old milkers. Three and a half months on the road they should be quiet. Ben,' she said shyly, 'Come over to my swag when you finish your watch later, I want to talk to you.'

Then she disappeared in the darkness towards her blankets. Ben had become an accepted member of the crew and took a turn at watch each night — the midnight watch. Now he rolled into his swag for a few hours sleep before he was called. But he was still awake, staring up at black clouds forming when third watch rode in to wake him.

'Come over to my swag later.'

It was all he could think of as the night-horse plodded slowly around the bullocks. Then a flash of lightning alerted him to the coming storm. A few of the bullocks became restless and sniffed at the wind and a big old piker stood up and lowed softly. Ben rode over and faced it. 'You get back to sleep, old man,' he soothed.

Then it was time to wake his relief. He stayed on watch with the man a few minutes.

'Come and get me if that storm gets 'em up,' he called as he rode in. He could barely see the fire. It was almost out and the tea billy was cold.

'Damn third watch,' he muttered. He hung the night horse up to its tree. 'Too lazy to stoke the fire.'

He dragged up two logs and lay them together on the coals. Smoke billowed up.

'Hell! I've near put it out.' He fanned with his hat until a tiny flame appeared. 'That's better. In half an hour she'll be blazing again.'

He walked off into the darkness where Rusty was camped. She was wide awake, waiting.

'Get in the swag, Ben. It's cold.' She pulled the cover aside. She was lying fully dressed. He slid in and lay down beside her.

Suddenly there was a loud crack of thunder. Ben sat bolt upright. 'I better get back to the cattle.'

She held him back. 'No need. Dad always goes out when there's a storm. Anyway, they won't rush. Been too long on the road for that.' She put her arms around him. 'Lie back, sweetheart, we got a lot to talk about.'

There was another crack of thunder, louder this time and a sudden roar as the cattle leapt to their feet and rushed towards the camp. There was no fire to split them, only the wagon.

Mick heard the news a week later as he passed through Anthony's Lagoon. Everyone at the station was talking about it. 'Bad cattle smash over on the Queensland Border. Two drovers killed. One a woman.' More news came through the next morning. 'Jim Halloran's plant. Daughter killed and one man. Ben Bright. Died in their swags, cattle trampled over the top of them.'

No-one talked about how they were found, arms locked around each other.

Jim buried them back at the Twenty-Mile Mill.

'That's where they met,' he explained later. 'And I couldn't bear to leave them out in the middle of nowhere.'

When Lester stopped speaking, Jack looked up in surprise. 'Is that all?'

'How you know there's something else, Jack? I can't hold anything back from you, can I?'

Jack laughed. 'Reckon I've heard enough of your stories to know when you haven't finished. Come on, what else is there to know?'

Lester looked at him seriously. 'I know there's a phantom wagon out there on that Barkly Tableland, Jack. Near that mill. Lots of drovers seen it. Full bore, charging through the mirage, with Rusty drivin' and ol' Ben Bright sittin' on the tail-gate. Shriekin' with laughter at Rusty's red hair streamin' in the wind. You don't want to be passing by with cattle. Cattle will take off quicker than lightning when they see that wagon comin'. Lots of drovers won't water at that mill any more. They'd rather dry camp.'

'I don't know that I go for all that phantom stuff, Lester, but she was some girl by the sound of her.'

'There's a lot of things happen out in this country, Jack, that people can't explain. But that don't mean they never happen. I haven't seen that wagon, but I've seen a lot of other peculiar things.'

Lester stood up. It was full daylight now.

He looked out the kitchen door.

'Look at Phil's windmill, Jack. Spinnin' around an' not a breath of wind. That's what them drovers say happens before Rusty's wagon comes flying.'

Jack left the table and walked across to the doorway.

'I can't see the mill spinning, Lester.'

But Lester wasn't listening. He was busy pummelling at a lump of dough and crooning an old stock route song.

"Ten Thousand Dry Gullies Later" Jack Vitnell at age 40 with ringer Lockie McKinnon shortly before Jack's death.

Jack Vitnell competing in the campdraft, Victoria River Downs Race Meeting, 1950. Jack later won the Sandford Cup, riding at 13 stone in a stock saddle. He immediately gave away the trophy, a large mantel clock. "This won't fit in me watch pouch. Here, you take it, Doug (Scobie)."

9.

Just a Lend of Lulu

Old Mick's skin was roughened bark,
Like a speckled bloodwood tree,
His face was a crumpled wrinkled mask,
White hair straggled free,
But she was fresh as this year's grass,
With skin a soft smooth brown,
And Lulu rode in her skimpy dress,
With black hair tumbling down.

They were out on the run at last. Six musterers — Phil Hanlon, two black stockmen, and the three blow-ins from Camooweal — and Lester Kerrigan and a lad cooking and horse-tailing.

It was a small stockcamp but that was all they needed. There was no frenzied galloping over the ranges, requiring two and three horses a day. The musterers followed the storms and pounced on the cattle as they came in on the green shoots.

'You ever see open bronco done, Jack?' Phil asked first night camp out from the station. 'Well, we do a lot here. Only got a few yards but there's bronco panels all over the run.'

Next day Jack took part in the action. They picked up a mob of around forty head browsing on some new grass and moved them along a couple of miles to a small clearing in the timber. A bronco panel sat in the middle. It was simply two strong timber yard panels constructed in such a way as to allow cattle to be dragged up by horse and held firmly until men on the ground could leg-rope and pull them down. Then they could be easily branded, earmarked or whatever.

'We got more men than cattle,' Billy Yeomans laughed. He was used to big stockcamps handling mobs of five hundred branders at a time.

'Maybe so,' Phil answered. 'But we got no yard to hold 'em. We got to hold 'em in the open and brand 'em same time. That's why we need the men.'

Three men held the mob together, Phil rode in and roped the cleanskins and Jack and Billy did the branding and cutting. It was constant work.

'Where's all your musterers?' Don Kirk asked Phil later.

'Gone walkabout. I can't hold 'em once the storms come. They're off after bush tucker. Won't come back till next season. By then they'll be glad of a bit of white man tucker.'

There were plenty of horses. One of Jack's string was a big black mare that reminded him of the high climbing black on Connmara. The one that had given him such a hard time his first day. But this Seven Emu mare never gave up. She was ready with a vicious buck every morning. Jack found her no trouble to ride. 'She don't like that. Me being able to ride her. Keeps trying to get me. Got a nasty streak in her that mare.'

It took her a week. He had her saddled ready to mount one morning when Don Kirk called. As Jack turned his head the mare spun around and kicked him both barrels in the chest. The force knocked him off his feet. He lay there ghost white, unable to move, gasping. They crowded around him.

'Kicked him over the heart,' Don said. 'Don't move him, his ribs may be smashed. They'll puncture his lungs if he moves.'

Right from childhood Jack had been tough. He never appeared to feel pain but this time it was showing. How many ribs were cracked no-one ever knew.

'Get me onto my swag,' he finally got out. 'Leave me. Go and start the muster. I'll be right.' He was still lying on his swag at sundown when they arrived back at camp.

'Never eaten anything all day. Had a sip of tea is all,' Lester told them. 'I think his chest bad hurt.'

He lay there a week. Then they rode past the camp one afternoon with cattle to take on to the yard nearby. He was still prone. Suddenly a big roan bull broke and rushed for the scrub. Billy Yeomans was closest and raced his horse towards it. The bull spun around and charged. Don Kirk galloped up the other side and it spun around and charged him. Instead of galloping off in fear it was standing its ground. Unless they could get it running and wind it, it would be difficult to pull down.

The bull was too cunning to run. It had too often seen its mates run down and captured. It was not going to let them do the same. It would stand and fight. The six stockmen were soon grouped around dodging his charging horns.

'What a mongrel of a thing!' Don Kirk yelled. 'Did you ever see anything like it? How we going to pull the brute down?'

Suddenly a horse burst on the scene, stunning them for a moment. It was Jack, full gallop. They looked in astonishment. He set his horse straight for the bull, leapt off and grabbed its horns, twisting its neck in a headlock. Then he hung there, knees up to his chin, pulling down with all his weight. Suddenly the bull fell over, legs up in the air. Jack let go of its head and grabbed the tail, thrusting it between the bull's legs and using the tail as a rope to hold it down.

The others were too astonished to move.

'Well don't sit there!' he yelled at them. 'Get down here and cut his horns off!'

As soon as they had the animal secured he stood up and hobbled off to his swag. Every man hung his head in shame.

'Showed up by a cripple!' Phil Hanlon muttered. 'A fella half dead!'

Two days later Jack buckled on his spurs and caught the kicking mare. He swung on and struck her hard in the shoulders with the spurs. She leapt high, twisting and bucking furiously. He sat her, spurring hard, till she stopped. Then he lashed her with the reins. She squealed in rage and climbed high again, cow-kicking and twisting. Jack kept lashing till she stopped. Then he galloped her, hard through the timber. When he brought her back she stood head down, beaten and mastered. She never bucked with him again.

By the time the monsoon rains rolled in a month later, they had branded four hundred cleanskins.

'May not seem a lot,' Phil said, 'But it's four hundred scrub runners we missed during the season. If I can turn them off as fats in four years' time, it will be worth it.'

It was useless to keep mustering in the constant rain. Within days there would be grass all over the run, scattering the cattle. So the men packed up and rode back into the station, glad to be dry at last.

'He good man that Phil Hanlon,' Lester told Jack later. 'Would have been easy to slip in and brand McArthur River cattle next door but he don't work that way. We didn't even need to go out this time of year. Got enough branders during the season to keep him in tucker and stuff. Know why he do it? Pride! Don't want any cleanskins runnin' on his place!'

'You and Smokey wouldn't have worked that way,' Jack grinned. 'Wouldn't want to be your neighbours!'

'Me an' Smokey never had any country much. Only enough to register a brand. There was no neighbours for hundreds of mile. But we never touched battler's stock. Only big stations. Big stations deserve to lose everything they do. The owner ain't there. What the manager care? When he leave that place he just living under a tree same as the rest of us!'

Jack was getting restless. They had been back at the homestead a month now, repairing the saddles and harness gear and making hobbles and ropes out of sides of greenhide.

'Where's this Borroloola?' he asked one morning.

'Ride there in under a week,' Lester told him, 'But not now. River's up. Water everywhere.' He could tell Jack was itching for action. 'How old you now Jack?'

'Must be seventeen now.'

'Old enough to drink, eh?'

'I been drinking since I was fourteen, Lester. They got a pub in at that Borroloola?'

'They got a pub all right! Wildest in the whole of the Territory!' He watched Jack's eyes light up. 'Phil always takes us in before the season starts. We'll get in there directly.' Lester started up another of his stories...

You know how that place get its name? One time the stock route to the west run through this country. Before they put the bores down across the Barkly. Way back last century. Those drovers used to follow the Gulf around until they hit the Roper. Then they run the Roper up to where it heads on Mataranka Springs. There was a drover's store at that place but nothing between there and Burketown.

So a fella called Monty Smith decided to open a store on the McArthur. Luggers used to come right up the river those days to a place called The Landing and that's where he built it. Just a rough bush hut sheeted with paperbark. He could get stuff in by boat from Darwin or by wagon out of Burketown.

He wasn't a very likeable fella and he surely wasn't the most honest rooster so it's not surprising he got the name of Soapy. He had most everything a drover could want in that store, from flour to horseshoes.

First thing you stumbled over when you walked inside was Soapy's bed. That was to let you know he camped there an' not to come round after dark peeling off the bark. The next thing you saw was a shotgun sittin' on the counter. Then you might see a sickly white facing staring at you. That was Soapy. If he knew you he smiled. If not he glared.

There was no shelving. Things like bags of flour and sugar that would rot on the dirt floor were piled on sheets of corrugated iron. Old Soap was a good man at rotating his stock. But that wasn't to give you fresh stuff. If he didn't shift it around on the iron every month the white ants would get at it. Stuff he didn't sell every day hung off the rafters. You couldn't move for the packbags and saddles an' things hanging down.

After every Wet he had to re-build half the store. That's how bad the ants were. Only thing piled on the ground was horse-shoes and iron water tanks. If he didn't watch out the white ants would build tunnels up the outside of the tanks and take a short cut to the rafters. Most of all, though, Soapy sold rum. From a nine gallon keg on the counter. His stock of kegs was the counter.

There was an old bagman knocked around that Landing country those days. He was that old his skin had gone all spotty. He didn't look sunburnt any more — just a wrinkled old white fella covered in brown blotches. But he had a young woman. Black of course. Lulu her name was and the whole countryside was hanging their tongues out for her. She was some woman — long black hair and devil eyes. When she shot you a glance it made you forget any other woman you might have known. It was a look full of promise but it also came with a little sad smile that said, 'I would but I can't!'

Isaac the fella's name was that owned her. Isaac Issacs. He swapped her for a bag of flour and a pound of nicky-nicky tobacco from an old salt-water blackfella he met up with one time down the mouth of the Limmen. Old Isaac watched her like she was a prize show heifer. He never left Lulu in camp. He went out doggin', she went out doggin', he rode into town, she rode into town. The Landing was the last place old Isaac wanted to take Lulu, with all those rough woman-starved drovers about. But he wasn't game to leave her behind while he rode in for tucker. He wasn't worried she would run off. She reckoned times were good with old Isaac, no chasing after bush tucker and being treated like a slave. No, he was worried someone was going to sneak up an' take her up on that roving eye of hers.

Lulu had been Isaac's for about six months before he brought her in to The Landing. He only come in because he was forced to. The flour run out, he got her grinding seed. The sugar run out, he sent her out for sugarbag. Tea run out, she boiled up coonkaberry leaves. But when the tobacco run out he had to bring her in. He made camp a bit out of town and in they come.

Old Isaac never had money. Had no use for it. He traded dog scalps for whatever stores he needed. They were worth seventeen and six a piece those days. Old Isaac had two sugar bags full. Enough to buy all they wanted plus a new dress for Lulu. She'd been gettin' about in a dress stamped Brunton's Flour since she'd met up with Isaac. Lot better than being naked but she wanted a proper dress now she was with a white man.

There was two big mobs of cattle being tailed around the Landing at the time. Drovers spelling their horses a bit and having a few nips of rum before heading out further. A heap of them were sittin' around outside the store as Isaac an' Lulu rode up. She never looked at any of 'em. She was pretty nervous with all that company about. Isaac just nodded and in they went.

Ol' Soap was in a rotten humour. Seems every time anyone walked in lately they fronted up with shin plasters, dud cheques or dog scalps. When Isaac tossed the two bags of scalps down on the counter Soapy just give him a sneer and turned away and found himself looking straight at Lulu. She looked at him a moment and then up at a row of floral dresses hanging an inch from her nose. Then she flashed her smile.

Soapy turned back to Isaac. 'How far you come to get here?'

Old Isaac looked at him real sorrowful like and wheezed out, 'A long week's travellin' — a long hard track without tucker.'

'Well,' said Soap, 'You'd best have a drink.' He twisted the spigot of the keg on the counter and half filled a pannikin.'

Old Isaac downed it in two gulps. Black, treacly overproof rum. Soapy poured another. Isaac was having trouble focussing. There were two Soapies grinning at him and three Lulus. Suddenly they all started whirling around ...

When he woke up he was in the dark. His throat was on fire, his head was pounding. He saw vague shapes of pack-saddles above his head and thought he was in his camp. He staggered to his feet searchin' for the water canteen and bumped into a keg of rum. Now he remembered. He was in Soapy Smith's store at the Landing. On the counter was an empty pannikin. He picked it up and hobbled around the counter to the spigot ...

Next time he woke it was full daylight. There was no Soapy in the store and no Lulu. Lulu! He staggered to the closed door and pushed it open. Half a dozen drovers were squatted outside yarning by the verandah posts. They scarcely looked at him as he burst out of Soapy's front door.

'Lulu!' he croaked. 'Lulu! You fellas seen Lulu?'

'Lulu? Never see her today. Seen her yest'y' someone answered.

'Yesterday! Where?'

'She an' Soapy Smith was walkin' down to the creek.'

Isaac looked like he was going to cry. 'He's stolen Lulu!' he wailed.

'Not stolen, Isaac,' a grinning face answered. 'Just borrowed her a while!'

The local wag walked up. 'What's all the ruckus?'

'He's gone and borrowed Lulu!' Isaac wailed.

'Borrowed Lulu! Well, we better put a notice up!' He took a piece of blacksmith's chalk from off the outside forge and wrote up on Soapy's door.

Missing! Lulu! Stolen or borrowed?

All information to Ike Issacs Esq.

Old Isaac was so upset he just stood there mumbling, 'Borrowed Lulu! Gone an' borrowed Lulu!'

After that, whenever drovers were referring to the Landing they would say, 'You know the place. Where Soapy borrowed Lulu!' And the name stuck, right up to the present!'

Jack laughed. 'You expect me to believe that, Lester?'

Lester pretended to be hurt. 'It's true, Jack. Everything I tell you is true. You know what happened when Soapy brought her back? Old Isaac didn't say anything, he was so pleased to see her. Soapy just walked past Isaac and into his store like he'd been out fetchin' the horses.

'Bring your tucker packs in, Isaac,' he called. 'These are pretty fresh looking dog scalps, I'll take 'em.'

So Isaac got his tucker an' a flask of rum and Lulu got her dress. But all the attention unsettled Lulu. Went to her head, I guess. Within a week she left Isaac and run off with a drover. Isaac carried on dogging and still came in with scalps from time to time. Him an' Soapy became quite good mates. Then the next year after that he never come in. Whether he died somewhere bush or moved on no-one knew but he was never seen around The Landing again. Lot of old fellas passed on that way.

10.

Borroloola

He was six foot three, hard and lean,
And his eyes were black and fiery,
His face was long with an axe-like jaw,
His frame was tough and wiry,
And he leaned at the bar and gazed enthralled,
At the reflection he made in the mirror,
A suitable pose for one who was called,
The infamous Darwin Terror!

The Darwin Terror gazed in the mirror behind the bar and reckoned he had never looked better. The tall, lean, work-hardened frame. The dark sun-tanned handsome face. Black fiery eyes so many had cowered from. The square, rock-hard thrusting jaw. No one was watching and no-one was near. He smiled at the blood red bandanna around his neck and doffed his black bull-shooter's curled brim hat.

There was no-one near because the drinkers gave the Terror plenty of space. He was not the most pleasant of men and had no mates. He could be talking quite rationally in his strange hoarse voice then suddenly lash out at random with a fist. There was a rumour he had fallen drunk down the hatch of a ship when doing a spot of wharf-labouring at Darwin Harbour and landed on his head thirty feet down. It was improbable that he fell that far but it added to the mystique and legend of the man and at least gave a reason for his unpredictable behaviour.

No-one could remember the Terror having a fight for a while now. He was fifty-five and looked as though he had lived through at least seventy drunken, fight-filled years. Nowadays he menaced people with his reputation, aloofness and size.

There was a good crowd in the bar of the Borroloola pub this afternoon. Drovers passing through to pick up cattle, ringers having a final fling before the long hard season ahead, a croc shooter,a fisherman and Phil Hanlon and his Seven Emu crew.

Phil was well known and liked in that part of the Territory and was now moving slowly around the bar, with a smart looking young fellow in tow, renewing acquaintances.

Suddenly the Terror heard his name.

'This here is Randell Smith.' The Terror faced the voice. 'This is a new man of mine, Terror. Jack Vitnell. A man after your own heart. Likes a bit of action.'

Jack was in great form. He had sunk two rums and was feeling greatly at ease amongst this rough motley mob of Territorians. And here in front of him was another. A poser, yes. Jack could see that. But he took a man as he found him. If the fellow was dinkum to him ...

'Good-day mate. What you drinking?'

The Terror looked at Jack as though he was inspecting the dirt under his nails. He gave the merest nod to Phil, glanced again at Jack and with a sneer and twist of his thin lips, turned back to his drink. This young ringer of Phil Hanlon's was not worth knowing.

Jack raised an eyebrow and looked at Phil. Phil tapped the side of his head with one finger and moved on. Jack stood still, quietly staring at the Terror's back.

Then he said in a loud voice, 'Who's this cowboy-like remnant in front of me?'

There was silence in the bar. No-one had ever addressed the Terror in such a manner. Every face in the bar turned on Jack. And the Terror? Randell Smith could not believe that what he had heard was meant for him. For was he not the Darwin Terror? He must have misunderstood what the young fellow had said. He would ignore it.

Then Jack moved. He was now fully matured, almost six feet and weighing thirteen stone. He was so strong he could take a door edge in his hands and swing himself out at arms length from the door, horizontal to the ground. He could hold himself out in that position for a full minute.

Now he reached up and grabbed the Terror's hat. The Terror turned to see it being drop-kicked through the open doorway. He stood blinking in surprise for a moment, wondering what was happening.

Then Jack tackled him around the knees and brought him thudding to the floor.

As he was struggling up, Jack jumped on his back and started to belt his ears with his hat.

'Yahoo!' Jack yelled. 'Yahoo! Ride 'em cowboy! Look at this horse buck!'

The Terror stood, stooped with Jack's weight. The crowd watched in amazement. Jack sat firm, legs gripped around the Terror's waist, still slapping him around the face with his hat. Then he slid down and faced the Terror.

'Here I am, mate! Hit me!'

The Terror swung in an agony of shame. There was no-one in front of him.

'Here!' the voice called. 'Around here!'

The Terror turned.

Jack rushed in, grabbed him by the shoulders and spun him around. Then he held the Terror at arm's length by his waist, lifted him high in the air and dropped him.

The Terror stumbled forward, trying to keep from falling. Jack gave him a shove that sent him toppling on his face. Then he grabbed hold of the Terror's boots and swung him around in a circle an inch above the floor.

When the Terror's head came opposite the bar for the fourth time round, Jack let go of his boots. Randell Smith slid across the floor and crashed head-first into the timber bar.

'Yahoo!' Jack yelled again. 'Look at that cowboy fly!'

The Terror lay dazed for a few seconds then slowly caught hold of the bar and hauled himself upright. He turned and faced his tormentor with a sickly look. 'Get it over with mate. Take me out.'

Jack walked up close and spoke in a quiet voice that only the Terror could hear.

'I'm not going to hit you mate. You're too old for fighting. But don't ever take Jack Vitnell cheap again!'

Jack was aware of the silence and the eyes watching.

'Everybody have a drink,' he yelled. 'I'm shouting. Me an' the old Terror's finished our bit of skylarking! Come on Terror, let's get a rum down!'

But Jack did have a fight that day. The croc shooter became jealous of all the attention paid to Phil Hanlon's young new ringer. He walked over and planted himself in front of Jack.

'Let's see how good you really are.'

Jack could see Don Kirk grinning at him further down the bar. 'I'll try a Don Kirk special!'

He swung an uppercut, missed and took a smash to the face.

'Damn you, Don!' the crowd heard him yell. 'I'll do it my way!'

His opponent was standing off, smiling, ready to move in again. Jack took two quick steps forward and threw a left right combination. The croc shooter came to later on the floor.

'There was no need to sink the boot!' he complained, feeling his gashed cheek.

'He didn't kick you, Crocodile,' someone laughed. 'That was the floor giving you a goodnight kiss!'

It was a long lonely ride back to Seven Emu after the excitement in town. Phil Hanlon and Don Kirk were suffering too much from the three day rum binge to talk. Jack and young Billy Yeomans felt little effect and rode ahead leaving the two older men to hunt along the two pack horses. Jack and Billy had only ridden that way once and from the opposite direction heading in to town, but both were natural bushmen.

There was little talk between them as they looked out for landmarks and watched for sign of their previous tracks. But Jack learnt that Bill also came from New South Wales. His father had owned a small block of dirt towards Mudgee but had sold out.

'He's still there somewhere, I reckon. I haven't wrote for a while and he don't know I'm up this far. But I'll go back one day. I left two year ago to follow the rodeo circuit but haven't got around to it yet. Don't you miss the buckjump show, Jack?'

'Not a day of it. It lost its challenge. Same thing all the time. And I don't know I'd want to stop ringin' in the one place for long either. I like this moving about seeing new people and places. When you first come to a station all you see is a hut in a patch of scrub. You don't know what's out yonder. Then off you go, mustering. There's rivers an' ranges, wild cattle racing, cunning old bulls to throw and good horses to ride.

'I don't know anything better than that. Galloping after a mob of cattle and wheeling the lead, bulls racing off and taking half the mob with 'em, fellas ripping after 'em, shouldering them back or jumping off and pulling 'em down. And it's real stuff, Billy. It's not the show ring. One slip out here and you're gone. Under your horse's hooves, horned by a piker or tossed onto the stone by some mad-headed horse bucking and catching you asleep.

'It's wild, Billy. Hard and rough. It's all out there going it's own way. It don't want us around. We got to go and get it. Bend it to our will. But it's always trying to get us. Chuck your swag out and camp, it'll rain on you if you're lucky. Luck's out, a river'll flood and drown you. Get in too close to a gallopin' bull and he can hook you in the thigh and rip your horse's guts out. Any boss that pays me is a mug. I'd do it for nothing!'

Lester was pleased to see them back and smiled at the story of Jack and the Darwin Terror.

'You were right how you handled that, Jack. Man don't want to earn a reputation beating drunks or old men. But he could fight once, that same man, don't worry an' he was a good ringer with it. But terrible unpredictable. You never was sure what old Terror would do. It seemed to come in runs. He'd be fine a while, then bang! Off he'd go doin' something silly.'

'Was he always like that, Lester, or was it the result of an accident like someone told me in Borroloola?'

The question started Lester off telling the story of the Darwin Terror ...

Always the same, Jack. He got that way no-one would give him a job on the stations, so he went into Darwin and got work on the wharf. Fellas there reckon that fall down the hatch sent him off, but they didn't know him before. Might have got a hit on the head somewhere else one time.

I remember one time over in the west a drover called Mick Coombes gave The Terror a job horse-tailing. First day out Mick said, 'Make sure you pick a good camp tonight, Randell.'

Mick was a very polite little fella, always fussin' over his bullocks. Good drover. Later that afternoon as he and his men were bringing the bullocks along, Mick decided he'd best ride ahead and have a look at the night camp Terror had picked.

Mick had told the Terror to keep well off water. Cattle filing past in the middle of the night on their way to drink can stir a mob as you know. Mick was pleased when he topped a rise and saw a neat little clearing amongst the trees well off the creek.

Then he noticed the stumps. He was droving Lissadel bullocks and was still only eight mile from the station and here in front of Mick was a place where the Lissadel wood cutters had been in action. There were stumps knee high all the way across the clearing. You imagine in the black of night if your mob gets frightened and takes off in that sort of country. The bullocks are rushing blindly, scared out of their stupid wits because some silly looking steer saw a dog and thought it was a devil come to get it or whatever comes to get bullocks in their imagination.

Next the man on watch has to set off after 'em. The other men have to jump out of their swags, climb on night-horses and follow. So the whole bang lot's galloping full pelt, in the dark, with two foot high stumps all over. They'd get cut to pieces. A stupid, dangerous place to camp.

It was close to sundown now, too late to shift. The horses had been hobbled out other side of the creek so they wouldn't disturb the bullocks camping, swags were unpacked, supper was ready by the fire. They would have to stop.

Mick rode over to the Terror and told him what a bad blunder he'd made and to make sure he did better the next day. The old Terror was pretty upset. He'd wanted to make a good showing his first day on the job. Mick rode back to where his men were bringing the cattle along, nice and slowly, letting 'em get a good bellyful before camping. They were about half an hour gettin' up to the rise overlooking Terror's camp when suddenly the lead bullocks started milling around like they were scared of something. Next thing they started breaking back.

'What the Dicken's is going on?' Mick said to himself.

Up he rode to take a look. There's that silly lookin' Terror with a crowbar and shovel, diggin' out a stump! The whole plain was covered in 'em and he's diggin' out one! Anyway, the bullocks camped okay that night and next morning off they went on their way again. Old Terror packed up in fine fashion, eager to make amends and pick a good night-camp. About mid-morning he and the horse-tailer caught and passed Mick and the bullocks, heading down the route.

Mick watered at a big shallow stretch on the Ord about dinner-time and was poking 'em along quietly a bit later when he spotted the Terror. Canterin' along on a horse. He had something over his shoulder, 'Look like a shovel!' Mick thought. He sung out, but the Terror just waved and kept going back towards where they were camped last night. About an hour later, Mick saw him coming back.

'Hey!' he yelled out. 'What are you doing? What did you go back to the old camp for?'

Old Terror rode over with a big grin on his face, very pleased with himself. 'I got a good camp this time Mick. Don't worry about that. But I got to thinking about that camp of ours last night. You were right, that was a silly thing I did, to camp amongst all those stumps. But you never know, another drover might come along and say, well, ol' Mick Coombs camped here. Must be a good place. Then how would I feel if the cattle did rush and some poor devil's horse fell down that hole I made digging out that stump? So I just rode back and filled it in.'

That silly lookin' bugger! The whole ground was covered with two foot high stumps. Hundreds of 'em. What did a single hole matter? After that Mick put him with the bullocks. Wasn't game to let him loose on his own.

Mick reckoned he had a pretty rough trip of it. Watchin' toey cattle at night and the Darwin Terror during the day. Mick Coombes is still out in that Kimberley country. You ask him when you run across him, Jack, if he knew a fella called Randell Smith. That's one name Mick won't forget no matter how long he lives. The Terror got the boat up to Darwin when they delivered the cattle to the 'Works in Wyndham. Wasn't long after that he had that thirty foot fall down the hatch.

When Mick heard the news he said, 'Thank God for that! That might knock a bit of sense into the silly coot!'

11.

A Saddling Lesson

And if any travelling bagman,
Met Jack along the track,
And said that home's Dajarra,
Well, then he'd cop some flack,
Jack would laugh and ask him,
Who saddled up his mare,
Sure stockmen from that country,
Only learnt to ride 'em bare.

Suddenly the steamy wet season was over. It was as though someone had pulled up a blind. The banks of grey disappeared and all was blue.

'Time to get the horses,' Phil Hanlon said.

They were in the saddle shed, greasing the last of the gear. There were new head ropes, leg ropes, hobbles, neck straps, bull straps, all twisted or plaited from greenhide — cow or bullock hides stretched over old heavy wagon wheels when green and left to dry in the sun. Every saddle and pack-saddle had been counter-lined and repaired and the heavy breaking-in and bronco gear had been checked over and pieces renewed. All was ready for the new season.

'You want us fellas to move on now, Phil?' Don Kirk asked, indicating himself, Jack Vitnell and Billy Yeomans.

'No way! You blokes got a job for the season, you want it. All found and Queensland rates.'

'Queensland rates! I thought you paid Territory wages out here.'

'So I do, but you fellas are worth more than seven pound ten a week. What they paying inside now?'

'Nine. Ten for head-stockman. It's been sneaking up since the war finished.'

'Well, I might pay ten. Depends how many bullocks we get. I generally take in two mobs of five. But not to the rail-head. This ain't fattening country. Only reason I got it was because no-one else wanted it. But I turn off good stores. I take 'em down to old Boy Beaumont's place near the Isa. Boy's got more country than he knows what to do with. He fattens 'em down there. We were partners once.'

'With all these bulls Jack and young Billy going to throw,' Don grinned, 'I reckon we'll make up another five hundred mob of stags. You'll be paying that ten quid for sure!'

Jack, Billy and old Lester took the first mob. There were only five of them. Three with the cattle, Lester and a black horse-tailer in the lead with the plant.

Boy Beaumont took delivery.

'Four hundred and ninety-nine,' he called. 'You lose one?'

'Dropped one. A bullin' one. Damn thing was driving 'em crazy. What you reckon that is, Boy?'

'Some sort of a smell that gets on their rump, I don't know what. But they ride the poor buggers to death, hey.'

'They were chasing it around so much we cut it out before it took a dozen of 'em off into the scrub. Your four horses are here, Boy, and your packs. We owe you one.'

'You don't owe me, but you can do me a favour. Take a small mob of breeders down to Moonah Creek out of Dajarra. I got 'em sold to that Ken Doherty fella but I'm short of men this season.'

It was a slow trip with the cows and calves. Phil was in the middle of mustering back at Seven Emu, but he would want them to help Boy. Most days the cattle were strung along for almost a mile as the drovers allowed them to feed along at their own pace. Darkness caught them out one evening, coming down a jump-up. Thirty sneaked off into thick scrub and were not missed until the next morning.

'I'm not delivering short,' Jack told them, taking charge as usual. 'And we haven't enough men to go back for 'em. We'll pick some up.'

It was his first poddy-dodging venture. There were no fences so cattle roamed at will. Stations here had only a horse or bullock paddock at best so the steal was easily accomplished. They picked up a small mob of cows and calves and slipped them into the mob. No-one was keeping track of their movements, it was not a stock-route, they were cutting across country.

'What's the chance of this Ken Doherty spotting the different brands?' Jack asked Lester.

'No chance. He's no cattleman. Books about all he good for. Think he a good cattleman. Tells people he a good cattleman. I don't know how some of them blokes get manager jobs. Because they married, I reckon. That's the only qualification he got. And he'll take delivery for sure. Won't let anyone else count 'em. His men will be out on the run, he don't like seeing the stockcamp in till October. The horse-tailers come in for the fresh horses. He was tellin' Boy last time we come what a smart counter he was.'

Jack had a quiet word with Billy Yeomans. 'When we get there I want you to hunt these cows and calves through the gate like they were bullets ripping out of a machine gun. Lester reckons this bloke can count, we'll see!'

Jack had counted the mob the previous day. They were three down on number, four hundred and seventeen in all.

Ken Doherty saw their dust and met them at the bullock paddock gate. He was dressed like a country squire and seemed unimpressed with the dusty drovers. 'Where's Boy? He always brings my cattle.'

'Ol' Boy's crook,' Jack said. 'You got a good mob here, we brought 'em along nice and slow.'

'How many you delivering?'

'Four hundred and forty,' Jack replied. 'We'll see how good he counts,' he thought.

'And how many did Boy send?'

'Four hundred and fifty. We lost a few in the scrub.'

'Lost a few! Lost some good cattle along the way! I'm not surprised. You men don't look like you've done much droving.'

Jack flushed but made no reply. Doherty opened the gate and Billy got them running.

'Hundred!' yelled Jack after a few minutes.

'Hundred!' yelled Doherty, immediately after. He had lost the count after the first thirty had galloped through. Now he was in the dreadful predicament of having to lose face and ask for a re-run or take the young drover's count.

The cattle were flying through the gate in a cloud of dust.

'Hundred!' Jack yelled again.

'Hundred!' Doherty called straight away. He couldn't bring himself to ask for a new count. He sat his horse on the opposite side of the gate to Jack, head down, pretending to count.

'Hundred!' Jack called, for the last time. 'And forty!'

'Four hundred and forty it is,' Ken Doherty agreed, forcing a grin. 'Well, cheerio, young fellow, you'll learn to be a drover one day, I can see that!'

'And you'll learn to count and read brands one day if you live long enough,' Jack grinned to himself as he rode away.

'Jack,' Billy asked, riding back to camp. 'Did you really get a count of that mob?'

'Course I did. Think I'd be game not to count in front of a top cattleman like Ken Doherty? And Mister Doherty don't know it, but he's going to shout us a day's boozing at the Dajarra pub before we go home. I'll get it out of Boy later, twenty three cows worth of grog! All for him being smart!'

They camped just out of town, on the Common, near several other drovers. Dajarra was a railhead town, mostly for Territory and Kimberley cattle being trucked east.

'Hey!' Jack called to Lester who was squatting rolling a smoke and talking to Phil's two boys. 'You blackfellas can drink in Queensland. They got a different law in here.'

They grinned. They knew him well enough to know he was only poking fun.

'You want to come to town with me an' Billy and get outside some good cold beer?'

Blacks and half-castes were not allowed alcohol in the Northern Territory or Western Australia unless they had a 'Dog Ticket'. This was a piece of paper, difficult to come by, which stated that the bearer was entitled to the benefits of full Australian Citizenship. There was a six months mandatory gaol sentence for any person, white or black, who was caught supplying liquor illegally.

'I'm not interested in boozing, Jack,' the old coloured man answered. 'I tried it once, sent me mad. And I seen it send a lot of you white fellas mad, too. We might walk down the truckin' yards later and have a yarn with some of them Territory boys.'

The hotel bar was surprisingly empty. There was only one group of stockmen sitting quietly down one end. Jack bought the drinks.

'This is the money Phil gave me to buy more tucker with. But we got enough left ... I think! What the hell are those blokes over there saying? They can't get a saddle on a horse! Well, strike me roan, Billy, did you ever think you'd hear that from ringers? Let's go over and join 'em.'

Jack was looking for action. He quickly sized up the five ringers seated on bar stools. They were not drovers. Their clothes were too clean for that. But their sweat-stained faded hats, worn leather belts and cuban-heeled boots pointed to long days in the saddle and sun.

'We just come in with a mob from the Territory,' he told them. 'Where you fellas from?'

'Out the Georgina. Headingly. You camped on the Common? Well, look out a big black don't run your mares off, he's a real mongrel. He's one of ours an' needs a good work-out to quiet him down.'

'Well, what's stopping you?'

The ringer looked at the grinning face. 'Can't get a saddle on him. Nobody can.'

'Real hoorang mate,' another ringer chipped in. He pointed a finger. 'Tommy Morrison's tried and if he can't saddle him, no-one can!'

Jack looked at Tommy Morrison. 'You're a ringer and you can't saddle a horse!'

Tommy reddened. 'I can saddle a horse all right, mate. Don't you worry about that! But I can't get near that cow-kicking, biting, striking coot. Nobody can!'

'I can!'

They stared at Jack.

'I can saddle him and ride him because I need some drinkin' money and because I've never seen the horse I couldn't saddle. Seen a few horses I couldn't ride first up but none I couldn't rig. Anybody want to put a brick up?'

'You got ten to cover it?'

'No,' Jack answered truthfully. 'But we got five. Come on, Billy let's get this outlaw no-one can saddle!'

Tommy Morrison rode out with them. 'That's him, runnin' over there.'

He was a fine-looking animal. Trotting along, tail held high.

'Why, he's a rig!' Jack said. He could pick a horse in an instant. 'He's just running proud. We'll fix his little play around.'

They ran the horse that couldn't be saddled to a set of yards and chased him into the pound.

Jack turned to Tommy. 'We'll see you back at the pub. Line your mates up outside and be ready with my fiver!'

There was some breaking-in gear hanging over the rails. Jack selected a head-rope and threw it over the rig's head. Then he looped the other end of the rope around the bottom rail of the pound yard and reefed hard. The black lurched forward. Jack reefed on the rope until the horse was close to the rails. Then he gave it a tremendous jerk.

The loop around the rail acted as a pulley and brought the animal to his knees, nose crashing hard against the bottom rail. Jack allowed the horse to regain its feet. It shook its head and trotted unsteadily to the other end of the small pound yard. Jack reefed on the rope and repeated the performance. He then climbed over the rails and jumped into the yard. The horse stood still, trembling.

Jack walked over, patted its neck, and slipped the rope off.

'Give me a halter, Billy.'

He fastened the halter and jumped on the horse, kicking it hard in the ribs. It cantered around sedately.

Jack slid off and led it outside.

'Here, Billy, lead him down to the pub and we'll show these Dajarra ringers how to saddle a horse!'

The ringers in the bar had been joined by some drovers. Now there were a dozen or so squatting on the verandah as Jack and Billy rode up.

'Here he is!' Jack yelled. 'Take a look at him! The horse no-one can rig!'

He pulled the saddle off his horse and carried it to where Billy held the black.

'Give him here, Bill.'

The animal stood quietly as Jack held it loosely by the end of the rope halter. He held the saddle high over his head and slammed it down on the horse's back. The horse staggered a little and gave a kind of groan, but made no other move. Jack buckled girth and surcingle and sprang into the saddle. He didn't bother with the stirrups.

'Git up, outlaw!' he yelled, lashing it with the rope.

The stockmen stood gaping, not knowing what to make of this wild young drover who took a rogue horse so cheaply. With only a halter and no bit or reins, it could have made a bolt, but it made no attempt to deal with this man who had treated it so harshly and disdainfully.

Jack wheeled the horse around and galloped back to the pub.

'Take a look at him, you Dajarra ringers! Take a look at the horse that can't be saddled!'

Jack was in full flight. It had been a long slow trip with the cows and calves. Now he was back in action! He slipped off the horse, collected his five pounds and shouted the bar. He kept away from the Headingly ringers.

'Bloody jackaroos!' he snorted.

As the day wore on, a good crowd of Territory drovers stopped by. Jack listened to their tales of cattle rushes, the Murrunji scrub, the wild galloping stock camps of Victoria River Downs... Each new group heard the story of the horse that couldn't be saddled. 'That's him! Young fella over there!'

'Let's see you saddle this black that can't be rigged,' someone would yell and out Jack would go, rip the saddle off, throw it on again and gallop the black up and down the road. He was getting drunk now, but was still in control. Somebody, envious of all the attention he was receiving, told the policeman.

'There's a fella down the pub galloping a horse up and down the road that don't belong to him.'

The policeman strolled down. He had long been around these rough towns.

'Where's this stolen horse!' he shouted out in mock anger.

'Comin' down the road,' a voice called.

Jack galloped up, reefed on the halter and jumped off. Billy walked across and said a few words.

'Is that right!' Jack said in a loud voice. He stripped off his saddle, loosened the halter and belted the animal across the rump. As it galloped off he gave a final mocking yell. 'Where's that stolen horse that can't be rigged?'

Jack visited Dajarra several times over the years. He knew that country bred stockmen as good as anywhere, but he never forgot those ringers in the bar on his first visit. Neither did some of the drovers. They ranged wide over the Territory and back of Queensland, meeting and talking with many people. They told of the wild young ringer Jack Vitnell who showed the Dajarra ringers how to saddle a horse. The saddling episode became an embarrassment for the ringers around Dajarra. Someone strung a line of verse about it that was often recited in the pubs and cattle camps of the west.

By the following season Jack's name was mentioned in cattle camps as far away as the Kimberley in West Australia. It was always to be the way. His notoriety preceded him and men were waiting to meet this dare-devil ringer. From now on he did not need to seek out boisterous times or challenges. They came to him and he revelled in them. And wherever he went he met the best — horses, bulls, men.

Some were content to know and enjoy his company, exchanging stories of incidents in their adventurous lives. Others were keen to meet him to prove they were better ...

12.

Brunette

Cammy smiled as he stood by the outlaw's head,
Ready to make his attack,
Then deliberately kneed it hard in the gut,
As he swung up high on its back.
It was bucking a fit before he got set,
But he laughed and grabbed at its flank,
The crowd gasped in awe as it twisted and rose,
Yet to Cam it was only a prank.

The morning after the saddling episode, Jack and his mates were packing up at their camp on the Dajarra Common when they were visited by one of the drovers who regularly brought in Territory cattle.

'Splinter Prendegast's the name, fellas. Seen you in action yest'y, Jack. You sure showed them Headingly ringers up. That Tommy Morrison struts round town when he comes in like he was a gun. You going back north now? Can you take a mare back to Boy Beaumont? Gawd, he's a good hearted bloke, lent me his best cuttin' horse last year at Brunette Races and got drunk an' left without it.'

'When's those races, Splinter?'

'September this year. Should be August. You goin'?'

A race meeting. That was the place to find a little action! 'Could be, if I can get there.'

'Phil Hanlon ain't been the last few years. You want to all go. It's a good meeting but I won't be there this time. Got another mob from VRD to pick up.'

'That's where I'm heading soon,' Jack told him. 'You reckon I'd get a camp?'

'Might. They got six. Mt Sandford, Pigeon Hole, Moolaloo, Montejinni, Gordon Creek an' the Centre Camp — the one at the homestead. Hartley Magnussen's always lookin' for good men.'

Head-stockman on Victoria River Downs! Largest cattle station in the world. Jack was ready. He would ride every rough horse and throw every scrub bull on the place.

'Splinter, if I wasn't obliged to go back with this plant to Seven Emu I'd come with you now!'

'You goin' to leave us, Jack?' Lester wanted to know later, as they rode back to Boy Beaumont's.

'I'm not going to sit around for another Wet listening to all your lies again.' He grinned. 'Don Kirk might stop. Reckon me an' Billy will both push on.'

Billy Yeomans, slightly built and quiet, was an unlikely companion for the boisterous Jack Vitnell, but since mating up in Camooweal the year before they had stuck together. Jack could always depend on Bill and knew he was as good a ringer as was in the country. If Bill ever tired of being in Jack's shadow, he never complained. He would be one of only three close mates Jack ever made.

The return journey did not take long. They averaged thirty miles a day and camped wherever there was good feed for the horses. There was no need to camp by water. They filled the canteens every day at tanks or waterholes when the horses watered.

'We don't got much tucker left, Jack,' Lester told him as they pulled the packs one evening. 'Wasn't we supposed to get more at Dajarra?'

'Phil gave me the money, yes, but me an' Billy drank it. We'll borrow a bit off Boy when we get there.'

It never occurred to Jack to lie. If people didn't like what he did or said that was up to them. Jack would be ready for whatever play that came.

There was no-one at Boy's place. The house and even the store were wide open. Jack took a bag of flour. He didn't bother with a note. Boy would find the mare in the horse paddock and know someone had dropped it off. If he missed the flour he would reckon that was fair payment for delivering the mare.

There was no-one at Seven Emu either, when they arrived home a week later. Just a note from Phil on the kitchen table.

'When you bunch of drunks are sober, I'm out at Yellow Creek yard.'

'Thinks we been on the grog in Isa, just as well I've got a bottle of rum in the packs for him.'

It was more than a bottle, it was a gallon. Six bottles of Bosun Overproof Jack had ticked up at the Dajarra pub on Phil's account. They sat under a big white carbeen on Yellow Creek and drank it down in two days. Jack, Billy, Don Kirk and Phil. It was Jack's first, heavy bush-boozing session.

They laughed and talked, argued, cursed, recited verse and sang cowboy dirges. Billy warbled off an ode called 'Captain Kettle and his Crew.'

They all knew and joined in the chorus.

Bosun Rum and here is Bose,
Grinning from the label,
Watching as we pass him round,
Or slip beneath the table!'

The first two of many verses went:

The Bosun used to peer at me,
With grinning, woolly head,
I remembered what my father said,
'Rum will kill you dead.'
But I had that old rascal fixed,
He never bothered me,
I stuffed him in my tucker pack,
And Bose? He smiled to see!

Suppose I must have been eighteen,
A rugged wiry lad,
I used to have a nip each night,
Same as dear old Dad,
But sometimes if I found a mate,
I had a second nip,
And that old woolly Bosun?
He curled his knowing lip!

The song went on to detail the young man's lengthy slide into alcoholism. He believed by changing brands that things would be better....

Now Captain Kettle was my skip,
I lived to take a pull,
And as that bottle emptied,
Toiled to keep it full,
But when I woke up in the night,
A helpless, shivering wreck,
I sometimes saw the Bosun,
And Kettle walk the deck.

Eventually he succumbed to the DT's and was taken and confined to an institution. Later he recovered and kept away from his old companions as the last verse tells.

Now I'm strictly sober,
And keep much to myself,
Aware that where the boys are,
There's rum upon the shelf,
But I'm not going to buy it,
I'll leave it there for you,
And see if you can beat them,
Captain Kettle and his crew!

It was traditional for boozers to bellow out the last four lines as loudly as possible then toast the bosun's health amid roars of raucous laughter, not accepting that it could possibly refer to them. None of them were drunkards! The third morning Jack and Billy Yeomans caught their horses and joined the musterers. The older pair could not move off their swags.

'What's wrong with those fellas, Billy? Are you okay?'

'I'm a bit squirmy, Jack, but okay. Rum knocks you around when you get on a bit. Old fellas can't take it like us young blokes. Kills some of 'em.'

'Kills 'em? Well, it ain't killing me! If I ever get as bad as those two, I'll give it away!'

The six bottles of Bosun Rum lay empty, scattered along the bank of Yellow Creek. Already the labels with the grinning face of the old bearded bosun were fading in the harsh sunlight. Cracking. Curling at the edges. It was as though they heard and understood Jack's words. They weren't grinning any more. They lay on the dry yellow grass where the creek gurgled as it flowed slowly over a rocky bar and leered. A mile away, riding just behind Jack, Billy saw Jack give a sudden shudder.

'Somebody walk over your grave, Jack?'

'I'm not going to any race meeting,' Phil told them when they talked about it later. 'That rum we had back at Yella Creek will keep me going for a while. You lot can go. Take the boys, they know the way and need a spell.'

Only Billy and Jack decided to go. 'Me an' Billy might move on after the races, Phil. You won't need us now, the mustering's mostly done. Be a good chance to get a lift to somewhere else, there's a lot more of this Territory I want to see.'

Don Kirk headed back to the Isa. 'Me knuckles are missin' them miners!' he laughed.

'You comin' back one day, Jack?' Lester asked hopefully.

'Too right! Reckon I'll miss your soggy dampers after a while. And those stories. I never did find out why you came over to Seven Emu to die.'

'I'll tell you when you come back, Jack. But don't leave it too long. I ain't going to be here forever!'

The race meeting at Brunette Downs was a fairly primitive affair. It was held on a grassy plain by a bore, well away from the homestead, to cause the least possible disruption to the everyday running of the station. The only amenities were a few roughly erected bough sheds and the single railed oval course itself. There were no yards. The campdraft was conducted in the open like a genuine bullock draft and there was no crush available to assist riders get mounted on the buckjumpers.

Wason Byers was at the races that year. He was a hard man. A solid six foot three in height, he had seldom been beaten in fights around the back of Queensland and the Territory. Opinions on him varied. Some swore by him, others at him, but always behind his back. He first appeared as a drover from somewhere back 'inside'. No-one asked where he came from and few were told. A man came west to lose his past.

Nowadays he leased a block of country near Brunette. He and Jack soon got into conversation at the bar. An old hard case, fifty years of age, on his way down and an eighteen year old tearaway on his way up. Jack felt at ease with this rough, colourful man. That Wason was a good horseman and cattleman Jack had no doubt. Jack would always gravitate towards the top hands. His own kind. And the wilder the better. The also-ran-would-be-but-can't fellows were too boring for Jack.

There was a host of cattlemen on the course, crowding the bush timber bough shed that served as a bar. A publican from Tennant Creek had won the rights this year to supply the beer. He had brought in eight ton and by the second afternoon was wondering if he had trucked in enough.

The meeting ran over three days. The second day was the 'off' day when they had a simple rodeo. Flag and barrel races, a camp draft, a blackfellows' horse race, bullock ride, feature horse ...

Jack was with Wason Byers and Billy, watching the entertainment from the shade of the bar. He noticed a little stockman quietly sitting on a stool drinking with a pair of weather-worn ringers. Jack could not make his mind up if the little fellow was a sunburnt white or had a splash of colour.

'They're ringers from Lake Nash,' Wason told him. 'Down the desert. Breeds good horses that country. Good as any I've rode.'

'Good place to work?' Jack wanted to know. Wason laughed. 'Who said anything about working there? I just said they got good horses! They lose some at times, to drovers passing through. Bloody thieving drovers!' He laughed again.

Jack understood. 'How do I get a ride on this feature horse?' he asked.

'Can't. Ride's took. Cammy Cleary, that little fellow there.' Wason pointed to the little Lake Nash ringer Jack had been eyeing.

'Thought he looked a horseman. Any rate suppose I can get a ride on a bullock?'

'Sure can. I'll go and fix it for you now.'

Cammy Cleary was standing now. Jack had heard Cammy's name spoken as the Territory's top rider. 'Should be able to ride,' Jack thought. 'He's all legs.'

They were announcing the feature horse ride now.

Cammy finished his drink.

'Ghost he's a quiet one,' Jack thought. 'Don't think I saw him speak once to those two mates of his.'

Wason came bustling back as Cammy Cleary walked slowly out where two officials were holding the feature horse. 'You're set, Jack. Bullock ride's next, after Cammy.'

'Little fella's looking nervous, Wason, don't tell me he's running scared.'

'He's scared, all right, but not of the horse. Cammy hates crowds. He'd rather be anywhere but here right now. He never nominated for the ride, his mates stuck him in the hat.'

'I hope you're right,' Jack thought. 'Hate to see another frost like that gun ringer at Dajarra who couldn't saddle his horse.'

There was no need for a surcingle to make the animal buck. It knew what was expected. As soon as the rider was on its back and the blindfold pulled, it would go into action. There was no bell or pick-up man. The rider would ride the horse to a standstill or come off. The crowded bar had emptied. Everyone was lining the rails to watch. For the last three years this same big chestnut had thrown the three riders who had tried.

Cammy spoke to the ringers holding it. One of them carefully pulled away the shirt covering its eyes. There was a murmur from the crowd.

'Going to get on it without the blindfold!'

Cammy stood by the chestnut's shoulder for a moment seeming reluctant to step on. The ringers seconded as stewards, stood either side of its head, grasping the bit.

The rider took hold of the reins.

'Let him loose!' he called.

He thrust one boot in the stirrup and then he did the unthinkable. As he swung up, he deliberately kneed the animal hard in the belly. It was bucking before he swung his leg over the pommel. He had no chance of finding the off side iron. It lifted high in the air as the horse came down from its first buck. It appeared Cammy would come off at any moment. He was all over the place. Forward on its neck, backwards on its rump, two foot above the saddle as it twisted and turned. It was only when he spoke, that those who hadn't seen him in action before, realised he was in control.

Suddenly he turned his head to the crowd and drawled in his soft sing-song voice, 'This-is-how-you-ride-a-buck-jumper!'

Jack couldn't believe what he was watching.

'And I thought I could ride!' he muttered. 'I couldn't do that!'

Jack could have ridden the horse, but not in the same style.

No-one who rode up north ever sat a bucking horse as casually and loosely as Cameron Cleary. He was born in Alice Springs and reared on Lake Nash cattle station and had even less schooling than Jack. And rode as well. No-one could separate them as horsemen, two men with greatly different styles and temperament.

Cammy rode long and loose, Jack rode gripping tight with his thighs, spurring hard. A balance rider and a grip rider? Maybe. Either way, there was no-one around who could match them. Cammy was the original quiet-man-in-the-corner. Jack loved devilment and fun. And if that led to fighting, so be it! In years to come they would meet at many different places and become good mates. But at this meeting they barely spoke. Jack was always the centre of attention, Cammy on the edge.

Jack had no trouble riding the bull he was allotted. But it didn't buck well and disappointed him. A pig-rooting poddy was his comment. He was still looking for action when a bullock broke. A ringer took off after it and attempted the bulldog. It was a wild looking bullock with big untipped horns. The ringer leant over his horse, ready to make the leap, then lost his nerve.

Bulldogging was still largely an American rodeo event and most of the crowd hadn't seen it. Only some were aware of what the ringer was attempting. Then a horse raced up shoving the ringer's horse aside. The crowd gasped as the rider closed with the bullock and jumped off. It was Jack. He grabbed the horns and swung the bullock crashing to the ground. As it lay there stunned, he casually sat on its head and drew on his half-dead cigarette. Then he stood up, puffing out smoke and swaggered towards the crowd.

Two days ago Jack had arrived unknown. Now everybody knew the name Jack Vitnell and wanted to shout him a drink. Someone lent him a horse to enter the camp-draft. It was just an average cutting-out horse. But the way Jack rode it, it performed like a champion. He won. The Brunette ringers mustered up another outlaw and led it up to the Course. Jack rode it to a standstill. Someone hollered out for Cammy Cleary but it was too late. Cammy was on his back, down one end of the bar, passed out.

Wason Byers invited Jack out to his block.

'Can't afford to pay you anything, Jack, but you can stop as long as you like and take a look at the country and the way we operate.'

Billy Yeomans tagged along.

They stayed a month, branded some cattle, learnt how Wason helped himself to his neighbours' cleanskins and witnessed him get the flogging of his life.

'I never touch branded stock or anything not weaned,' he told them. 'And it's no use riding into someone else's country and just branding any cleanskins you come across. That only starts a war. I got big stations on my boundaries and they could rip the hell out of my stock. But those places always knock off mustering come October.' Wason grinned. 'That's when we move in. Anything they miss, we brand and bring back here and stick in our bullock paddock if there's plenty of grass like now. Next season they're the first ones on the road.'

They were out a week and brought back a good sized mob.

'Everywhere I've operated the same way and never been hassled.'

Wason was a man known to be hard on blacks. His blacks hated and feared him but were too frightened to leave. Too often they had seen what happened to other runaways. Wason followed, brought them back in chains and flogged them with his whip. Sometimes the floggings went on for days. None of this happened during Jack and Billy's stay. Wason was careful to be well behaved.

But his treatment of his station blacks as well as his cattle-duffing activities had been noted by the local police. Later he faced court on both counts. But to date nothing had been done. Then a relieving constable was sent to Anthony Lagoon. He heard about this station man so handy with his whip and decided to pay a visit. Billy Yeomans and Jack were shoeing a horse when he rode up.

'Which one of you is Wason Byers?' he asked.

Jack pointed.

'Neither. That's him riding up now.'

Wason wondered who the stranger was. He looked a horseman the way he sat his mount. Then Wason got a clear view of his hat.

'A copper!' he sneered. 'What do you want here!'

'I'm lookin' for the bloke who thinks he can use a whip!'

This was no ordinary policeman. This one had spent many years outback in a variety of jobs before joining the Force. Wherever he went, his hair got him the nickname of 'Snow'.

'I'll give you whips!' Wason snorted and loosed a long, greenhide plait he was carrying. It cracked an inch above the policeman's hat.

'That's the mistake Billy The Kid made,' sneered Snow. 'If you're going to shoot, shoot!'

He loosed his whip and ripped Wason's shirt from his back in two chops. Wason sat stunned for a second then bellowed in rage. No-one had ever treated him with such disdain. He lost control and pulled his revolver. Most stockmen carried a revolver in a holster on their saddle to stop rampant bulls.

'You mongrel!' he roared.

Snow's tracker yelled a warning. Snow sent the gun flying with a flick of his wrist.

'Use your whip, you critter!'

Wason did, plying savagely, slashing at the mocking face.

Snow spurred his horse and dodged out of the way. Then he moved in, whip snaking, ripping flesh from his opponent's exposed back.

'That policeman's going to chop him to pieces,' Billy said. 'He can really use a whip.'

'Wason's going to get no more than he deserves,' Jack answered. 'He should never have pulled that squirt.'

Suddenly Wason's whip was torn from his grasp and fell to the ground. There was no chance to dismount and retrieve it with Snow's whip whistling around.

He could either stay and face a flogging or gallop off. He chose to stay. Wason Byers had never run in his life. He sat there, bleeding and in pain as the policeman flogged him with his whip. Then it was over.

'Get his gun,' Snow called to the tracker.

Snow snapped it open. It was empty.

'If there had been a bullet in here I'd have taken you in for attempted murder. You're lucky. But you listen. One more complaint about you and your whip and I'll come back and really flog you. After that, when you're able to ride again, I'll take you in and get you two years.'

Wason looked at the hard blue eyes.

'What's your name, copper? I like a man who talks tough and can back it up.'

'Snow will do.' He gave a crease of a smile. 'You were dead unlucky sport, I cut me teeth on whips!'

'Wonder where that copper learnt to swing a whip like that?' Jack asked later.

'Dunno where he learnt,' Wason growled. 'But wherever it was, I hope he goes back there. He sure didn't learn to use a whip like that at no Police Academy!'

13.

Gordon Creek

When a Queensland man joins a Kimberley camp,
It's said he's from "inside",
They wonder if he's galloped stone,
And how well he may ride,
But there's men "inside" can lead the way,
And mix it with the best,
And show the old hands in the west,
They're equal to the test.

Lockie McKenzie had spent his life up North. He had arrived years before the First World War and always said he learnt more about the war by reading about it afterwards than he had ever learnt when it was on. His father was a Kidman drover and Lockie had been his horse-tailer. When he was seventeen they had travelled up to a Kidman owned station out of Alice Springs to take a mob back to the channel country. Here they had argued over the horses and Lockie had ridden off, swearing he was finished with horse-tailing forever. He rode north and never saw father or family again.

For nearly fifty years he had worked on stations from the Gulf to the Kimberley. For the last twenty he had been on Victoria River Downs, largest cattle station in Australia. He had droved their cattle, built stock-yards, dug wells and run their stockcamps. Now he was at retirement age but still working, camp cook at the outstation, Gordon Creek.

All old ringers finished up camp cooking if they stuck to station work. It was a key position in any stockcamp and meant much more than just cooking. The cook travelled with the horse-tailer, ahead of the stockmen, and set up the camps. These were regular camping areas, usually close to yards but the exact location any one year depended on availability of water and feed for the horses.

On arrival at camp, the pack-horses had to be unloaded and everything stacked away neatly. Then water had to be carted up from the creek or rock-hole, wood gathered and chopped, a fire pit dug and fire lit and all the host of jobs done to ensure the hungry team of stockmen were fed at sundown. Bread was baked or drums of already kneaded dough knocked back, buckets of salt beef were cooked, tea billies readied, clean sugar bags laid out on the ground for a table, a scrounge made through the tucker packs to find some custard powder or sultanas for a brownie ... It was no job for a lazy man.

And no matter what the weather or the state of the stores — fresh, weevily, run-out — the men had to be fed as well as possible. But the most irritating part of the job Lockie found was watching another man run his old camp. Lockie had run the Gordon Creek stockcamp for eight years and always mustered the required branders and bullocks. Now he had to watch lesser men struggling to make their quota. But not this year. This new man was as smart a man as Lockie had ever seen.

They had finished the horse muster and were now drafting. The horse muster. Wow! Had that fellow led the way! Lockie had never seen riding like it.

'Thought I could ride when I was young,' he mused, 'But I wouldn't have kept up with this bloke. Could have hacked it with his little mate, Bill. Good all round ringer like the rest of us. But this new head stockman Jack! No matter what he was on, he hit the lead and that Big Bruno, didn't he set him first night out ...'

'What's that half-caste doing, camping with the blacks, Lockie?'

'That's what they do here, on VRD, Jack. If you coloured, you camp with the blacks. That's where he's always camped and he's a proper trouble maker, too. I reckon he's why Johnny Silver went drovin' this year. He didn't want another year with Bruno white-antin' everything he did.'

'Well, he won't be white-anting me.'

It was sundown and they were at the first night camp out from the station. Fifteen black stockmen, Lockie, the new head stockman, Jack Vitnell and his mate, Billy Yeomans, plus the half-caste. Jack had looked across where Big Bruno was sitting cross-legged at the stockboy's fire a hundred yards away. He was talking loudly and from time to time pointed to where the three whites stood by their fire.

'I'll fix this bloke,' Jack had said.

He had walked across to the other fire. The stock boys looked at their boots. Bruno stared defiantly at his new boss.

'You black or white?' Jack had asked.

'Can't you see! I'm a yella fella!'

'No you're not! Not in my camp. You're white. Get on your feet when you're talking to me.'

Bruno was so stunned at being told that he was white he just sat there.

Jack kicked him hard on the sole of one boot.

'Stand up!'

Bruno jumped to his feet. He was head high over Jack and heavier, but he was a bully who liked the odds his way. He had heard about this boss man and his fists and saw a tiger ready to spring.

'I don't want no trouble with you, Jack.'

'Get over to our fire then or roll your swag and get! You understand what I'm saying? You don't camp with these boys anymore. You camp with us. You don't even talk to these boys. I talk to these boys. You got anything to say in this camp you say it to me. Now get your swag and I'll teach you how to act like a white man!'

It was Jack's first experience with the colour bar. Elsewhere he had worked half-castes were treated as whites. But he would run this camp his way. Since then Bruno had been a different man.

'It's going to be a good year,' Lockie smiled as he sat on the pound top rail of the drafting yard. There were two hundred horses to sort out. Six horses would be drafted off to each stockman, his mounts for the next month and a half. After that the camp would return to the station and muster a fresh plant of horses. Then they would pull the shoes off their jaded mounts and bush them. Depending on the constitution of each horse and its condition, it may be ridden again later in the season or not until the following year. It was hard country on horses.

The head-stockman allocated the horses, but because Jack was new and Lockie knew every horse, he sat next to Jack and assisted. He gave a brief description of each horse's capability as it ran into the pound.

'This one good horse, Jack. Whitefella horse. You or Billy want to take him for sure. He can really go. Top cuttin' mare this one, won the campdraft at the races last year. Blackfella horse, this bloke, he can buck too. Night horse this one.'

Then a big, black horse ran in and trotted around, head and tail held high, amid yells from the stockboys.

'Bush gate this 'un! ... Lookout! Here the killer horse ...'

'What's wrong with them?' Jack asked.

'Bad horse. Anybody get on him he rears straight up and comes over backwards. He's a killer all right. Tries to flatten anybody gets on him. Wants shooting. Nobody can ride him now. Good horse one time.'

Here it was again. An unrideable horse. This time a horse that chose not to be ridden any more and had found a way to frighten men off its back. Jack's eyes gleamed.

'Get a bridle on that black, I'll fix his little game!'

'Don't try it, Jack ... ' Lockie turned and started to say, but there was no-one there. Jack had jumped down and was outside the yard walking towards a heap of rails stacked on the ground. There were always a few rails, new and broken ones, around a yard. Jack selected a solid broken one about three feet long.

'What he going to do with that?' the stockboys whispered as he walked back to the pound. 'Knock him on the head? Kill the bugger?'

Jack wasn't about to kill it but he was going to remind this rogue horse man was its boss. He climbed through the rails into the pound where the black was bridled and standing quietly. A stockboy held the reins. Another was walking towards it with a saddle on his shoulder.

'Put the saddle back on the rails, mate,' Jack told him. 'More better I ride him no saddle, what I got to do.'

If Jack had to slip quickly from the animal he didn't want a saddle to tangle with. It was nothing for him to leap on a known buckjumper without using the stirrups. They could flap all he cared. He held onto a horse by gripping it with his powerful thighs. Mounting a horse without saddle or stirrups was simple for Jack. During his time with McConville's Wild West Show he had nightly leaped on and off circling cantering horses in the show ring. To spring on this animal bare-back holding a three foot club was nothing.

But to the stockmen watching, it seemed incredible that any man would take this animal so cheaply. Billy Yeomans wasn't surprised. The last two years riding with Jack had taught him his mate could do anything with horses. He wasn't sure how Jack was going to tame this Horse-That-Topples-Over-Backwards but he was quite certain he would come out the winner.

The stockboy holding the reins passed them over and quickly left the yard. Jack was on his own. He was holding a fine looking animal, big and powerful. If it sensed this man was here with a challenge, it gave no sign and stood meekly as he slipped the reins over its head. It would get rid of this rider same as all the others. Jack took a handful of mane and sprang on. Immediately the black reared straight up on its hind legs, front legs pawing the air.

Jack held on firmly with his legs and took one end of the club in both hands. He raised it high above his head and leaned forward. At the moment it seemed the horse must fall over backwards, he brought his club crashing down on the animal's forehead. It fell forward and stood on four legs, shaking its head in pain and shock. Then up it reared again. Jack lifted the rail and struck it hard on the forehead once more. Down came the horse on all fours again. This time it took a few hesitant steps.

'That's the fella,' Jack said. 'Now let's see you step out.'

Jack hooked it in the shoulders with his spurs. The horse gave a few half-hearted pig roots and broke into a trot around the pound.

'Open the gate!' Jack called. He cantered it around the Big Yard.

'Now the bush gate!'

The outside gate swung open and away they went, galloping across the flat. Jack took the horse in a wide circle around the big set of drafting yards. Then he brought it back through the gate and jumped off. The stockboys stood around and looked at him in awe. They had never seen a man like this before.

'Here!' Jack called to one of them. 'He's your horse now. Saddle him up and work him hard. If he looks like rearing again, grab a stick and do what I did. Let him know who's boss!'

After that, there wasn't a man in the camp who wouldn't have followed Jack Vitnell through the eye of a cyclone.

They were mustering a belt of limestone country. It was dangerous to gallop, flat and slippery, with random sink-holes that could swallow a horse. Scrub bulls were everywhere indicating it was hard country to muster clean. Rogue bulls charged off soon as the horsemen were sighted, heading for scrub or stony ridges. Others less cunning could be more easily chased and pulled down. The stockmen worked in pairs, selecting a bull and giving chase. They were big, heavy animals unused to moving quickly and could be easily overtaken by a fast horse. The trick was to pounce on them before they became exhausted and aggressive.

The lead rider kept his horse close in towards the beast and when ready, quickly reefed on the reins and jumped off. He was now a few paces behind the fleeing bull and needed to run quickly to overtake it. Then he would grab the tail, and when the bull was momentarily off balance, with both hind feet off the ground, pull down hard on its tail. Down it would come, rolling as it fell, over on its side, stunned for a moment. That was when the stockman secured it by slipping the tail between its legs and levering backwards, using the tail as a rope to hold the animal down.

The stockman's mate would have galloped alongside, leapt off his horse, ready to play his part. He would grab a horn and saw it off with the special saw carried on his saddle. When both horns were cut off he would take his knife and castrate the animal. Meanwhile, the thrower still held to the animal's tail preventing it from rising.

The horses were well used to this activity and used the free minutes to chomp a few tufts of grass and take a breather. As soon as the animal was dealt with, the man with the saw caught his horse and rode it back to the bull, leading the other animal. Then the thrower let go of the tail and sprang on his horse.

Up the bull would get, furious at the treatment, and charge the nearest horse. It couldn't understand why the animal made no attempt to flee. It kept butting at the horse, covering it with blood from the sawn-off horns. Now it could easily be managed.

If the stockmen were mustering bullocks for the drover and wanted to take the animal along, they would make sure there was a mob of previously mustered cattle, called coachers, close by. They would chase the bull across to this quiet coacher mob where it would soon settle down and become part of the mob, though sore and sullen for a time. If there were no coachers about the beast would head back to the hills minus its horns and be easily mustered next time the camp came past.

Billy always worked with Jack, throwing bulls. Often each threw a bull at the same time. They carried a heavy leather belt slung over their shoulders and used these to lash the thrown animals hocks. Then they could leave one and both work on the other.

This day two bulls broke from the scrub. Both men whipped up their horses and took after them. They leapt off at the same time and Bill quickly had his by the tail and thrown. But for the first time Bill could remember, Jack missed. Just as he was about to grab the bull's tail, Jack stumbled on a rock and fell hard on his back. The bull should have kept running but for some reason this one decided to attack the man lying helpless in the dirt.

In a flash it wheeled around and charged.

Jack saw the bull coming and knew if he attempted to rise it would rip him to pieces. His only chance was to lie still. It took a great deal of courage and discipline to remain quiet and watch half a ton of furious bull charging. Bill had no chance to help because if he let go of the bull he was holding there would be two rampant bulls to worry about. He sat watching in horror, fifty yards away.

Jack lay where he fell, on his back. His elbows were bent, hands partly shielding his face. He took a deep breath and closed his eyes. The bull lowered its head and struck hard with its horns. One horn thudded into the ground to the left of Jack's chest, the other to the right. Bill could see the bull standing right over Jack's body. Then with a toss of its huge head it was gone, galloping for the hills.

Bill still squatted, holding his bull by the tail. Jack had not moved.

'By God,' he thought wildly, 'It's killed him!'

Then slowly he saw Jack's hands unclench.

'Bill,' he called, in a low voice. 'Did you make your throw?'

'Yes! I've got him down. Are you okay?'

'Let him go!'

Bill let go of the tail and jumped up. The bull sprang to its feet and rushed after its mate. Jack was still lying on his back. Then he sat up and slowly got to his feet. He didn't look at Bill but walked stiffly off towards his horse cropping the grass. Bill mounted and followed.

'You all right, mate? By God I got a fright. I thought he had you!'

'So did I. He slobbered all over my face. I don't want to go through that again.'

They rode back towards the musterers without another word.

'That was the coolest thing I've ever seen,' Bill thought. 'How did he manage to lie there like that without moving? Anyone else would have jumped to their feet and been horned. He nearly was horned! It was only luck saved him.'

That night as they sat drinking tea around the fire, Bill said to Lockie and big Bruno, 'What would you think of a bloke who fell asleep when a bull was charging him?'

They looked up with interest. Jack shot him a fierce look then quickly turned to them.

'Bill beat me at throwing today, that's what he's talking about. First time. Slipped when I grabbed the tail and off he went, that old bull, full bore!' He laughed. 'Luckiest bull on the ridges, still got his horns!'

Not a word of his close encounter. He looked at Bill with a strange look.

'Why,' Bill thought, 'He's ashamed! Ashamed he missed the throw. Doesn't want anyone else to know. Why didn't he tell me not to say anything?'

But he knew the answer. Jack's pride wouldn't allow him to ask. Jack was furious with himself for tripping over. And to make it worse, someone had been watching. Jack didn't want to talk about it, no matter that he had shown great courage by lying doggo and taking his chance.

'Strewth,' Bill muttered. 'He always has to win. By ghost he does!'

They had completed the final bullock muster. Twelve hundred head for Queensland. 'Who's taking this mob, Jack?' Bill asked.

'Supposed to be that Elmore Lewis, the bloke who owned that horse I rode in Camooweal. Soon know, he's due to meet us tomorrow at Dashwood Yard.'

Two Kimberley head stockmen. Lloyd Cravigan left, Don McLachlan right.

Waterloo stock camp setting out for the bullock muster in the very dry season of 1954. Don McLachlan left, Jeff Tribe, The Mongrel from Mungindi, on right.

View of the cattle ramp, holding yard and The Bastion mountain from the Knocker-Down's perch on the Killing Floor, Wyndham Meatworks, 1954.

George Fogarty, Jack Vitnell, Don McLachlan, with Six Mile Hotel barmaids, Wyndham Races, 1954.

14.

The Dashwood Yard

The shadow of the night-horse,
Is with me as I sleep,
His muffled shuffling hoofbeats,
Make another sweep,
The fire at the camp-site,
Winks warmly at the night,
A thousand restless bullocks,
To guard until daylight.

Dashwood Yard was the place Victoria River Downs handed over cattle to the drovers —and what a sight it was. Just an ordinary set of drafting yards on the Victoria River up from the Pigeon Hole outstation but when the Gordon Creek stockcamp arrived the whole plain surrounding it was covered in cattle and horses. Bill had never seen so many in one place before. Six or seven hundred head of horses hobbled out and over ten thousand head of tailed cattle.

Five of the VRD stockcamps had already arrived and Jack and his crew made the sixth. There was George Bates, head stockman of the outstation Mount Sandford and all his men, Tex Moar and his crew from Moolooloo, Buck Buechester, Pigeon Hole, Gilly Gilbert, Centre Camp, and Dan Thorne and Co. from Montejinni.

The stockcamps set up well away from each other. The cattle had to be held separately because each camp's bullocks were to be handed over to a different drover and there was a lot of work to do before that happened. The drovers camped apart as well. There was Doug Scobie, Splinter, Slippery and Claude Prendegast and Johnny Darcy.

There was a heap of men. Each of the stockcamps had around twenty and each drover six or eight but there was little opportunity for getting together. The camps were too busy cutting-out, tailing and at night, watching their mobs. Jack had been told to have fifteen hundred head of bullocks ready for the drover to take into Queensland but like the other camps, had brought in closer to two thousand. That meant five hundred of the poorest would be cut out.

Their drover, Elmore Lewis, arrived the next day. The Miniature Stockman, who had shown the Camooweal men how to ride a buckjumper while standing in the stirrups, was with him astride a huge pie-bald horse. They didn't wait to set up camp, but rode straight across to the Gordon Creek camp and grinned their 'good-days'.

'Guess who's carrying the canteen pack, Jack?'

'I can see him, Elmore. Ol' Kruger. You're as good as your word. He gave me a tough ride just the same.' Jack and Elmore continued talking as Bill Yeomans walked slowly amongst the drover's horses. Miniature nudged his mount forward. 'Good plant, hey Bill?'

'Gawd he's got some pretty little horses, that Elmore. Reckon he must make a hobby out of it. How was the trip out?'

Miniature shrugged. 'Nothing wrong with the trip and Elmore's a good bloke to get on with but I'm ready to quit. If there was anyway of not going back with the bullocks I'd take it. Droving don't suit me, Bill. It ain't what I come north for. Too quiet, give me the stockcamp any day.'

'How would you like to swap places?'

Miniature stared at him. 'With you? Fair dinkum!'

'Yep. Restless, that's what I am. Soon as I saw these drovers here yesterday my feet began to itch. I need a change, Miniature. Gordon Creek's a good camp and Jack's a top boss but I got the urge to move on. I've spent a season here, that's long enough in one place for me. Don't say anything about it now, let me talk to Jack. Okay with you?'

Miniature nodded.

'Of course. I've heard about this Victoria River Downs all my life and always wanted to work here. Soon as I saw that big Bulls Head brand on a bullock the other day I reckoned this would do. And especially working with a man like Jack Vitnell.'

That night Miniature rode over to the Gordon Creek camp to take a turn on watch.

'Well, look at this,' Jack called. 'If it ain't Johnny the drover! What you done with Johnny the buckjump rider?'

Miniature grinned. He was expecting a bagging. It was unusual to find a buckjumper in a drover's camp. Poking along steadily behind mobs of cattle soon quietened even freshly broken colts.

'He's been asleep, that's what, but I reckon he's about to wake up. You got a start for me?'

Jack shook his head.

'I already got my man, Bill here. These stations out here won't allow more than two white blokes in the same camp — sometimes only one. Say they can't afford 'em. They can get all the blackfellas they need for five bob a week — and they're damn good stockmen most of 'em.'

The next evening when Bill saw Miniature riding towards the camp he called to Jack, 'Look at that poor little bugger. Can't keep away from the stockcamp. He's terrible browned off with that droving. A man ought to change places with him seeing we can't put him on.'

Jack cocked his head.

'What does that mean? You want to go back droving?'

Bill shifted his feet uncomfortably. They had become good mates by this time.

'Well, I do and I don't, Jack. Seeing these drovers has unsettled me a bit. I wouldn't mind doing a bit of travelling again.'

They stared at one another for a moment. There was no hint on Jack's face of what he was thinking but Bill could tell he was annoyed. His eyes were grey. Mostly they were blue, but they would change according to his mood at the time. Look-out if they went black!

'Go then,' he suddenly snapped. 'It won't make any difference. One ringer's as good as another. Clear it with Elmore and it's okay with me.'

He made no attempt to change Bill's mind. To Jack, that would have been asking a favour and he would never do that.

Once the campdrafting was finished, the cut-out cattle — the culls — were taken bush and let go. Then the road cattle were yarded and inoculated against pleuro for the long, slow, cold trip across the Barkly Tableland. Each bullock had to be run through the crush of the big drafting yard to have a seton soaked in vaccine run through its tail and each mob had to be kept separate from the others. Everyone bogged in and helped and this was the first time the men had been able to get together as a group. Bill was given a job forcing cattle up the race. It brought him in contact with the Centre Camp head stockman, Gillie Gilbert.

Bill had noticed this man the past couple of days when campdrafting. Riding into a mob and cutting selected beasts out took a great deal of skill and it was also a good chance to do a bit of showing-off. But unlike most of the men, Gilly Gilbert went about his job as quietly and off-handedly as he would have amongst his own men in his own territory. There was no wild, flash riding. Mostly he left it to the mare, as smart a camp horse as Bill had seen. She never let a beast past but twisted and turned, always on the bullock's tail, and Gilly Gilbert's boots never sat more than half-way into the stirrup irons the whole time.

'Wouldn't say he was better than Jack on a camp-horse,' Bill thought. 'But he's about as good and that's saying a heap.' And it was true. Gilly Gilbert had gun ringer stamped all over. He stood out even in that company.

They were squatted around the fire at the yard at dinner-time that first day's inoculating when Jack noticed a mud fat chestnut horse trot by. It was running with the Centre Camp horses and he could tell it had not been ridden that season.

'What's wrong with that horse?' he asked Gilly. 'Why hasn't he been worked?'

'Oh, they reckon he can buck,' Gilly replied. 'I was going to ride him but never got around to it.'

'That so,' said Jack. 'Well, if you haven't rode him by now you're not going to. How about give him to me and I'll use him in the Gordon Creek camp. He's too good a horse to leave roaming around unworked.'

Gilly stared at Jack, sort of looked him up and down but not in an insolent way, more like he was trying to work out if Jack could handle the horse and was as good a man as he'd heard. Finally he said, 'Well, I'm pretty used to seeing that horse running about and I wouldn't like to part with him, but you can take him for a gallop if you want. But he's not easy to get on. In fact there's not too many around has ever got on him to find out how good he can buck.' Well! That was enough for Jack. He would have paid to ride the chestnut after Gilly told him that.

'Can he be caught or do we need a rope?' Jack asked.

'Oh, we can catch him okay,' said Gilly with just a hint of a smile. 'In fact I reckon ol' Greasy Back will be glad of a bit of attention.'

With that he called to one of the horsetailers to catch the chestnut and fetch it over. While the horsetailer was rigging it with a saddle, the Centre Camp stockboys drinking tea at their fire a short distance away, grinned amongst themselves and sneaked amused glances towards Gilly and Jack. If Jack noticed he ignored it. He didn't hesitate when the horsetailer arrived with the chestnut but sprang straight on. A blink of an eye later, he was standing in the dirt, reins still in his hands, with his back to the horse. Bill had not seen the horse move, it happened so quickly, and thought for a moment he had been imagining things and that Jack had not attempted to get mounted.

The chestnut was just standing quietly, looking at Jack, and Jack was standing just as quietly eyeing the chestnut. Then Jack sprang for the horse again. This time

Bill saw a flash of movement. A smudge of chestnut horse, blur of Jack's blue shirt and then he was looking at Jack again, standing on the ground in front of the horse, reins in hand. No-one spoke, least of all Jack. He was so astonished he just stood there with a look of amazement on his face, trying to work out what had happened. Then he leapt on again.

'Hi, ho, Silver!' he yelled. 'I'm here this time!'

And he was. Jack told Bill later that as soon as he placed his foot in the stirrup the chestnut dropped its head to the ground and flung itself sideways. A difficult and unusual move for a horse to make. But by his third attempt Jack had worked out what to do. Instead of trying to throw his leg over its back, he clung on to one side of the saddle until the horse stopped moving sideways. Then he swung on.

Soon as Jack was set, he grabbed the horse with his spurs, sitting bolt upright, right arm flung out, in his usual style. The chestnut bucked, twisting and turning but it was all in vain. The rider never looked like coming off. Finally when it slowed to a pig root Jack lashed it with the reins and set it galloping across the flat. Then he brought it back and jumped off, his eyes sparking.

'A bit hard to get on! He's the trickiest thing I ever tried.' He looked at Gilly. 'You teach him that or did he come up with it himself?'

Gilly just smiled and shook his head. 'No, I'm not that smart. He's done that from colt time. I broke him in and he don't do it with me but anyone else tries to ride him that's what he does. I don't know why.'

Maybe Jack believed him, Bill didn't. There was a lot more of Gilly Gilbert that Bill would liked to have seen but next morning Elmore took delivery of the bullocks and was ready to head off — fifteen hundred head and a thousand miles to go. Elmore had been as indifferent as Jack, to Bill and Miniature swapping places. Each man was sorry to leave the Dashwood camp — it had been a chance to meet others of their kind and see them in action. But before Bill left he made an enemy of Tex Moar, head stockman of the Moolooloo camp. Elmore had the bullocks in hand and was about to head off when Bill slipped away to say goodbye to Jack and Miniature.

On the way he passed the Moolooloo stockcamp packing up ready to leave and saw that they had several of Jack's Gordon Creek prize night horses. Jack and Miniature were busy checking the pack bags when he rode up.

'I'm off now, Jack. See you back in Camooweal sometime, hey?'

Jack grinned to where Bill was sitting his horse and reached his hand up. 'Look out you don't get lost in that Murranji scrub. Keep close to Elmore.'

Bill smiled, then he said, 'You give any of your night horses to that Tex Moar?'

'No,' Jack answered. 'He got some?'

Bill was reluctant to squeal on Tex but Jack was a mate and he was annoyed that Tex was cheeky enough to take some of his horses.

'Six, I reckon.'

'Come on then, 'Jack said climbing on his horse. 'Let's get 'em back.'

Tex Moar was a tough rangy fellow, a top stockman, not frightened to knuckle if the occasion arose. Jack rode across to where he was standing in his camp watching and came straight to the point.

'You got six Gordon Creek night horses here. I want 'em.'

'Oh,' said Tex, with a grin. 'Have I now. I thought I was working on Victoria River. They the only horses I got, Victoria River horses.'

Jack grinned back. 'Nice try, Tex, but they belong to Gordon Creek and I'm taking 'em. You aim to stop me?' Tex shrugged, he knew he was in the wrong. 'Help yourself, Jack, but how about let me keep half. I'm damn short of good night horses.'

Jack gave him a nod and called to Bill. 'Give me a hand to cut three out, mate. Then you better catch Elmore up or he's going to sack you on your first day.'

They cut out the three best and the last Bill saw of Jack was his back, as he hunted them towards his camp. Tex Moar gave Bill a savage look as he rode back. 'You'll get yours, dobber!'

It took Tex a few years, but he got square. Bill was passing through Pine Creek and called into the Commercial Hotel. Inside he saw Tex Moar arguing with another ringer. Finally they started fighting and the publican called the police.

The officer who answered the call was a young fellow new to the town and the ways of the North. Instead of stepping in swinging his baton, he attempted to break the fight up. As he wrapped his arms around Tex Moar to pull him away, Tex threw him heavily to the floor. Before the policeman could regain his feet, someone from the crowd rushed in and kicked him. The young policeman was not hurt, quickly regained his feet and Tex was promptly arrested. However, before he was led away, he yelled out to Bill Yeomans who was amongst the crowd watching, 'Thanks for trying to help, Bill.'

Before Bill realised what had happened he was arrested too. Tex Moar was fined for fighting but Bill received three months in Fanny Bay for assaulting a police officer. But all that was a couple of years in the future. For now, Bill kicked his horse up and cantered after Elmore. There was a mob of bullocks to be taken into Queensland. He was on the road again!

'I'll never find another mate like Jack,' Bill thought as he caught up with the cattle. 'But sooner or later I got to strike out for myself. If I keep riding with Jack I'll always be in his shadow. Time I got away and run a camp myself, or got a droving plant together. And I'll meet up with him again.'

His heart quickened a little as he thought of something else.

'Why don't I admit it? I've got a girl on my mind. If I don't get a rope on her someone else will. No good talking to Jack about those things though. He knows as much about women as I know about market gardening. And he's about as interested. All he thinks of is wild cattle, rough horses and new places!' Bill kicked the big piebald after a bullock that had stopped behind to linger on a particularly sweet clump of grass.

'Suppose we're much the same,' he grinned. 'Just as well this girl's a drover's daughter. She's going to be doing a lot of travelling out west!'

Six weeks later they were passing Newcastle Waters.

'We need more flour, Bill,' Elmore said. 'We'll camp early tonight and you an' me can take a pack-horse over to the store and get some. But no boozing. That's on hold till Dajarra.'

The station was a regular stop for Queensland-bound drovers. As they lugged the flour out they could hear raucous singing coming from a nearby hut. They stopped and listened.

'By jings, Elmore, it don't take 'em long to make a song up in this country. You recognise that?'

Then Jack led him up to Elmore,
Said, 'Matey, here's your nag,
I thought you had an outlaw,
Not this broke down old stag,'
And climbed the pub verandah steps,
And joined me in a toast,
When I said I'd been in Alice,
Time he rode the Guyra Ghost ...

'Me an' Kruger!' Elmore was tickled. 'No doubt about them fellas, they smart all right to come up with that!'

'But Jack ain't been to Alice Springs, Elmore.'

'Oh, them poet fellas always balls something up! Must have needed something to rhyme with toast'.

'But he'll get there, an' he'll ride that Guyra Ghost if he ever comes across it. There ain't nothing that Jack Vitnell can't ride!'

15.

Death in the Men's Quarters

Only a black girl, Sally by name,
A chattel for one of her tribe,
And traded around to any who came,
And offered a worthwhile bribe,
But pearls were never as lustrous,
As the teeth in her laughing replies,
And bullets were never as dangerous,
As the flashes she sent from her eyes.

Jack was in at the head station. It was nearly Christmas and the Wet was close upon them. He had left the Miniature Stockman and Lockie Mackenzie behind at Gordon Creek on their own. The stockboys had all headed off walkabout soon as the mustering was finished. Big Bruno, the half-caste, had stood miserably by as they strode off across the flat.

'They my people too, Jack, no matter I whitefella now.'

Jack had smiled. 'You can go, Bruno. Holiday time now. Go with them. Tuck-out on plenty goanna. Do you good.'

Bruno had looked at him, uncertain if he was joking.

'Go! Hurry and catch 'em up, but Bruno, you remember this. Next year in the stockcamp you proper white man again and camp with us!'

Jack had come in to load up with stores. It would be the last chance to top up until after the Wet. Soon the station roads would be impassable. Jack had loaded the old three ton Dodge but got no further than the single men's quarters. One of the Centre Camp stockmen had received a parcel. Officially alcohol was banned on the station, but when the mustering season was over Hartley Magnussen, the manager, pretended not to notice when the odd parcel arrived in the mail. It was never called a gallon of overproof rum, but a 'parcel'. A wind-down for the men after the long cattle season camping out.

Jack was starved for new company. The only men he had spoken to that year apart from those in the stockcamp had been the group at Dashwood Yard during the handover of the cattle to the drovers.

'It's good country,' he reflected. 'I like it. It's rough and wild and so are the cattle and horses. And the men too, I guess. But by God it gets lonely. I'm not cut out to bury myself in the bush.'

Jack was in his element with the others of his kind, drinking rum and yarning. He had never been one to sit back and just listen. He had experienced many interesting adventures and been to many different places in his nineteen years and revelled in recounting them. He didn't dwell on his own wild exploits. He didn't have to. The grapevine took care of that. He was already becoming a legend.

There were six stockmen enjoying the parcel of rum, sitting cross-legged on the verandah.

'Where's Colin the saddler?' Jack asked Roley McPherson, the Victoria River Downs horse boss.

'Down in his shop keepin' an eye on his little piece of black velvet.'

'What's wrong with those blokes? What they want to get mixed up in all that for? Give 'em a quick prod if they want to, but falling in love with some blackfella's missus is beyond me.'

'Colin calls her husband, Big Charlie, his brother. He's always giving him tobacco. Got a proper skin name too. Chungala. All the blacks call him Chungala now.'

Jack shook his head. He would never understand how any white man would allow himself to get tied up like that. He changed the subject. 'Sorry I missed Hartley Magnussen. Didn't know he took holidays. When's the new boss due, Roley?'

'This arvo's kite. He'll be another parcel-post bloke, I'll bet! I don't want nothing to do with him.'

They couldn't have been more wrong about the relief manager. He was a Queensland ringer from way-back, who had ridden the rough string at Dalgonally in his time. Now he was back on a cattle station after six years at war and trying it for a while on a sheep place. His wife and two little children were with him.

'This is more like it,' he thought as he jumped down from the DC3. 'Glad I got that letter. Those sheep were driving me bonkers.'

He helped the pilot and the black driver of the station Jeep unload the parcels and mail bags and stow them in the vehicle.

'I'll take this one,' he said to the driver and placed it with his swag and their ports. His wife looked at him inquiringly.

'Bottles.' He read from the label. 'Roley McPherson Esquire, Victoria River Downs, NT. I reckon old Roley's either down the Quarters drunk or waiting to get his hands on this and get drunk. And get every other white bloke they got here on it.'

'Arthur! You can't take his parcel. That's against the law. Interfering with the King's Mail.'

'Honey, there's one thing you got to understand. Out here I'm the law. I'm king and this is my little empire. That's what's often wrong with these places. Get a tyrant and he can make it miserable for everyone.'

'King!' his wife sniffed. 'Then I shall be Queen!'

'Yes, my love. Of the kitchen and house girls. Come on let's get settled in, I want to look around this big run they got here before the Wet sets in proper.'

The Boozers were almost out of grog. They had been having such a great time, travelling around Australia on the men's quarter's verandah, with stories, ditties and songs, they had forgotten it was a day since the plane had called.

'Me parcel!' Roley suddenly yelled. 'We got more grog! Another gallon! I'm going down the store to get it.'

'Hang on,' Jack told him. 'They having dinner down there now. Get it later, we got some left. Here's one called 'Gone Dingbats', about a bloke that went into the horrors.'

'Won't have to sing about it soon, Jack. Ol' Roley will give us a demonstration on going ding bats any moment now. We had to rope him down last time. Tried to castrate the Chinese cook with his cuttin' knife. Reckoned he was back up the Islands again with them Japs.'

Jack started the song. They had all heard it before and joined in.

Woke one morning early,
Heard a rasping wheeze,
The Ghost of old Rod Riley,
Was shivering in the breeze,
I looked around the doss-house
Weren't no-where to hide,
It called me to the window,
Said, 'Let me come inside.'

Its face was grey and shrunken,
An old hat on its head,
Its breath steamed out in whistles,
To wake the restless dead,
Said, 'Hope I didn't scare you,
Me hands and toes are numb,
I been laid out in the mortuary,
By cripes I need a rum!'

'I need one, too!' said Jack. 'Anything left in that bottle?'

'Jack,' Roley said, peering drunkenly across the verandah, trying to get him in focus. 'I never could understand that song. What does it mean at the end?'

'Well, Roley, this bloke's laying on his bunk in the horrors. An' he thinks two old mates of his have come back from the dead to get on the grog with him. It finishes up with someone taking the poor bugger before the Beak and getting him dog-acted and stuck in a home for six months to dry him out. They do that a lot inside, to blokes who can't handle their booze.'

'By ghost, Jack, them Beaks would be busy out in this country. What's the use of gettin' on the grog if you don't do it proper? Give me that end bit now. I might get it this time.'

He strapped me in a jacket,
Canvas made and tight,
And took me to the Justice,
Who said I looked a sight,
He begged him for a sentence,
To keep me off the street,
And told him my mate Riley,
Was with me on the seat.

He handed out a Sixer,
'That should be enough,
Take him to the Rat-House,
Poor coot's done it tough,'
And as they led me cellwards,
I covered up my eyes,
And left my two old comrades,
Boozing with the flies.

'It was too much for him, Jack, he's passed out!'

Roley lay stretched out in the calm repose of oblivion, head lolling on the wooden floor. They laughed and drank his health ...

Colin Secombe scarcely used his single room up at the men's quarters. Most nights he slept in his swag down the saddle-shop and most nights Big Charlie brought his wife, Sally along and left her for a few hours. But Colin wanted more time.

'You can leave her all night?' he asked as he handed over a tin of best Ready Rubbed.

Colin lay sleepless and miserable every time Sally left and went back down the blacks' camp to her husband. Now it was agreed Charlie would leave her every other night, all night. Soon even that was not enough. Colin wanted her with him all the time.

He was a Queenslander, as good a saddler as had come out west. He was twenty six and had been on Victoria River Downs for four years. He had never been away for a holiday and seldom mixed with other whites his age. He spent all day in the station saddle shop, repairing the huge amount of gear required to run the largest cattle station ever. He ate in the kitchen with the other men when they were in at the station but mostly they were out on the run and there was only the old cook and blacksmith for company.

He had always been introspective and now he became more so. This was his world. He was happy here. All he wanted now was to have his woman by his side. Another man's woman. A black man's. He could not have her. The station people, black and white, would not allow it. He would have to run off with her.

A week after he made his decision, Colin had everything ready. His Bedford van, with the homemade plywood body everyone laughed at, had a full petrol tank and there was another forty-four of petrol loaded inside. His saddling tools, swag and suitcase were stowed and his Greener three-quarter bore shotgun stood ready in the special brackets by his seat. There was also an empty forty-four gallon drum for Sally to hide in until they cleared the station.

Now it all depended on Charlie, but Colin was sure he would bring her up tonight. He wasn't at all nervous. He knew where he was going, a track that led over to West Australia. Things would be different there. He would say Sally had no boy and marry her in Halls Creek and then no-one could take her away. If anyone on VRD tried to stop him, well, he had the shotgun.

Sally's mother, Amy, worked for the saddler, teasing horse hair for the saddles. She had seen the situation building up and decided it was time to tell the boss. She would not speak to him, but to his wife. Amy liked the new missus. She smiled at people and spoke to the kitchen girls in a friendly manner. Not like some of the white ladies Amy had known. At dinnertime, Amy walked up to the kitchen window to pick up her piece of bread and beef and smiled as the new missus brought across a pannikin of sweet tea. 'How are you, old woman, okay?'

'Me gottem guts-ache, Missus. You can look?'

She walked off to the empty laundry behind the kitchen, the new missus following.

'I got no guts-ache, Missus. I frightened that man see me talk to you. He going to steal mine daughter tonight. He got 'em shotgun an' everything.'

'The saddler?'

'Him. Colin good man but he got no right to do that. You got to see boss, stop him.'

There was a police station on VRD. It had been established years before when blacks and whites were warring. Arthur drove the two miles down river and spoke with George the constable.

'I wouldn't involve you, George, but looks like the poor bugger's not thinking straight over this and he's prepared to use his gun. He needs a good long spell out of this country to get things back into perspective.'

'You're right there, Arthur. Seen it with a lot of young fellows who come up here and get involved with black women. If I had my way I'd make them get off the place every year for a while, but they won't go. The stations can pay them off, tell them there's no job till next season and they sit the Wet out down the creek frightened to leave in case someone takes over their stud. Any idea which way he's likely to head?'

'Sally's mother heard him talking to one of the men about how the track was through to the west.'

'Good! That means he's got to drive right past here. Thanks, Arthur. Go home and forget about it. I'll be waiting for him.'

'What about the gun? Don't you want a hand?'

The constable laughed. 'He might pull it on you but the only ones who draw on coppers are blokes right off their heads and Colin's not that bad. Yet!'

George saw the car lights coming at eight o'clock that night. He was sitting in his jeep waiting. He let Colin drive past and followed. Colin had to stop at the Home Paddock gate a mile further on. He was aware of the lights following and knew it must be the policeman but decided he had no option but to keep on. He had never been in trouble before and was close to panicking. He pulled up at the gate and stepped out.

George was right behind. He left the motor of the jeep running and the lights shining on the barn doors of the Bedford. He had come alone. He had decided not to involve his tracker. The fewer people who witnessed Colin's humiliation the better. If he could minimise the event to just a silly indiscretion, the less people would talk and the more hope the saddler would have of getting over it. On the other hand, if he charged him and got him six months up in Fanny Bay, that would get the young fellow off the place to sort himself out. But it would leave a stigma that would follow him everywhere up north.

'It's a difficult one,' George thought. 'I got to do my job but up in this country you got to skip a few pages of the rule book. Charge a bloke down south and who knows? His family, couple of mates. Maybe a neighbour or two. But up here the whole country finds out. And he's a pretty sensitive sort of fellow. Could really harm him. I better have a long talk with him before I decide anything.'

Colin stood by his open driver's door not sure what to do.

'Hello, Colin. Mind if I take a look inside?'

The saddler walked up with a resigned expression on his face and opened the rear doors.

George noticed a peculiar gleam in the young man's eyes that disturbed him. He shone his torch towards the front of the vehicle. The shotgun was securely in place in its brackets.

'Hop inside and let's take a look.'

Colin crawled into the rear of the Bedford. The policeman followed shining his torch around. There was only one place to hide anything as big as a woman. George tapped one of the two forty-four gallon drums. Full. He tapped the other. It didn't sound the same.

'What's in here?'

'Teased hair.'

George placed his hand inside the drum and removed a bundle of teased hair. He put his hand back and dug deeper.

'What's this?'

He shone his torch inside. Sally was hunched up, head down, absolutely petrified. Colin burst into tears.

George walked to the front of the Bedford, reached in and removed the shotgun.

'Jump in and turn your bus around, Colin, and take this woman back where she belongs. Then come up to the station for a drink of tea. We need to have a chat about things.'

It was daylight and the sound of dry-retching came from the men's quarters. The relief manager heard it as he walked down to the kitchen for an early drink of tea. The cook had heard it too and was grinning knowingly as Arthur came in.

'It's cruel, ain't it, boss, the way some fellas punish themselves.' He was a tall, wrinkled old fellow with a face that told of a thousand trips up dry gullies.

'I give that OP away years ago. Now if me hide's crackin' I fly up to Darwin and get on the amber stuff. I'd rather be dead than go back on that bullock's blood.'

It was Arthur's third morning on the station. He still hadn't met any of the stockmen but he was wise to the ways of boozers. He would gain nothing by going over to the men's quarters and attempting to stand over them. Besides, they had worked a hard long season and deserved a little time off. He was waiting until they ran out of grog. Then they would come to him.

'They coming across for a feed at all, those blokes?'

'Couple. Others too busy boozing. Must be about cut out now!'

The screen door banged open and Roley McPherson stood blinking at them. He staggered to a long low wooden flour bin and flopped down.

'Lord God, I'm crook. Going to die this time for sure. What time does that miserable looking manager coot get up, he's got my rum!'

Arthur looked sternly at him.

'He's got it all right! And he's keeping a hold on it too. When you've got some tucker inside, you can go down to his office and he'll shout you a nip, but only if you got gravy stains down your shirt!'

Arthur walked out.

Roley looked at the cook, perplexed.

'Who in hell was that?'

'The new manager. He's not a bad bloke. Old digger too. You better do what he says and get outside a feed or he won't give you a nip. He don't say much but I wouldn't want to stir him.'

Arthur walked over to the quarters. Five sunburnt stockmen, looking decidedly pale, watched him climb up the verandah steps.

'Good morning men! Axes sharp? We'll be cutting a few yard posts today. Truck'll be ready straight after breakfast. Don't take your dinner, we'll only work half a day. Got to take things easy after a bender. Who's the bloke from Gordon Creek?'

Jack nodded, grin on his face. This fellow was all right.

'How would you like to take a saddler back with you? I think Colin needs a change of scenery.'

'Okay with me, boss. That's his room yonder if you want to ask him.'

Jack pointed to the last of the eight rooms that comprised the single men's quarters. Arthur walked down the verandah and looked in.

'Christ!' he called out. 'Come and look at this!'

Colin lay on his bunk fully dressed. He was on his back and there was blood all over his shirt. His throat was slashed. The stockmen crowded into the room.

'Don't touch anything,' Arthur said, 'And don't step in that blood.'

There was a large pool of congealed blood beside the bed. In the centre of the pool, and on top of the blood, standing neatly where they had been placed, were Colin's riding boots. A large curved barber's razor lay alongside.

'The silly bastard!' someone muttered. 'All over a little harlot every man in the camp's been through!'

'Keep everyone out of the room, will you Jack? I'd better get George right away.'

He was back with the policeman in a matter of minutes. 'What do you make of that? His boots on top of the blood?'

George walked into the room and had a good look. Then he asked a few questions.

'If I was anywhere but here, I'd have to say someone cut his throat for him. But I think he made the cut while he was sitting on the edge of the bed. Then for some reason he pulled his boots off, placed them down and fell back and died. Sounds stupid, doesn't it? But that's the sort of things blokes do when they're out of their mind. I didn't like the look of him last night when he left my place. But I never dreamed he'd do anything like this. He was upset but seemed to have himself in hand.'

'That's what happens when blokes stay too long in the bush,' Jack told Lockie and Miniature when he arrived back later at Gordon Creek with the stores.

'He never said anything. Those ringers thought there was going to be trouble over the girl one day but none of us knew he'd tried to run off with her or been down to see the copper. He never came near us that night. Don't even remember him going to his room, we were busy yarning down the other end of the verandah.'

'You sure he didn't get a hand to cut his throat, Jack?'

'Who? One of us? Why would we want to?'

'A blackfella?'

'Never! Would you go and kill Father Christmas? That's what he was to them. They all got a share of Charlie's tobacco. Jealous? Charlie was happy with the arrangement. All the tobacco he wanted and anything else he asked for, I suppose. Charlie was big time amongst the other blacks with a cudea brother. No. He did it himself, poor little beggar. Thank God he wasn't in on the rum drinking, we would have got the blame then.'

They finished unloading the stores and walked down to the kitchen.

'You know something, Jack? Blokes do crazy things in grog but they don't act half as crazy as those poor buggers who go off their head over a woman.'

'I don't know anything about that, Miniature, and I don't aim to find out. There's more to life than chasing after women.'

'And drinking rum!' Miniature didn't say it, but he thought it as he followed Jack.

Sometimes he worried about this wild mate. 'He just don't give a damn about anything. Got to give everything a burst. Full bore!'

16.

Midnight Valley

At the end of the season the horses are bushed,
Free to gallop and roam on the run,
All year they've been ridden, relentlessly pushed,
To finish up saddle-sore, jaded and done,
They'll wander at will by wide river banks,
Thick scrub, hilltop, ridges and plain,
To rejuvenate backs and fill out their flanks,
Ready next year for riding again.

Jack was restless. Another hot wet season was upon him. Another three months of sitting down and doing up the gear. This time at Gordon Creek.

'Whoever came up with that expression was right,' he thought. 'Sitting down. Doing up the gear. That's a saddler's job, not a ringer's. But what else we going to do? No wonder that Colin got tangled up with the wrong woman. He had to be half mad to cope. His whole life was one wet season.'

He gazed up at the late afternoon sky. The cloud masses were rolling in again and the red ground was still wet from the morning's rain. He left the saddle shed where Lockie had taken a break from cooking and was watching Miniature sewing up a kneepad and sloshed across to the stockyard carrying an axe.

'I'll chop out a few rotten rails and replace them tomorrow no matter how much it storms.'

Something moved in the timber behind the yard. Jack kept walking, pretending he had not noticed.

Then he saw it again.

Someone was hidden in the trees, watching him approach. Jack reached the yard and walked along, tapping at the rails with the back of his axe listening for a hollow one.

The figure strode forward. It was a black. He was naked except for a grubby cloth narga knotted around his waist. Across his chest were three white ochre streaks.

The native got closer.

Jack smiled. It was Bruno, the half-caste of the stockcamp on walkabout.

'What for you come back, gun ringer? Had enough of that bush tucker already?'

Bruno grinned sheepishly.

'No, Jack. I come to talk with you.'

'Well, what you hiding bush for? You could have come down to the house.'

'I shamed, Jack. If that other two man see me like this they going to laugh. I know you can't laugh.'

Jack stared at the man who lived in two worlds. The blacks' camp where he was reared and the white stockcamp where he had been forced to spend the season.

'Don't be ashamed of your colour, Bruno — or your people. You got two lots of blood in you. They not mixed up. You always going to be part black and part white. But if you want to get anywhere — be a head stockman and eat better tucker and wear better clothes — you gotta be more white than black.'

Bruno's eyes had not left Jack's face. Now he spoke.

'That's why I come in, Jack. You been treat me decent, now I tell you something. Somebody been stealin' all our horses. We saw their tracks.'

Jack's eyes shone. Here was some action. This would take him away from the homestead.

'How many, Bruno, and which way they been travelling?'

'Big mob, Jack. Might be one hundred. Headin' for that Baines River country.'

'Anybody in that country, Bruno? Man got a station there?'

'Man there all right. That Judd Joyner. Proper smart stockman. He can take 'em, he done it before.'

Jack's eyes widened.

'Done it before? How you know that?'

Bruno looked at the ground.

'You can't tell anyone, Jack?'

'Nobody. Nobody going to know anything — only you and me.'

Bruno raised his head, but his eyes were on Jack's chest.

'I know he done it before, Jack, because one time I worked for Judd Joyner. Every wet time we rode in and took Victoria cattle. Some years we took horses as well. But,' and now he looked Jack directly in the face, 'we never took big mobs of horses like this one. He gone and took too many this time.'

Jack couldn't help smiling.

'So if he only took a small mob you wouldn't have told me, Bruno?'

The half-caste grinned happily.

'That right, Jack. Victoria River Downs got plenty horses. They can't miss a few. But no good anyone take big mob. That not fair.'

Jack thought for a moment.

'Did you pass any horses as you came through the horse paddock?'

'There's a mob hangin' on the fence about a mile off. You want me to run 'em in?'

'In the morning Bruno. Have 'em in the yard by daylight. Come down now and I'll get you some clothes and we'll tell Lockie and Miniature about the tracks. Then we'll start packing up, ready for the morning.'

It was a full day's ride to where Bruno had found the tracks. The four stockmen camped beside them and were on the trail by sunrise. Bruno led the way. The three whites could track but not as well as the half-caste. Bruno could follow tracks as well as a full-blooded native. Now he rode confidently, at a trot mostly, across stone and soft ground alike.

Suddenly Jack saw the tracks cut out — washed away by a storm. But Bruno kept going. A stony ridge loomed ahead. Bruno did not hesitate. He urged his horse towards it and rode halfway up. Then he turned and followed the ridge. Jack could see nothing. The ridge was covered in boulders and clumps of spinifex and there had been a heavy storm

'He's not on the tracks,' Jack thought. 'He knows where Joyner's heading and just pretending.'

Two miles further Bruno abruptly swung to the left and rode down towards a shallow sandy creek. There were the tracks, still faintly discernible, leading to the water's edge and up the far bank. The three whites exchanged glances. No doubt about this Bruno.

They camped that day just before sundown in the mouth of a gorge.

'What name you call this one?' Jack asked.

'He got no name, Jack, but he got a brother. Jasper Gorge, a long way further down.'

Lockie Mackenzie was just about to tell Jack that Jasper Gorge was where the bush blacks used to pelt stones down on the early drovers, when there was a tremendous crash in the gorge ahead.

'Boulders!' Lockie growled. 'Someone up ahead seen us coming. That's a warning if ever I heard one.'

Jack bounded to his feet and ran towards the crash. He looked up at the cliffs. There was no sign of movement, only a wisp of dust rising from the gorge floor.

'So!' he muttered. 'Mister Joyner wants to play it tough. He'll want to look out when I catch up with him.'

He walked back to the camp.

'What the hell was it, Jack?' Miniature asked.

'A boulder fell down from the top of the cliffs. Maybe it was an accident, but I don't think so. More likely whoever took those horses was keeping a watch for anyone following. It was a warning not to ride through the gorge.'

Jack turned to Lockie.

'What's through this gorge, Lockie? Is that where Judd Joyner's block is?'

'Yes. Midnight Valley. Our cattle never go that way, it's all rough country. He does a bit of duffing. What do you reckon, Bruno? Could be old Joyner?'

The question was put casually but Jack noticed Lockie was watching Bruno carefully. Perhaps he knew of Bruno's past.

The half-caste nodded. 'We don't have to go through the gorge, anyway. There's another track further up that leads into the Valley. It's a long way but we won't have any mad bugger throwing stones down on us.'

He looked over at Jack. 'You want me to take you that way tomorrow?'

Jack's eyes blazed.

'What! Turn tail? No way. I'm riding down that gorge tomorrow no matter what they start tossing. You blokes go the long way if you want, I'll find my own way to Joyner's.'

Sunrise found them packed up and heading into the gorge. Jack started to lead off, the others following. Bruno rode up. 'I not letting you lead, Jack. That my job. I not frightened with you along but we want to keep a lookout just the same.'

Judd Joyner and his twenty-five year old quarter-caste son, Dempsey, watched them from the cliff top. Dempsey had a length of solid timber in his hands waiting to prise another boulder loose.

'Say when, Dad, and I'll let 'em have it.'

Judd peered down for a few minutes, then growled.

'It's not worth risking, Dempsey. We're not going to frighten them fellas. We start dropping any more rocks we're really going to stir 'em up. And they got

Bruno and Lockie Mackenzie with 'em. They'll know it's us. If they want the horses that bad they can have them.'

'Who's the big white fella in the lead with Bruno?'

'Must be that head stockman fella, Jack Vitnell. They reckon he can fight.'

'Wouldn't be too much for me an' you to handle, Dad. We could double-bank him easy.'

'Don't be too sure of that Dempsey. He cleaned three of 'em up at Top Springs last year. One after the other. Big Gerry Birtles was the third bloke. When he seen his two mates go down Gerry tried to back out.

'Don't worry, Jack,' he says. 'I'm not looking for fight any more now.'

But Jack says, 'You was lookin' for it before, Gerry. What change your mind now?' Then he barrelled him, same as the others.

Dempsey looked sour. 'Well I don't want to know him, anyway. And if he comes nosing around our place it will be different. On our own dung-hill we can do as we like.' He patted the Winchester nestled in the scabbard on his saddle. 'Exactly as we like.'

Judd looked at his son and shook his head.

'Why risk having every trooper in the Territory gunning for us? There's an easier way than that.'

'Like what?'

'Like Jinny. If any one of 'em comes knocking Jinny can look after him.'

'Ain't she got enough to look after now, Pop?'

Old Judd leered.

'One more ain't going to matter to Jinny.'

He saw a pained look on his son's face.

'Don't tell me you're jealous! Hell, she's only your sister. It's not as if you're married or anything. Come on, get back to the house. I'm going on to the Valley to pull the wires out of the fence. I should just beat them there. Then with any luck the horses will poke off by the time they get there.'

The four Gordon Creek stockmen followed the tracks through the gorge and out the other side. Then they lost them amongst a tangle of scrubby hills. There had been another heavy storm and the tracks were washed out completely this time. The men split up searching, but circled around in vain.

Bruno rode up to Jack.

'I can take you to where Judd Joyner plants his stolen horses, but what about them two fellas? The hideaway's nowhere near his homestead and they going to think I been there before if I lead you straight to it. That Lockie a good bloke but

I don't want him to know too much. He's seen what old Joyner gets up to and knows I rode for him.'

'You leave Lockie to me, Bruno. He not going to say anything. You'll have to pretend you're on the tracks again. None of us will know. We can't see what you can see at the best of times. Just take it slowly and make it look like it's a tough job following 'em.'

Jack was riding in the lead with Bruno when Bruno said quietly, 'That hill over there, Jack. The one that look like a policeman's hat. Hat Hill it's called. The Joyner homestead right there but we're going to those ranges yonder. That's where he plants the horses. We'll get there dinner time.'

'What sort of a bloke is this Joyner, Bruno?'

'He was smart ringer one time Jack, but he gettin' old now. I got on all right with him, he's decent enough. Got a mongrel son, but. Dempsey. Jealous of any man workin' around the place. Tried to get me the sack couple of times. Ol' Judd got a good missus, a half-caste woman. But she don't say much. Too frightened I reckon. Judd's a bit hard on her but if it wasn't for her he wouldn't have anything. She the one kept the place going.'

'I've never even heard of the man, Bruno. He been up here long?'

'Might be twenty year. Worked on a few places, head stockman and that, but nobody see him much these days. The family do all the work now.' He laughed. 'They never put a man on in my place. That Dempsey would rather do two men's work than risk having another bloke around. He got a younger sister, Jinny. Judd's other kid. Creamy piece, proper good-looker, but terrible ki-eye. Always chasing after men.' Bruno winked. 'She don't need to chase far. Seems that Dempsey stop her from roaming!'

Jack shuddered as they rode on. 'Jesus! His own sister. That's the trouble with this country, Bruno. People get too much on their own.'

It was late afternoon before they reached the hideout. It was a valley tucked away in the ranges with a narrow entrance between two bluffs of rock. Across the entrance was a row of fence posts.

'But there's no wire!' Jack exclaimed.

Bruno pointed to the ground.

'See the boot tracks, Jack? Someone's been here not long ago, pullin' out the wire. If those horses aren't fenced in how can anyone say they're stolen? Nobody holding 'em. They free to go any time.'

Jack followed a set of fresh horse tracks towards one of the bluffs. Hidden among the rocks were four large coils of wire. He had a feeling he was being watched and looked up quickly at a cluster of huge rocks halfway up the hillside. Nothing moved. He rode back to the others.

'It's too late to do anything now. We'll give our horses a spell and camp here for the night. Then first thing in the morning we can muster up and head for home.'

Every horse found in the valley belonged to Gordon Creek. There were ninety four. Jack had understood all the time that they were on the trail of stolen Gordon horses but now that he saw them in a mob, he was furious.

'That bloody Joyner! I'm not letting him get away with this. You blokes can take the horses back, I'm riding into Midnight Valley to give Joyner a thumping. I'll make him think twice about coming on to Gordon Creek country again while I'm in charge.'

'Don't go on your own, Jack,' Bruno pleaded. 'More better we all go. We can take the horses that way and back you up same time.'

'He'll clear out, Bruno, if he sees us a mob of us coming. Better I go by myself. Wait for me at the end of the gorge where we camped. If I don't catch you up by tomorrow night you can come looking for me. But you won't have to. I'll be there.'

By mid afternoon they were abreast of Hat Hill.

'See you tomorrow,' Jack called and rode off alone. He had no swag. He would sleep on the horse's saddle blanket. In his shirt pocket was a johnny cake. That and a drink of creek water would do for sustenance.

An hour later he rounded the hill and gazed down at the Joyner homestead. It was surprisingly neat. There was a corrugated iron hut with a wide verandah and a small kitchen off to one side. Next to the kitchen stood a large bough-shed eating area complete with bush timber table and stools. A solid post and rail fence surrounded these buildings and further off Jack could see two large sheds and a set of yards.

He rode up to a double swung front gate and hailed the house.

There was silence, then a figure stepped through the hut doorway and crossed the verandah. It was a girl wearing a green and white candy striped dress. A young girl, of about twenty, with a smooth sallow complexion. She was tall and pretty and had long black hair.

'Who are you and what do you want?'

Jack murmured to himself. 'Jinny Joyner. Wow! She's a looker all right.'

He called out to her. 'Jack Vitnell. Head stockman from Gordon Creek. Looking for Judd Joyner.'

'Dad ain't here, but git down and come in. There's a drink of tea brewing.'

Jinny drawled her words in a flat, nasal voice and when she said, Dad, she pronounced it *dead.*

Jack dismounted and looped the reins loosely around the top rail of the fence. He opened the gate and walked in. Jinny had disappeared. He sat down at the table in the bough-shed and waited. Two women came out of the kitchen. One was Jinny, the other an older version. Darker and heavier but still with a hint of beauty.

'Ah'm Mary,' she said, looking at Jack's boots. 'An' this is mah daughter Jinny.'

Jinny smiled and looked frankly into Jack's eyes. Then she minced across, hips swaying and took his hand.

'Wow! You must be a hard worker. How you going to feel a girl with hands like that?'

Jack grinned. So this was the way it was going to be! He had been a long time without a woman. There were bold young black girls back at the station he met down the creek from time to time, in the time honoured fashion of ringers up north. A quick guilty encounter behind the coonkaberry bushes and an exchange of tobacco. But this was different. This woman was almost white, with a proper dress and wearing high heeled shoes — even with a hint of perfume. He felt a surge of excitement and pulled Jinny close. She gave a gasp and fell against him.

'Oh, Jack! You're so strong!'

Jack kept his arms tight about her. 'Who else is on the place?'

'Nobody, only Mum and she won't come out again.'

Jack gave a little push and Jinny fell back. He lowered her to the ground.

From inside the kitchen Mary heard a scuffle and peeped out the window. 'Holy Mother of Jesus,' she whispered. 'If she ain't got him already!' She gave a sudden giggle. 'He's still got his spurs on. Ride 'em cowboy!' She looked away, feeling sudden guilt and a wisp of dust far across the flat caught her eye. Was it a whirly wind or Judd coming home? Or Dempsey? She walked to the door and called softly in her native tongue. 'Take him down to the saddle shed, Jinny girl. Your father could come home any time now.'

Jack gave a start at the voice and shifted his weight. Jinny wriggled away and scrambled to her feet. 'Pull your pants up, Curly Jack, an' follow me. It's too crowded this-a-way.'

She led him towards one of the big sheds. Jack looked around. There was no sign of anyone else, but down in the yard he could see two horses and a few head of cattle. Was there anyone with them? He couldn't quite determine. He grinned at a sudden thought. I came here to give that Judd Joyner a hammering, instead I'm hammering his daughter. That's not a bad way of cracking even.

It was dark inside the saddle shed after the harshness of the bright sunlight and Jack could just make out a heap of teased hair for counter lining saddles. Jinny flopped down on the heap, on her back, facing him. She smiled up at him and raised her knees. Her dress slipped up around her waist and she parted her legs a little.

Jack unbuckled his belt.

Suddenly Jinny's eyes widened and she looked in fear at something behind Jack. Jack tried to turn his head but he was too late. A heavy steel shoeing rasp crashed against his hat, knocking him to the floor.

'What did you want to do that for, Dempsey?' Jinny screamed, bounding to her feet. 'Dad going to kill you when he finds out. You know he said to leave any nosy strangers to me.'

'This is one bloke you ain't gettin' your hands on Jinny Joyner. Now or ever. You say one word to Dad about this tomorrow and just you look out. He going to be hearing about a whole lot of things!'

Then he leered down at the prone body.

'Three at a time man, eh? Met your match this time, slugger.' He nodded to his sister. 'Give me a hand to get him on his horse. Then you can take him for a little ride. I'll point the way and be right behind. Me an' a little mob of splay footed cows.'

Meanwhile, Miniature and the others had not waited for Jack but had gone on, back to Gordon Creek. There was a blood stallion with the mob. For the whole of the trip it had tried to make off bush with some of the mares, so the three stockmen decided it was best to press on.

Miniature was worried. It was a Friday, when Jack had ridden off alone to Joyners, and now it was sunrise Monday and Jack was still not home.

'Me and Bruno's heading back,' Miniature told Lockie. 'There's something wrong.'

Within the hour they were on their way, with three spare horses and a packhorse. It was a good two days' ride to Joyners. They would do it in one.

But early Tuesday morning found them riding away in frustration from Midnight Valley. Jack had not been sighted. The Joyners knew nothing about him.

'That old woman knew something, Miniature. She was trying to tell me something when that Dempsey walked up.'

'What did she say to you, Bruno?'

'She said "Follow the cattle!" Then Dempsey came out of the hut and she shut up.'

'Follow the cattle, eh! That's what I been wondering. Why they been shifting a mob of cattle this time of the year. These tracks here. You notice them too?'

'I see 'em all right. Maybe they just yarded a few head up at the station to get a killer. You think Jack's gone this way?'

'Could be Bruno. Let's get after 'em. If them Joyners come after us they better look out. I didn't pack this Winchester for nothing!'

'I don't think Judd knows anything, Miniature. He would have said if he did. But that don't mean nothing's happened to Jack. Got to be some reason he ain't come home.'

They followed the tracks until they came to a small, circular plain. The ground was bare of grass and streaked with deep erosion channels. Breakaways. Miniature saw something moving.

'What's that? Over there by that dead tree. Looks like an eagle flapping around on the ground.'

Bruno looked where Miniature was pointing.

'Jeez! That's no eagle. It's a hat. Someone's waving a hat!'

They galloped across and saw a horse on its back. It was Jack's horse, legs up in the air, jammed tight in one of the narrow breakaways. It was dead. Sticking out from under the horse was an arm with the hand clutching and feebly waving a hat. They jumped off their horses and looked. Jack's face grinned weakly up at them. There was barely an inch clearance between his chest and the carcass of the horse.

'About time you blokes turned up,' he croaked.

Miniature and Bruno tugged at the horse. They could not move it. It was jammed tight. Bruno grabbed a nearby log of wood and together they used it as a lever to prise the horse up. Then they were able to pull Jack free.

They helped him across to a tree, propped him up and gave him a drink of water from one of the neck bags. His throat was so dry he could scarcely talk.

'What happened?' he rasped.

'Looks like you took a buster mate. Your horse must have come down, flipped over on its back and got jammed in that breakaway. You've took a terrible whack on the head, there's blood caked all over it. Lucky we come looking, you wouldn't have lasted much longer. Remember what you were doing? Where you'd been?'

Jack shook his head.

'Nothing. All I recall was a mob of horses. I've been blacking out and coming to the whole time. This morning a bunch of crows turned up but I got an arm out and belted at them with the hat. Wasn't long after that I saw you blokes coming. There was no way I could budge that horse. It was a good while before I worked out what was on top of me.'

Bruno gathered some wood, started a fire and put a billy on. Miniature walked over and looked at Jack's horse. There was a mark on its neck. A fresh scar. It looked like a rope burn. He circled the breakaway eyes to the ground. He looked towards the fire. Jack was leaning against the tree, eyes closed. Bruno had caught the packhorse and was busy at the packbags getting out some bread and beef.

Miniature strolled over to Bruno and whispered, 'Do you remember if you walked on the far side of that breakaway when we were getting Jack out?'

Bruno shook his head.

'Neither did I,' Miniature muttered. 'But go take a look. I'll take the tucker to Jack. I can see tracks there and I don't think they belong to you or me.'

Miniature squatted down with Jack as he picked at the food.

'I don't feel hungry. Suppose I should be. How long was I stuck there?'

'Far as I can make out, about three days. You left us last Friday to ride to Joyner's. You remember going there?'

'No. Only a mob of horses. I was with a big mob of horses.'

'That's right, we all were. Gordon Creek horses we found up the back of Joyner's block. But don't worry about it now. It'll come back to you later. You want to camp here today or head home?'

'I'll be right soon as I get some tucker into me. Feel a bit groggy that's all.'

He tried to stand, but stumbled.

'Give me a leg up on the horse, will you. I'll be okay once we get moving.'

Bruno led the way. They didn't go near Joyners, but cut straight for the gorge. Jack rode slowly, hunched over, and by late afternoon was swaying in the saddle. They made camp and Jack was soon asleep. Then Miniature was able to ask Bruno the question he had been holding back all day.

'What did you make of those boot tracks?'

'They weren't ours. Or Jack's. Look like somebody saw Jack there but wouldn't help him.'

'Could be. But it might mean something else. What happened to those cattle tracks we were following? Did you notice? I was too busy with Jack to look.'

'I followed them for a spell when I got our horses together. They just petered out. Whoever was tailing that mob just let 'em go.'

Miniature stared at him.

'So! So what does that mean?'

Bruno looked surprised at the question.

'I dunno what it means. They were just shifting 'em from the station yard out to where they come from I guess.'

'Well, I don't think so. I reckon them Joyners done that to Jack. That's what that old Missus Joyner was trying to tell you. She saw them carrying him away on his horse. Then they mustered up a mob of cattle to hide the tracks. 'Follow the cattle tracks and you'll find him'. That's what she was trying to say when that Dempsey mongrel come up. They took the cattle that way to cover their tracks.'

Bruno stared at Miniature, wide eyed.

'Christ! You mean they tried to kill Jack?' He thought for a moment. 'Maybe they got fighting and thought they'd killed him and got scared and decided to hide his body.'

'You reckon Judd Joyner would do that? Not from what I've heard you say about him. There's one thing I can do, Bruno. Pick a liar. Judd Joyner was telling us the truth when he said he hadn't seen Jack.'

'What are you saying, Miniature?'

'I'm saying Judd wasn't home when Jack called. I reckon he was out at that valley where we found the horses. Where he pulled the wire out of the fence. He was probably busy running the wire back, ready for next time. Dempsey done that to Jack. Caught him unawares and jumped him.

'Then they loaded him on his horse and carted him out to that breakaway. That horse of Jack's never fell and broke its neck. That horse was strangled. Someone threw a rope over its neck and choked it. Then they shoved Jack down the breakaway and rolled the horse on top.'

Bruno looked at Miniature dazedly.

'You keep saying they. Who the hell is they?'

'There's only two it could be. Dempsey and Jinny.'

'Jinny! She wouldn't do that.'

'She would, Bruno, if that Dempsey hoo-er forced her.'

'Jeez, Miniature. What we going to do?'

'I tell you what we're not going to do. Tell Jack. He'd ride over and shoot the lot, old woman included. I've only seen Jack do his block once and I never want to see it again. I'm just hoping he never remembers. I hate to think of that Dempsey Joyner getting away with it, but I'd rather that than get an invitation to a hanging up in Fanny Bay!'

17.

Cattle Duffer's Son

If you could girth a skittish horse,
And slip upon him on the stone,
Sink your hooks and hang up tight,
Without a show of getting thrown,
Spur him while he's at his best,
Climbing higher than a tree,
You'd stand a chance to get a start,
In Vitnell's camp on VRD.

A few days after Jack's rescue old Judd Joyner rode in to Gordon Creek. It was raining heavily at the time. Bruno had returned bush to catch up with his relations. Miniature and Jack were at work in the saddle shed, Miniature working harder than Jack. Jack was still recovering and his head pounded if he concentrated for long. Jack looked out the door at the weather and saw a rider.

'Who's this coming?'

A man on a horse leading a packhorse was letting himself through the homestead gate. Miniature peered out through the rain.

'Can't say who it is but it's a wet day to be travelling.'

The man rode up to the saddle shed and dismounted. Water dripped from his hat and his cloth coat and moleskin trousers were soaking. He stood in the rain and looked in at them.

'Judd Joyner,' Miniature whispered.

Jack walked to the doorway and eyed the man who had stolen their horses. He saw the open, weather creased face of an old stockman.

'I'm Judd Joyner. You can tell me to git if you want.'

'You got a hide coming here. I've been waiting to catch up with you.' Jack glared at him for while then growled, 'Well, come in out of the rain. I can whack you just as hard in here.'

Old Joyner gave a weak grin and stepped into the shed.

'You must be Jack Vitnell. I been riding around two days lookin' for you. Found a dead Gordon Creek horse in a breakaway, then my missus told me you'd called.' He spat on the floor. 'That Dempsey never told me.'

Jack was impressed.

'So you went looking for me. This fellow here, him and Bruno, found me. With all this rain about I'd be lying drowned in that breakaway but for them. What are you going to do about taking our horses? You cost us a week's riding. If it hadn't been for you I wouldn't have been stuck under my horse. I ought to bust you one right now.'

'I'm sorry about your fall, Jack, but there's nothing I can do now. You've got your horses back.'

Judd looked at the heap of saddles that needed repairing and frowned. Suddenly he brightened.

'I can send my boy, Dempsey, over to do your saddles. That might help square things. Won't cost you. He's a good counter-liner.'

Jack did not want help. On the other hand, it would be a way of making the Joyners pay. This man was too old to fight.

He gazed out at the rain and darkness of the late afternoon.

'Okay, it's a deal. Send him over. You better camp here tonight. Pull your packs off and take your horses up to the paddock. Then come over to the kitchen for a feed. It's too late to be moving off now.

A few days later Dempsey arrived. Jack directed him to the saddle shed.

'You can camp in there. It's drier than out in the rain mustering other people's horses. When you hear the bell, come over to the kitchen. Then you come back here. Understand?'

Dempsey gave no trouble. Jack eased up on him. Soon he was staying on in the kitchen after meals for a yarn. One night he asked for a job.

'I've never had one before, Jack. Always been working at home. Haven't even earned one pound.' He grinned wryly. 'Well — I've earned it, but never got it.'

The first morning he proved he could ride a horse.

The stockmen were drafting horses for the first round muster when a brown gelding trotted into the pound. Jack looked at it, then called to Bruno.

'How come I never saw that horse before?'

Bruno smiled. No doubt about this man. He knew every horse on the place already.

'Might be we missed muster him last year. He no good anyway. Run backwards all the time. Ever since he bolted one time and got tangled up in a fence. He buck backwards too. Never seen a horse like it. No-one can do anything with him.'

Jack was stunned.

'Goes backwards! What are you talking about?' He glared at the men around the yard. 'I'll get him going frontwards, by ghost I will, but I'll need a rider. Who's going to try him?'

Dempsey was first into the yard.

'What you want me to do, Jack?'

'Get me a stick, then climb on bareback. He won't want to feel a tight saddle first up. Slip up on him and when he comes backwards I'll belt him over the rump with the stick. That will get him going. And he's going to buck. So look out! Then take him outside and gallop him.'

Dempsey sprang on and the brown immediately bucked backwards and crashed into the rails. Dempsey was thrown sideways but held on. Jack whacked the horse hard across the rump. It jumped, bounded forward, then propped. Jack whacked it again. It jumped again and took a few steps. Dempsey patted its neck.

'Open the gate,' Jack called and struck the horse again. It rocketed out the gate into the big-yard and charged across to the end of the yard. Dempsey wheeled it around and cantered it up and down the yard several times. Then he rode it back to where Jack and the stockboys were standing.

'He's right now, Jack. I'll take him outside.'

Jack opened the bush gate. Dempsey lashed the reins and galloped the brown across the flat. He brought it back a short time later and walked it sedately around the yard.

Jack scowled at the stockboys.

'The horse that runs backwards! Take a look at him you fellas. Didn't take much, did it? A good whack on the arse and he's as good as any.'

He turned to Bruno and Miniature.

'He's all right, that Dempsey. We might have a good man there.'

The two men cursed silently. They wished the brown had pelted Dempsey and splattered him all over the ground.

'Now Jack's going to think he's a great bloke,' Miniature complained. 'Like he always does if someone can ride. But he'll find out different. That Dempsey can ride because he was born to it and doesn't know anything else. But that don't mean he's a man.'

Miniature could scarcely bring himself to speak to Dempsey Joyner. Bruno was the same. If Jack noticed, he did not say anything. In fact it seemed to Bruno and Miniature that Jack was becoming more matey with Dempsey as time went on.

'If only Jack knew, Bruno, what happened at Midnight Valley. Or what we reckoned happened. Old Judd went looking for Jack and was game to come and face him. That proves he had nothing to do with it. But if Jack ever finds out about Dempsey ...'

Dempsey had been a competent stockman before he arrived at Gordon Creek, but now he became better. He followed Jack wherever possible and copied his ways. Jack did not mind. Now instead of Jack and Miniature riding together during the day's mustering, it was becoming Jack, Miniature and Dempsey.

Finally Miniature decided to ride with Bruno.

'It don't take three of us to throw a bull, Jack. You and Dempsey can ride today, I'll go with Bruno.'

Jack had just nodded and rode off, Dempsey following. That was the last Miniature rode with Jack for a good while.

They completed the first round and returned to the station for a fresh plant of horses and a few days spell.

The night before heading out again, Jack produced a bottle of overproof rum. Bruno and Dempsey eyed it speculatively. Being coloured, no-one had ever asked them to join in a drinking session before.

'Here, you pair of savages!' Jack grinned at them.

'Come and meet old Captain Kettle.'

He poured an inch in both their pannikins.

'Put some water in and take it steady. Old Kettle will put some fire in your bellies.'

The four men sat around the kitchen table. It was dark in the kitchen and the light from the carbide lamp shone eerily on their faces. Jack, giving a spirited account of some adventure, Miniature quietly listening, the other two inscrutable and uncomfortable. None had drunk alcohol for months and were quickly affected. Dempsey more than the others.

Suddenly he leered at Miniature and sneered, 'You're not a ringer. You're a bloody jockey.'

Jack banged the table with his fist.

'Hey! None of that. I won't stand for it. We're all mates here.'

Dempsey swung on Jack and snarled.

'I done for you once and I'll do for you again if you don't watch out.'

There was an immediate silence.

Then Jack said very quietly, 'What did you say?'

Dempsey realised his slip and was suddenly sober. He reddened and forced a laugh.

'I beat you throwing bulls once, Jack and I'll do it again. That's what I mean.'

Jack stared intently at him.

'I don't remember you beating me at throwing. Tell me about it Dempsey.'

'You remember. That day out on the stone.' He was making it up as he went along. 'I got my bull down just ahead of you.'

Jack looked puzzled. There was a strange expression on his face.

'I think you're telling lies and I don't like it. You better watch what you say or you and me's going to be stepping out where the bull feeds.'

Then he turned to Miniature.

'Get the cards out, mate. Let's get a game of euchre going.'

But Jack's mind was not on cards that night. Miniature saw him frowning at times and Jack played badly.

Next day they were off. Sixteen men and a hundred fresh horses. The horses bucked all around the flat as they set off. Even the packhorses were tight and cavorted around trying to dislodge their loads. The black stockboys rode off in a bunch, laughing and talking. The four rum drinkers rode separately, shaking off the effects of the liquor.

The station was soon left behind and they were bush again. Jack had been riding in the lead, now he hung back and let Miniature catch up.

'A bit seedy, this morning, mate?' the little ringer called.

'Head's thumping a bit. But no more than usual. I must have took a whack all right.' He rode closer. 'Something came back to me last night. I remembered sitting at a table talking with a girl — a coloured piece. We were talking and then she stood up and I walked off with her. You remember what Joyner's daughter looked like?'

'Ah!' Miniature thought. 'Jinny Joyner.'

'We never went in, Jack. Judd met us at the gate. I only remember seeing a bit of a house and a bough shed with a table and stools. And down towards the yard, a couple of sheds. But we saw a girl. She was standing in the doorway of the house watching us.'

'What did she have on?'

'A green and white dress.'

'Striped?'

'Could have been.'

'So!' Jack whistled. 'I was with Jinny Joyner while I was there.'

'What did you an' her get up to, Jack?'

'I can't remember. We were just talking. It's a strange feeling, losing your memory. Ever happened to you? Well, it's like waking up after a dream. It's clear but it's also muddled. Things come in flashes. But I can see that girl very clearly. Sitting at a table talking.'

'Can you see a yella fella? With a smart-arse face and an undershot jaw?' As soon as he had said it, Miniature regretted it.

'Dempsey? You don't like him, do you? You think he was there? I don't remember seeing any bloke.'

'No, I don't like him, Jack. And I don't know what you see in him. Maybe he's a good ringer but deep down he's got no ... oh, I dunno. I don't want to get talking about him.'

'Guts? Is that what you were going to say? That deep down Dempsey's got no guts?'

'I just feel if some day you needed him, he'd let you down.'

'You could be right, but until he lets me down I'll stick with him.'

A week later Dempsey ran from a charging bull. The running away didn't matter. Every man amongst them had run from a cranky bull. But not when the bull was attacking a mate.

Jack was still riding with Dempsey and they were out in the tiger country where the limestone was the most slippery, the hills the steepest and the scrub bulls the wildest. These big animals did not run as soon as they saw horsemen. They stood proud, tossing their heads, pawing at the ground. Only at the last, as the stockmen galloped up, would they race off.

This day Dempsey had made a throw and was holding the bull down by the tail. Jack was off his horse, freeing the horn-saw. Suddenly the bull wrenched from Dempsey's grasp and bounded to its feet. It wheeled on the man who had been holding it down. Dempsey called no warning but ran for a tree. The bull turned and charged Jack.

Jack was lucky. His horse whirled to face the bull and took the full force of its horns. Jack spun around and battered the bull's head with his hat. The bull unhooked its horns from the horse and charged the man. Jack dodged and grabbed it by the tail. It was too strong. With a snort and toss of its head it rushed off.

Jack looked around. Dempsey was nowhere to be seen. Then he dropped down from a tree. He didn't look at Jack. Jack turned to his horse. Blood was oozing from two wounds in its chest. Jack stripped off the saddle, bridle, neck strap and hobbles. Then he turned to his riding mate.

'Ride back to camp and get me another horse.'

He stroked the horse's neck.

'You saved my life, old fella, but I can't save yours.'

His revolver was still in its holster, tied to the saddle. He pulled it out and took a deep breath. Then he shot the horse between the eyes. Miniature found him shortly after, squatting against a tree. He looked up at the little stockman.

'You were right about Dempsey, mate. Deep down there's nothing there. Let me up behind, I wouldn't ride with that other thing — that Dempsey!'

'That's all he said,' Miniature told Bruno later. 'I don't know what happened back there, but I don't think Jack will be riding with Dempsey Joyner any more!'

Soon it was the bullock muster. Now when they mustered, the stockmen drafted off the bullocks and held them in a separate mob. The remainder of the cattle were then yarded and the cleanskins branded. These were then let go but the bullocks were taken along each day and had to be watched at night.

It was not like watching drovers' cattle. Drovers' cattle soon become quiet from the daily routine of feeding slowly along the stock route. At night they camped contentedly — full of feed and water.

It was different in the stockcamp. The bullocks did not get a chance to settle down. Fresh cattle were continually added and these the mob regarded with suspicion. They were strangers, from different country, and bellowed for different mates. At night the mob could hear those other cattle, missed by the musterers, bawling plaintively from the ridges. Sometimes, too, a testy scrub bull would run in to the mob, angry at these cattle who dared camp in its territory. Then the whole mob would be up and on their feet. The men on watch had to be constantly alert.

There was no truck or wagon for protection if the cattle rushed. It was a packhorse stockcamp. So at night the men camped behind the fire, few able to sleep soundly. Most nights there were shouts from the men on watch, 'Whoa, bullocks! Whoa. Steady boys, steady!' as the mob surged around. Sometimes there were two men on watch. Other nights three or four. On a really bad night, six men were needed to hold them.

When the cattle did rush — stampede off into the night — it was often when they seemed to be camping quietly. But the slinking form of a dingo or shadows cast from a rising moon could get them charging blindly in an instant.

It was a week before the drover was due and the stockcamp was holding eight hundred head. Lockie was baking bread in a long fire pit and a row of camp ovens sat hidden beneath heaps of smoking coals. He had some big logs cut, ready for the fire during the night ahead. It was early evening and the three horsetailers were on watch.

Jack was in good humour. He had been told to have at least five hundred head ready for the road and he had almost double that amount.

'They're camping quiet tonight. We might all get a sleep for a change.'

He sat by the fire with the other three and watched Lockie pick up a pair of wire hooks to remove a lid and test the bread.

'I saw something strange today when I was mustering up the river. Someone had built a hide. A stone wall about six foot high, made into a semi-circle, big enough to hide a couple of men. It was very cunningly located. It didn't have any roof but it didn't need one. No-one could look down on it. It was underneath a big sloping cliff wall. You ever see it, Lockie?'

'Plenty of times. It was built by Brigalow Bob. He was a bad man, old Bob. Used to lie in wait for bagmen riding past and shoot them for their packs.'

'Who'd be travelling down that river? It's way out nowhere.'

'That was a main route one time, Jack. Sixty year or so ago. The pioneers cut it, bringing cattle across to the East Kimberley. Later on, when gold was found at Halls Creek, any diggers who owned horses and were able to travel off the main tracks used it. It was a good short cut from Queensland across to the field.

'Old Bob busted out of jail some place inside and lit out for the Territory. Those cliffs are where he holed up. Did you see his hut? It's there still. A stone hut, a mile or so off the river. He lived there with a woman he'd stole from a tribe of blacks. Never went to town or anywhere near a station.'

Lockie chuckled. 'He didn't have to. All Bob's stores got delivered. Personally by packhorse. When he got low on tucker, he sat down in his fort and waited for some poor critter to come by. Then he would shoot him.'

Bruno knew the story.

'I'll take you next time we come this way, Jack, and show you the bones. He used to load the bodies on a packhorse and take them up to the top of the cliffs further down. Then he'd toss 'em down a big split in the rock. They reckon there's ten sets of bones down that crack.'

'What happened to him?'

'No-one knows.' Lockie answered. 'Nobody knew about the murders for years. Travellers went missing. So what? That was always on those days. Later they found the fort —then the hut and the bones. But they never found Bob. Only his name carved on a tree. I reckon the blacks got him.'

They yarned on. First watch rode in. They were the three horsetailers. They tottered up to the fire in their high heel boots for a warm-up and a drink of tea.

'How they camping?' Jack asked.

'They camping all right,' the boss one answered, a grey bearded old-timer who scarcely slept and would have had the horses on camp every morning at two o'clock if Jack had allowed it.

'But there's a couple of old pikers stirrin' 'em up. Anytime they see a bullock sleepin' they walk over and horn him till he gets up. We want to watch when that moon comes up bye and bye, Jack. It going to bring a wind. That going to stir 'em up some more, that wind, when it blows off their country.'

'How many night-horses you tie up?'

'Six. You want more? I can get 'em.'

'No, that's enough, old man. You go get some sleep now. Might be I go take a look at these cranky buggers.'

Jack walked across to the night-horse tree, unhooked a horse and rode out to the cattle.

'Jack will stop out there half the night,' Bruno grumbled. 'He never sleeps. I'm rollin' in.'

He walked off to his swag. Dempsey headed for his. Miniature sat by the fire until Jack rode in some time later.

'They're okay. But when that wind rises I'm going out again. Third watch will be on then, they may need a hand.'

Jack was out with the third watch men when the bullocks rushed.

Miniature and Bruno ran to the night-horse tree. Each snatched a bridle, swung on to a horse and galloped into the night.

Lockie was camped closest to the fire. He sprang from his swag and grabbed the long handled bread shovel. The bullocks were almost upon them. He swept the shovel into the fire and tossed a spray of glowing red coals high into the air.

The bullocks split, and thundered down each side of the camp.

There was an abrupt silence and a cloud of fine dust settled over the camp. Then off in the distance, came the sounds of the riders racing for the lead.

'Whoa bullocks! Whoa boys.'

No-one was hurt. Each of the men had been camped behind the fire. Within the hour the stockmen had the cattle back on camp. The animals stood wearily for a time, then one by one flopped down on the ground.

Men left the cattle and drifted in to the fire. The watch would hold them now. None of the men went back to their swags. They grouped around the fire, drinking tea and re-living the rush. Dempsey stood with them, out of it. He was one of a few who had not jumped on a night-horse to help. Instead he had run for a tree. The men ignored him. Each of them had a vivid tale to recount about their wild ride in the blackness.

Dempsey stole quietly away to his swag. It was not there. He searched around. It was gone. He was furious — someone was playing games. He strode back to the fire.

'Which one of you mongrels has taken my swag?'

The men stopped talking and stared at him. The fire hissed and crackled. Finally Jack snapped out, 'What the hell are you talking about?'

'My swag. It's gone. Someone's took it.'

Jack looked at the faces of the men. None were smiling now. It was the grey bearded horsetailer who answered.

'I bet I know who got him swag.'

He looked around.

'Come on you fella. Me show you.'

He walked off into the dark and pointed to a spot on the ground. Every man's eyes followed.

'Dempsey bin camp right here.'

He walked on. The others trooped after. A dozen steps more and he stopped again.

'Huh!' he snorted. 'Here the first bit.'

A swag cover lay on the ground. Dempsey ran to it. 'It's mine, but there's no blankets!'

'Huh!' the old chap snorted again, and moved off a little further. He pointed again. A blanket lay draped over a clump of spinifex. Dempsey picked it up.

'It's mine.'

The old chap peered ahead. 'There's another one.'

Then he turned.

'How many blanket you bin have?'

'Three. One under, two over.'

'Well, you go look at that tree.' He pointed. 'Might be you find the other one between here and there.'

Then the old man spat out, 'Because that's the tree you bin run to when the bullocks rushed!'

Dempsey looked at his feet.

The old man went on. 'You were in so much hurry, you never got out of your swag. It fell off as you bin run away.'

Jack snorted. 'Come on you blokes. Bugger 'im. Let's get back to the fire.'

By July the camp had completed the bullock muster. Three mobs had been handed over to the drovers. There was only branding to be done now.

'I'm not spending another Wet here, Miniature,' Jack growled one afternoon as they brought a big mob of cows and calves into a bronco yard. 'Soon as the last calf's branded I'm off.'

'You and me both, Jack. I'm not going to be hanging about either now Dempsey's here. Which way are you thinking of heading?'

'Halls Creek. The old gold field. Bet there's still plenty of gold left. It's a good time to scratch around for gold in the Wet. Anyway, don't worry about Dempsey. He'll head off home, I reckon, soon as the season's finished. If he doesn't I'll tell him to git.'

Since the night of the cattle rush the men had scarcely spoken to Dempsey Joyner. He had started the season off with a flourish, when he rode the horse that runs backwards and there was no doubt he could ride. But when things had got tough, he had let them down.

'I would like to have known that old grey bearded horsetailer in his prime,' Jack said one night. 'He would have done me for a riding mate. You hear a lot of talk that the blacks can't be relied on. But if he'd been my mate that day my horse got horned he wouldn't have run.'

Dempsey was getting more and more miserable. No-one would talk to him and there were several months yet before he could collect his pay and ride home. Thinking of home made him think of Jinny. And thinking of Jinny ... He sighed and tried to put her out of his mind.

That night there was no moon and after supper he walked off to his swag. Nowadays he camped away from the others. He couldn't put up with their laughter and talk. One time he had been part of it. He lay down on his swag and thought of Jinny. He rolled around restlessly then stood up and looked around.

Jack and the others were grouped around the fire. There were no cattle to watch and they were sitting yarning. Dempsey slunk across to the other side of the fire and carefully lifted a camp oven lid. He opened his clasp knife and cut off a large piece of bread. Then he crept towards the saddles and picked up his bridle. No-one saw him walk off into the night.

Next morning the stockmen rolled their swags and dumped them close to the packsaddles. They were moving on to muster new country. Lockie was limping about with the gout. Jack walked across.

'I'll get Miniature to stop behind and help you and the horsetailers pack up.'

Miniature didn't mind. He caught one of the pack mules and led her towards the saddles. The grey bearded horsetailer followed.

'Poor little bugger. Carryin' big load all day then man go an' humbug her all night. He all the same dog that fella.'

Miniature stared blankly at him.

'What fella?'

'That Dempsey.'

Miniature was puzzled.

'What you talking about? How's Dempsey humbugging the mule?'

The old horsetailer spat out a stream of tobacco juice.

'He doin' to the mule what he'd like to be doin' to a woman, that's what.'

'He's what?' Miniature stared at the old black man in disbelief.

'It's true Minichee. Every morning I see his tracks. Last night I followed. He led that little mule down into a breakaway then he hobbled her back legs. Next he went around and strapped up one of her front legs. Then he give her a piece of bread. When he climbed out of the breakaway that little mule was just the right height for him. I tell you, Minichee, it made me sick!'

Miniature felt sick too. He had heard about such things but thought they were just stories. He slipped the halter off the little mule and let her go. Then he turned back to the horsetailer.

'Who else knows?'

'All the boy going to know soon. Them other two horsetailer know. Can't keep a thing like that quiet.'

'I just hope Jack don't hear,' Miniature thought later as he rode off to catch up with the musterers. He heard a hail in the distance. It was one of the stockboys waving his hat from a ridge ahead. Miniature caught him up.

'Big trouble, Minichee. Man bin finish himself. He proper dead fella, you better come look.'

'Who?' Miniature cried in alarm. 'Not Jack?'

'No. That other man. Dempsey.'

They galloped down the ridge and across a limestone flat. Dempsey lay on his back close to a straggly tree. His horse stood awkwardly on three legs. Its off side front leg was dangling uselessly. Miniature jumped off his horse and bent down. Dempsey's head was twisted to one side at an unnatural angle to his body. Miniature pressed an ear to his chest. He could hear nothing.

'Better get Jack. He finished all right. What happened?'

'He been galloping after two cow. He was try to wheel 'em, then that horse come down right near that chellaloo tree. That man should have known better than to gallop close to that tree. Always that chellaloo grow alongside sink-hole in the limestone. That horse went straight down. Dempsey never. He went straight ahead. Through the air. Then crash! He never moved since.'

Jack was quickly on the scene. As soon as he verified that Dempsey was dead, he sent one of the stockboys to intercept the horsetailer and bring back a packhorse. Then he walked over and shot the horse.

'What we going to do with him, Jack?' Miniature wanted to know. 'Bury him out here somewhere?'

'We can't bury him here, mate. No-one's allowed to do any burying without permission from the police. We'll have to pack him in to Gordon Creek and send word up to the head station. Then anyone who wants to, can come and have a look at him. And we better get someone to ride over to Midnight Valley and tell old Judd. I'm sorry for his sake.'

He looked at the body, then at Miniature.

'Well ... he wasn't the Territory's greatest ringer but I guess he tried his best. I had a bit of time for him at first.'

He was watching Miniature closely.

'You never. Maybe you knew something, eh? Something I'd forgotten.'

Miniature stared at him.

'Like what?'

'Like he was the bloke that clobbered me in Joyner's saddle shed.'

He saw Miniature's jaw drop.

'Remember that night at the station we got on the rum? And what he said about doing for me once? That brought the girl in the striped dress back.'

Jack looked at the figure on the ground then at Miniature again.

'I told you I only remembered sitting at a table talking to her. That was true. Then. But later I remembered more. I did her over and then she took me into a shed and wanted more. So I got to thinking maybe that's where I got the knock on the head. Dempsey must have come in on us. Bruno reckoned Dempsey was hanging out of her. So he would have been watching us. Why didn't you tell me? Think I'd have killed him over it?'

Miniature nodded.

'No. A man will do anything in a fit of jealousy. I wouldn't have blamed him.'

He thought a moment and grinned.

'But just as well you didn't tell me. Anyway, how come I was able to get on my horse and ride away? That's what I can't work out.'

Miniature pointed to the corpse.

'That's how you got on your horse, Jack. I reckon he put you on it.'

Jack stared at Miniature.

'I'm not with you. If he put me on my horse I must have been okay. How did I finish up in that breakaway?'

Miniature pointed again.

'He put you in it. There was nobody else who could have.'

Jack's eyes rolled in his head. He took a step backwards and almost stumbled.

'What did you say?' he whispered. His face paled. Then his voice rose to a shout.

'What did you say?'

He lunged for the body. Miniature threw himself forward.

'Don't do it, Jack! Don't mark him. Those coppers will think one of us done it. I haven't kept quiet about it all this time to let you get into strife now. He's dead. Leave him. He's got what he deserved.'

Jack slumped to the ground. Miniature squatted beside him.

'It's all over now, mate. Get it out of your head.'

Jack made no reply. He kept staring at Dempsey. 'That mongrel! That rotten mongrel.'

Miniature touched his arm.

'Jack! Forget it. He's not worth thinking about. Tell you what. Let's get away from this place. Pull out. We been here long enough.'

Jack looked at him.

'How can we? We can't walk out. Who's going to run the camp?'

'Bruno. You've made a good man of him. He'll do the job. He's got Lockie to back him. You've got 'em their bullocks. There's only a bit of branding to do now. We ain't on contract. We can go any time. Let's head for Halls Creek via Ord River Station. I've always wanted a look at the Ord.'

Jack got slowly to his feet. Then he grinned at Miniature.

'Ord River, eh? I wouldn't mind a look at that place myself. They reckon those Ord horses can really buck!'

Bill Yeomans, Cloncurry, 1993.

Wyndham, 1952. Taken from the hotel verandah. Finlay's General Store and Gallon License (Later Vagg's) next to Gee Hong Yet's (Far right).

Old drover Mick Coombes, Wyndham, 1990.

Smokey's Underworld Retreat. From the entrance bluffs.

18.

The Kimberley Kid

Oh, they know a few tales of the Kimberley Kid,
I've been round for nigh twenty year,
They tell of the times after wrestling scrub bulls,
I'd climb on their backs without fear,
Yes, bulls were the fellows I specialised in,
I showed them a smart trick or two!
I'd pull them down by their horns or their tails,
That mustering horse fairly flew.

The Kimberley Kid was back in business, breaking-in horses on a station again. It had been a long time.

Time. He never wanted to hear that word again.

'Two years,' he thought, 'And should have been four. They could have made it one day. That would have been long enough to stop me ever going back. I owe this Joe Egan of Ord River one. Picked the right man when I wrote to him. He won't be sorry he took me on. He'll be able to climb all over these colts when I've finished.'

He walked over to the chestnut he had first caught two days ago. It stood quietly while he placed a bridle over its head and slipped in the bit. Then he rigged a collar rope and jumped on its back. The colt trembled a little but remained still. It was either used to this man or resigned to the restraint of the heavy leather collar-rope.

'I'll ride this bloke after dinner,' the Kid thought. 'He's going to be a quiet one.'

He girthed on a saddle and stepped lightly into the near-side stirrup. The colt didn't move. The Kid stood with all his weight in the iron and leant over its back. It remained quiet so he swung his leg over and sat down. It swivelled its ears back, waiting.

The Kid was pleased — hadn't lost his touch. The dinner bell rang and he unfastened the collar-rope, tied the reins back to the saddle and left the colt in the yard. When he came back later it was still standing quietly, mouthing the bit. He hunted it into the round-yard, untied the reins from the saddle and stepped on.

The chestnut walked slowly around the small yard. The Kid patted its neck and smiled. Then he kicked it lightly in the ribs and brought it up to a trot.

'Okay Jimmy,' he called to his black assistant. 'Open up the gate to the big yard.'

The colt trotted sedately out into the yard then suddenly exploded into a frenzy of high, twisting bucking. It caught the Kid off guard and he flew straight over its head and speared into the dirt.

'You bloody mongrel!' he yelled, climbing to his feet. 'What did you want to do that for?'

The colt stood a few yards away with its ears pricked forward. The Kid followed the direction of its gaze. A plant of horses was coming. A ringer in a blue shirt was in the lead, almost at the big yard rails. He was a young man in his early twenties, sunburnt and good-looking. He sat grinning and looking directly at the Kid.

'Just my luck!' the Kid thought. 'He saw me come off. Maybe that's what made the horse buck, he took fright at the horses coming.'

He walked across the yard as the ringer called out, 'He can buck mate!'

'He got me all right! I mostly stick on better than that but I'm a bit out of practice. I been...' he paused an instant... 'away.'

'I know Kid,' the rider said. 'We heard about it. You were dead unlucky. Vitnell's my name. Jack. And this here's Johnny Harrison, the Miniature Stockman. They told us on Limbunya you were back in the country breaking-in.'

The other rider nodded.

'Ghost!' the Kid thought. 'A jockey!'

'So you been working on Limbunya,' he answered.

'No, mate, Gordon Creek. Outstation of VRD. We only called in at Limbunya for some beef, but finished up camping the night. Me an' Miniature's travelling.'

Miniature cocked his head. 'That's the smoko bell, ain't it Kid? You better get back on that colt before we go. He might think he got you beat.'

Jack had been watching the Kid, sizing him up. About thirty or so. Got a few years on me. Looks a ringer. They reckon he can go, too. Well, he's too light for me. I'd eat him if it ever come to that. But he looks a good bloke. I'd like a crack at his chestnut colt.

'Come up and have smoko, Kid. Let me have a try at that fella when we come back. You look like a man who needs a good brew of tea. Come on!'

The Kid was a little peeved. He should be inviting them up for smoko. He worked here, they were just blow-ins, but he didn't argue. He was feeling stiff now and his leg ached. He tried not to limp as he followed them up to the kitchen, a quarter of a mile away at the station proper.

'Jack Vitnell,' he mused. 'Heard the name. Supposed to be up with the best. Good on him! I'm gettin' to be a has-been now. Be interesting to watch him in action on that chestnut. I can ride him but he can get on if he wants to. I don't have to prove anything. He certainly don't lack confidence this fellow!'

Joe Egan, the manager, joined them in the kitchen during smoko.

'You fellas pullin' the packs? There's a mile of feed in the horse paddock if you want to.' He gave them a sudden stern look. 'You young buggers can have the pick of the studs while the camp is out, I'm no shepherd, but none of that camping all night business!' He turned to Jack and Miniature and pointed to the Kid. 'Just make sure you do as he does.' He grinned. 'Or what I reckon he does! Give 'em a quick poke and bush gate. I don't want word getting out to the stock camp I've got a team of young white fellas in here rooting their women. My head stockman will never hold 'em. They'll all suddenly get flu-sick and troop back to the station.'

The Kid gave them a hand to let the horses go and string the saddles along the fence outside the men's quarters. They stacked the tucker bags and swags on the verandah.

'Let's get down the yard,' Jack said. His eyes were gleaming.

'Bet he hopes the thing bucks like Skuthorpe's Bobs!' the Kid thought as the three of them walked back. The chestnut was standing quietly. Jack let himself into the yard, the others climbed the rails and sat watching.

Jack swaggered across the yard. This was the stuff! A bad horse and an audience. The crowd was about the only thing he missed from his time with the buckjump show. But now he took the horse far too casually. He sprang upon it, ignoring the stirrup irons and dug his goose-neck spurs hard into its shoulders. Up it went, twisted and came back underneath him. The same kind of king buck Swanee had used. But this time Jack was quite unprepared and was left standing in the dirt. He was furious! The Kid's offsider, Jimmy, laughed and called out,

'He got you that time Jack!'

Jack swung around and faced the voice with a look as black as a midnight storm. Jimmy hid behind the brim of his hat for a moment, then slid down from the rails and slunk away. Jack turned his fury on the horse.

This time he used the stirrups. But swinging on, he deliberately kneed it hard in the belly. It was into its first buck before his right leg swung over but never looked like shifting him again. He was all over it, anticipating every move. When it stopped he twisted in the saddle, grabbed it by the flank and made it climb again.

The Kid had never seen riding like it. He turned to Miniature.

'Is he always like that? He's like a bloody tiger.'

Jack slid off the horse, smiling. The storm had passed.

'He'll make a good horse,' he called to the Kid. 'A bit of work and he'll be as good as anything they got around here. You got many more to break?'

'A few. Done sixty so far. Which way you blokes headed?'

'Halls Creek, going to dig up some gold. Still plenty there they reckon.'

'There's a lot of dirt mixed up with it too, Jack. You done any prospecting before?'

Jack evaded the question. 'My folks were all miners.'

'What they mine, Jack?'

'Coal.'

The Kid succeeded in not laughing. 'That's a bit different to looking for gold in the hills around Halls Creek, mate. Who was telling you about all the gold?'

'Lots of fellas. They reckon there's more in the ground there than was ever taken out of it.'

The Kid thought of the long, hard, hot weeks he'd spent one off-season, tramping the gullies of Halls Creek with one of the old pensioner prospectors. All they found was enough to pay their tucker bill at Bob Smith's store and buy a few beers at his pub. But it had been interesting. He could understand how some men spent their lives chasing the stuff. Always the next hill. The next gutter. The next creek. Next week!

'We can all go, if you like. You and your mate can help me finish the colts and I'll take you in and show you some likely spots. More chance that way than riding in cold. There's nothing but these colts holding me here. I'm not in love with any of the studs.'

That evening the Kid, Jack, and the Miniature Stockman were sitting in the cool of the verandah when Joe Egan the manager walked up. He was looking worried.

'A blackfella's just rode in from the stockcamp with some news. A heap of our calves along the Limbunya boundary have been branded TLP. The Limbunya brand.'

He looked at Jack. 'You fellas see the Limbunya stockcamp on your way here?'

Jack looked him squarely in the face. 'No. Me an' Miniature only camped overnight at the homestead. The camp was out mustering but we never sighted them.'

'Know who's running their camp?'

'Heard them talking about a new fella, Tom Waite. From the Gulf country of Queensland. He's head stockman. What's wrong with your head stockman, Joe? Why don't he ride in and teach him a lesson?'

'I got a good man running my camp, Jack, but he's a bit too old for that. He sent me word what happened and looks like that's all he's prepared to do. Ghost, I'd like to get over there and brand a heap of their calves!'

The Kid had been quietly listening. Now he looked at the manager.

'I don't know about branding their calves, Joe. That's a good way to start a war. But that Waite has got to be taught a lesson or he'll keep on doing it. The best thing is for me to ride back with that stockboy, find the Limbunya stockcamp and give him a hiding.'

'It's a good thought, Kid, but I don't want to mix you up in it. If anyone goes, it should be my man.'

'He's not going to. I've known him since I come up to this country. He's never been a fighting man and it's too late for him to start now.'

Jack had been standing grinning as the Kid had been speaking. Now he chimed in, taking over as always.

'That's a good idea of the Kid's, Joe. The three of us will go. The Kid's got a mob of colts finished, ready to deliver to the stockcamp. We'll take 'em out and do the other job at the same time. The Kid can make the play but I'll be there to back him. There'll be twenty of 'em in that camp. The black stockboys won't buy in but Waite could have another white bloke with him who might.'

It was agreed. They were two days reaching the Ord stockcamp. The head stockman was pleased to see them.

'He's old all right,' Jack thought. 'Too old for this tough job.'

He accepted the colts as being properly broken-in, then grinned as he learnt of their other mission.

'I never seen their camp, Kid, only my calves all branded. Reckon they'll be working their way along the border for another week yet. They should have told me and give me a chance to send a couple of men across to cut out our cattle. I hope you catch 'em at it.'

'I'm not worried about catching them at it,' the Kid told Jack and Miniature later. 'We know they've done it. There! Look at that.'

A small mob of cattle suddenly broke from a patch of scrub. The cows wore the 055 brand of the Ord. The calves at their feet, TLP of Limbunya. Later, when fully grown, the males amongst them would be turned off as Limbunya bullocks and add to that station's profit.

The following morning their guide, the black stock boy, was riding in the lead when he suddenly jerked his mount to a halt.

'Down there!' he called. 'Stockmen. That cudea Waite with 'em, I reckon.'

The three whites caught up with the stockboy and looked over the top of a low ridge. Four stockmen, three blacks and a white, were herding a small mob of cattle along a gully.

'Hey!' bellowed the Kid, spurring his horse. 'Who the hell are you blokes?'

The stockmen halted and the white man turned his horse and rode towards the Kid.

'Bloody puddin' arse!' the Kid muttered to Jack who had quickly come alongside. 'Should be on the end of an axe, not riding a poor bloody horse into the ground.'

The Limbunya head stockman was a hefty looking tough of about forty and sat his horse with the ease of a veteran.

He thrust his chin out and snarled back, 'Never mind who I am! Who are you lot?'

'The owners of them cattle,' the Kid snapped back. The Ord brands clearly showed. 'If you're Tom Waite, get off your horse. You've been branding our calves all week.'

The Kid slid off his horse.

'Watch him, Kid. He's a big one. More my size. Want me to take him?'

The Kid gave no answer. He was already shaping up. Tom Waite had just as quickly jumped off his horse. Waite made a rush, the Kid side-stepped. Then the Kid let fly. He crashed a left-right combination to Waite's face, then sank a ripping right into his belly. Waite fell to the rocky ground, clutching his middle and gasping.

'Get up you mongrel,' growled the Kid. 'I haven't even started yet! You're getting a broken bone for every Ord calf you've branded.'

Jack and Miniature still sat their horses, grinning. The Ord stockboy and the three Limbunya stockboys stood around in a group. They were laughing and talking excitedly, exchanging news, indifferent to the drama being played out on the stone.

'Get up!' The Kid called again, but Waite was finished. He was a bully, used to bluffing, not a fighter. The Kid was furious.

'I orta kick the shitter out of you! But I ain't done that to anyone yet and I'm not starting on a hooer like you.'

He looked around angrily then spotted Waite's hat. It was lying on a clump of spinifex where it had fallen after the first blow. He strode over and picked it up. He pulled out his knife and hacked at the hat until the brim fell off. Then he walked across and threw the crown at his still prone enemy.

Jack Vitnell nearly fell off his horse laughing.

The Kid walked to where his horse was nibbling some green shoots. Tom Waite climbed slowly to his feet. He didn't look at the Kid but walked towards his stockboys and cursed them for sitting around talking. Then he caught his horse and rode away.

The cattle had walked off, back towards Ord River territory. There was nothing further to do so the Kid swung on his horse and joined Jack and Miniature. That night they camped at a rockhole, halfway into the station. They were squatted around the fire yarning when Jack suddenly looked across at the Kid.

'Where you learn to box, mate?'

'School. Ex- pug used to come and give us lessons. Shilling a time. I pinched fruit down the markets and sold it to get that deener! Later that pug took me down to Grahame's Gym and introduced me to Bill Henneberry. Bill watched me box, then said he would make a champion out of me.'

'You win a title?'

'No. Main event was far as I got. Double bill in Brisbane. Then they found out I was only sixteen. Miserable coots barred me. So back I went where I come from, up north. The Feather who won the title later was a bloke I pasted twice. In and out of the ring. We hated each other. And he got the belt I should have won.'

'You come straight out this Kimberley country, Kid?'

'No. Spent a year in the Territory on the way through. With the buffalo shooters up the South Alligator first up. But I never liked that work. Galloping up an' poking a Three-Oh against some poor dumb critter's spine and pulling the trigger. And knowing it was going to lie there half a day before the skinners come along and finished it.

'Then I tried tin mining on Maranboy. Tin got up to a good price and we all made good money. But they were a bunch of drunks on that field. A drover come past on his way to Flora Valley to pick up a mob so I hitched a ride with him and left those alky tin-scratchers to it.'

Joe Egan was elated when he heard how the Kid had beaten Tom Waite.

'Kid, you got a job here for life. If you want it.'

'Matter of fact, Joe, I'm thinking of pulling out soon. Me an' Jack an' Miniature's going prospecting in to Halls Creek. Okay with you if the three of us finish the colts?'

'That's up to you, Kid. You got the contract. If you want to share your two quid a head, fine. It's good to see a bunch of young blokes together. Don't see enough of it out in this country.'

The day they left, after he had paid them off, Joe had a drink of tea with them in the kitchen.

'What you fellas going to do with all that money?'

The Kid looked at Jack. 'You tell him. He won't believe me.'

Jack grinned. 'After we dig up all that gold still hidden around Halls Creek the Kid's taking us up for a look at that Underworld country. We might even start a station up there.'

'And cows might come home by themselves,' old Joe thought as he watched them ride off.

'You boys are too wild yet to be settling down carving out a station from the bush. But anytime you do, God help your neighbours. They'll want to treat you decent otherwise they'll be in for a hot time!'

19.

The Mongrel From Mungindi

White women of the north, we never knew you well,
And mostly only saw you at the smoko bell,
You resided at the Big House, our swags lay in the Hut,
The division of the classes was firm and clearly cut,
White women of the Kimberley, you were just a faded dress,
Amongst green garden shrubbery, nothing more or less...

August was always races time in Halls Creek. It was towards the end of the cattle season and the major part of the branding and bullock mustering was complete. There was plenty of feed still on the Nine-Mile plain and the weather was not too hot — perfect for a three day race meeting.

The station people attended in mobs. Blacks, whites and all colours in between. Men, women, children, old grey bearded aborigines and young black girls with babes at the breast. Station managers and their wives and overseers and head stockmen. Stockmen, yard builders, well sinkers, jackaroos. This year there were even two single white women amongst the crowd of several hundred whites. But the really old people were back on the stations. You could be 55 and be really old in that harsh country.

Amongst the crowd attending, the Mongrel-From-Mungindi was ill at ease. There was no outward sign but his insides were churning. It was always that way when he came to town after a long spell out bush. He hurried up the outside steps of the ancient Halls Creek hotel, swaggered into the bar and called for a rum. Nothing like a nip of rum to build a little confidence.

He wasn't The Mongrel yet, he was Jeffrey Tribe, horsebreaker, stockman and general bush rouseabout, from Moree, NSW. But by the end of this Kimberley race meeting he would be The Mongrel.

He was six foot three and lean as a well trained greyhound. His hair, where it could be seen straggling beneath his black bull-shooter's hat, was ginger and his face and forearms were covered in large blotchy freckles. He had blue eyes and was altogether rather an ordinary sort of a young fellow. But people were to find he had a great sense of roguish humour, a ton of guts and the will to stick a tough job. He was twenty-two years of age.

The Mongrel had spent five months working as a stockman on one of the local cattle stations and had come to town in the station truck. Five months had seemed a long time to be out in the stockcamp galloping around the ridges mustering cattle and throwing wild bulls. But many people at this race meeting had spent their lives up north. Some were only ten year men, but nonetheless proud of their time. And some were only blow-ins like Jeff Tribe, unknown and yet to prove themselves.

The bar of the only hotel in Halls Creek was crowded. The few locals, mostly old pensioners eking out a living prospecting for gold, were pushed grumbling to one side. It seemed everyone else was a station man keen to catch up with others from the stations. For this was one time a year that mates scattered for several hundred miles around could meet up. No-one was anxious to speak to a lanky ginger-haired stranger drinking rum by the door.

The Mongrel felt isolated and uncomfortable and in desperation turned to an old-timer on a stool next to him.

'Where they find all the gold around here?'

The old chap fixed a pair of twinkling blue eyes upon him.

'Why, there's gold down there in that crik! Waitin' to be found right now! You come to town to look for gold?'

The Mongrel was wise to the ways of old timers. They said all kinds of things to irritate young fellows and test them out. He would give this old chap something to think about.

'No! I come to town to have a fight!'

Jake Puite, the old timer, nearly fell off his stool with glee. Oh, he was going to be a prize, this young fellow!

'Well now! You're just the man we've been looking for! None of these blokes here can fight. Some of them think they can. Some of them have had fights. Some of them have had fights and can't even remember having them. Others talk about all the fights they've had and haven't even had one. And nearly every one of them needs a good flogging. But a man who can fight — why, you're just the man we need!'

The Mongrel didn't feel he was being taken seriously. He ordered another rum and said, 'Who's the best you got in the bar?'

Old Jake didn't hesitate. 'The Kimberley Kid. Him yonder reaching across the bar now.'

The Mongrel smiled. The Best-In-The-Bar was about ten years older and six inches shorter. The Mongrel was so pleased he bought the old chap a beer.

Then the Mongrel spotted George Riley. He didn't like George Riley. They were in the same stockcamp out at Waterloo Station and there was great rivalry between them. So far George had handled the rough horses better and thrown more scrub bulls than the Mongrel. The Mongrel was a good stockman but there were many new twists to learn out in this wild East Kimberley country.

Once also, George had claimed he'd done a bit of fighting before coming north. They had wrapped shirts around their fists and had a reasonably good natured spar around the camp-fire. The Mongrel had thought then, George Riley wasn't anything special.

He ordered another nip of overproof. It sent his blood surging. His chest expanded and he felt his muscles twitching. He looked around. He towered over everyone. He gave a sudden whooping yell.

'What the hell was that?' the Kimberley Kid asked no-one in particular. He was drinking down the far end of the bar with his two gold prospecting mates, Jack Vitnell and the Miniature Stockman.

George Riley was standing nearby.

'That's an idiot from our stockcamp, Kid. Thinks he's the best ringer to ever come into the country. Not even a Queenslander. Comes from New South Wales.'

The Kid's mate, Jack, looked at him with a big grin.

'Hey! That's where I come from mate. We don't all carry on like him!'

The Mongrel was shaping up to the back wall of the bar-room now, throwing punches. He ducked, weaved and bobbed and attacked and countered with dazzling lefts and ripping rights. The man from Moree was invincible. Closer he came, down the bar towards George Riley.

'I can beat anyone in the bar!' he yelled suddenly.

Up till now the boozers had feigned little interest. Another young buck in from the scrub letting off steam. But here was a challenge that struck at every man. It had to be answered. All eyes turned to the Kid.

'Shut up!' the Kid said, in a quiet, flat voice. 'Get yourself a drink and shut up!'

'You're number two!' leered the Mongrel. 'George Riley, then you. Then anyone else who wants to try.'

The Kid had noted the way the Mongrel had snapped out his punches. Left, right, left. George Riley was game but he wouldn't stand a chance against this wild young fellow.

'Let me go first, George,' the Kid pleaded. 'He's too big for you.'

The Mongrel was half a foot taller than both of them.

'Too big for me! Why I've already tried him on. He's only a lightweight. Thanks Kid, but I can beat this hoon.'

The whole bar trooped out to watch.

The Kid held George Riley's shirt.

'Don't stand back on him, George. He's got arms as long as a gorilla. Get in close and swing one on his jaw!'

The Mongrel was warming up, shadow sparring around the circle of watching men. With his shirt off he looked less than impressive. His body was white, hairless and skinny, without any visible muscle. But his long sinewy arms were those of a blacksmith. He would pack a punch, no question.

They shaped up and the crowd thought George had a good chance. He was shorter but he was solid. If he had taken the Kid's advice and moved in at once, he may have scored a win. But he stood flat-footed as the Mongrel danced in. George was immediately knocked to the ground with a fierce blow to the face.

'Round one!' chortled the Mongrel, dancing and stabbing at the air with both fists.

George was straight up and then straight down again with a second blow to the face.

'That's it!' called the Kid. 'My turn now.'

He pulled off his Cuban heel riding boots but was stopped by the crowd.

'He's gettin' up. George ain't finished! Not by a long shot!'

But George was. There were only two more hits, both landed by the Mongrel who danced around his fallen opponent, hands clasped above his head in the boxer's salute, crowing shamelessly.

'Next!' he screamed. 'Bring 'em on! Bring 'em all on! The Tribe's just warming up!'

The Kid's shirt was off and he had loosened up his shoulder joints with a couple of quick arm movements. He was ready.

He walked quickly across to the Mongrel, shaped up, feinted with his left, ducked beneath the Mongrel's answering left and slammed a hard right to the Mongrel's heart. The Mongrel grimaced in pain and sagged slightly at the knees. The Kid followed with a left rip to the belly. The Mongrel's knees bent further. Next came a right uppercut to the Mongrel's jaw. It straightened him for a moment, to his full towering height. Then he dropped senseless to the ground like a falling wheat sack. It had taken less than ten seconds.

'Oh, nice going, Kid!' Jack Vitnell called. 'That was really neat.'

It was neat. But no more than the crowd expected from the Kid. He could really go and they loved him for it.

It was the second time Jack Vitnell had seen his mate in action.

'I'd still beat him,' he thought. 'But only because I'm two stone heavier. An' stronger too, I reckon. Kid's strong but he's one of those light-boned sorts, never be really powerful. A real gentleman. Not too many around like him. Hope it never comes to a clash, I'd hate to hurt him.'

The crowd had not seen Jack Vitnell in action yet, though some had heard of his reputation as the man even Wason Byers stepped around.

Now the Kid was helping the Mongrel to his feet.

'Come and have a drink, mate.'

The Mongrel followed, weaving slightly from side to side as he walked. It was the first time he had been knocked out. His famous long reach had let him down. He ordered a rum.

'Four beers!' called the Kid. 'Don't go drinking that poison, mate. It'll kill you. You got nothing to prove, you can hold your head up. You throw a good punch and will beat more than can beat you. But stick to beer and enjoy the races. We haven't come here to fight.'

The Mongrel adopted the Kid and his two mates for the rest of the afternoon and evening. He amused them with his rough and ready humour and his ignorant ways.

'Where you hail from, Jeff?' they asked.

The Mongrel thought for a moment. Moree didn't sound very exciting. People thought of Moree as the place where the bore water baths cured rheumatism. He chose a nearby town on the Queensland border with a more interesting name. All top ringers came from Queensland.

'Mungindi,' he said. 'That's a town in Queensland, full of us Tribes.'

The Mongrel was the first in the bar to succumb. It had been a big day. But he finished happy. He had fought twice and lost but once! And it took their very best man to beat him. He could indeed hold his head up. And now everyone knew him and respected him, he was sure. He lay contentedly on the floor and closed his eyes.

For a time, men stepped around him. Then over him. Finally they rested their feet on him. The Mongrel snored peacefully.

'Better shift him outside,' the Kid said. They grabbed his feet and arms and bundled him through the door to the wooden bench provided on the verandah.

Later in the evening someone called out, 'What have you blokes done with that Mongrel from Mungindi?'

For the three years he stopped amongst them, he was never called anything else.

Fred Terrone the barman hated Races Time. It put him right out of his routine. All these noisy beer guzzling station blokes. Fred forgot these days, he was an old station man, stockman, drover, horsebreaker, boozer ...

He felt beyond it all. He drank very little now and could only cope with the heavy boozing by ignoring it. The more the raucous voices shouted, the more demanding they became, the less chance there was of him hurrying. He walked at the same measured pace and poured the beers and nips as slowly and carefully as he did in normal times when there were only one or two in the bar.

He envied the old stockmen. How they could still swing onto a horse was beyond him. Perhaps they hadn't been smashed up as many times. Fred ached in every other joint and had done so for ten years.

'And what am I?' he thought. 'Sixty three, sixty four? That Charlie Swan's near eighty and still taking bullocks into Queensland!'

He had enjoyed the fight yesterday.

But Fred thought, 'If that ginger headed fellow hadn't been beat he would have been insufferable. Thank God the Kid was in the bar. But there were others too, who could have chopped him down to size.'

Jake Puite edged his way to the bar and winked.

Fred poured him a beer, opened the book and pretended to record it in case Bob Smith was watching. None of the locals ever paid cash. It was always strapped up in the book — the slate.

'Be back to normal tomorrow, Freddo. How's the Black Widow?'

The Black Widow was Bob Smith's barmaid. She had worked a year at the Kimberley Arms. She was a stunning woman, tall, dark and statuesque. Every single man who had come into the bar in the previous twelve months had fallen in love with her. She had ignored them all. She looked thirty but was all of forty and had been twice widowed and left plenty of money — or so the grapevine said. She never conversed with the patrons. She poured their drinks and withdrew to a seat close to Bob Smith's curtained-off office.

'She can handle 'em,' Fred answered. 'She's tough that woman. Treat's 'em all like they was rowdy school boys. Except the Kid's mate. She's always giving him the eye but he never notices.'

'Vitnell?'

'Him. Good looking bloke ain't he? Something special about him.'

'Something special the way he rides! He made that feature horse today look like a drover's night-horse. He can go too. Big blue down the creek last night. Two young Flora ringers looking for fight. They got it! He flattened both of 'em, one after the other!'

The next day the races were over. The tents were pulled down, the bar at the course dismantled and the heaps of rubbish picked up. Only the skeletons of the bough sheds and the single-railed fence of the course proper remained. The racecourse was a pathetic, desolate sight the day after the station people had gone home.

Even Fred found it quiet. The last of them had finally made it through the door, after the final, final, one-for-the-road and now there were but three indifferent locals to be served. The town was back to normal size, less than thirty souls.

The Kid and his two mates were in the transition from blow-in to regular. Every night and most afternoons now found them in the bar. Tramping up and down the steep hills and dry gullies, scratching for colours, carting pick, shovel and waterbags was becoming less attractive by the day. They hadn't found a leader for weeks. It was becoming a matter of who would give in first. The Kid or his two mates or Bob Smith. Currently Fred was still recording their drinks in the book. But their debt was increasing and the less time spent in the gullies meant the less chance of the debt being paid off.

No-one ever thought of slipping in behind the bar when Fred or the Widow were busy changing a keg and crossing out their drinks as paid. It was still an honest country.

'There she is now, Jack. At it again!'

Miniature was the first to notice.

'You like The Widow, Jack? Because she sure likes you. Never takes her eyes off you.'

'She's not looking at me, Miniature. It's the Kid! That's who she's got her eyes on.'

One afternoon when they came in worn-out and dejected from tramping the gullies she poured their drinks and lingered by the counter.

'What did you fellas find today?' She looked straight at Jack and smiled.

He grinned at her.

'What we been finding a lot of lately. Nothing! Reckon it's time we tossed in this prospecting and went back to breaking horses again.'

'Can you borrow a horse and take me for a ride tomorrow, Jack? It's my day off. I'd love to get out of here.'

Nobody had ever seen her take a step outside the hotel walls. But next day when Jack rode up with a spare horse, she was already waiting on the verandah in a yellow sun frock and large straw hat. Jack was surprised. 'Ain't you got a pair of pants to wear? Can you really ride a horse?'

The Widow laughed. 'I didn't intend doing any riding when I headed up north, Jack. But I can ride. My family's always had horses.'

She swung into the saddle and Jack was treated to a glimpse of white frilly underwear. His heart skipped a beat. Was that deliberate? Was something going to happen today, out in the hills? He wondered if she knew he met one of the young black kitchen girls some nights, up in the laundry. Those things always got around. He shrugged. It would be her play anyway. He would give her a quick stab if that's what she was after, but the last thing he wanted was to tie up with a white woman. No matter how casually things started, in the end it always came down to one thing with them. Marriage.

He led off, up the back of town towards the scrub covered ridges. 'You want to see some old graves? There's heaps up here from the gold days. Buried where they died, with only a rusted pick or wagon wheel on their graves to show they ever lived.'

By mid morning the Widow was complaining of sore legs. 'I'm sure the calves of my legs are rubbed raw, Jack. Can we get off and rest a while?'

Jack looped the horses' bridles around a straggly snappy gum branch and stripped the saddles. The Widow took the two sweat stained saddle blankets and spread them under another tree. She hitched her dress up and sat down, careful to leave the lace hem of her petticoat showing. The prickly clumps of dry yellow spinifex and red quartz streaked boulders scattered about mocked her femininity.

'It's harsh country, Jack,' she remarked, as he sat down beside her. 'Hard country for hard men. You ever feel like getting away from it?'

Jack shook his head. 'I come from down south and couldn't get away quick enough. This north is the country for me.' He grinned. 'Where every man has his day and every cat has its night.'

The Widow laughed. 'The men have their nights, too, from what I hear.' She was suddenly serious. 'You ever been with the gins, Jack?'

'Of course I have,' he snapped. 'Do you think I'm a monk? Are there any young white girls up here? There wouldn't be a white man in the country if it wasn't for the quee-eyes. Married men and all. You know something? Sometimes they're worst of all, the married station men. Gin shepherds we call them. Make sure the young ringers stop out in the stock camp the whole season. Then when all the stock work's finished, they pay 'em off and run 'em into town to spend the Wet. Frightened they may get amongst their favourite studs.'

The Widow was shocked at his outburst and his honesty. Whenever she had broached the subject with men before, they had always denied any knowledge of such goings on.

'I find that hard to understand, Jack, about the married men. Aren't their wives enough? What's so special about the gins?'

'Nothing special — except they're available. Just like there's women down south, too, available for blokes not satisfied with what they got.'

'And what about the single men. Do you think it's fair they go with white women after they been with the blacks?'

Jack was becoming irritated. 'Look Missus widda lady, I don't go along with all that black and white business. I work with the blacks, live with them, and sometimes I sleep with them. They're no different to the rest of us. There's good, bad, long and short. The only thing different is the law. If I shack up with you, the law says nothing, if it's a black woman I get a sixer up in Fanny Bay.'

They sat silently for a time and watched a kite hawk circling. I've done it now, the Widow was thinking. I should never have broached the subject. Now it's out in the open I can't pretend not to know what he gets up to out on the stations. It's this damn country. It's not normal for men to be locked away in the bush without their own women. She smiled. He's so straight. I might have known he'd tell me the truth. If I want him I've got to get him away from this north. There's no other way, no other hope for us, but how am I going to start things now? I'll feel cheap if I let him. She smiled again. And cheated if I don't! Oh, well, what the hell! He doesn't see anything wrong in what he's been doing. It's only me and my not understanding. She turned to him.

'I don't know what to think about it all, Jack. It's certainly a different world up here. I suppose it's because I'm a woman and we don't feel the same as men. I can go for months without ever thinking of a man — that way.' She stopped, then added slyly. 'But sometimes I get close to the right kind of man and all those feelings surface again. Did you know women feel the same way at times?'

Jack had never spoken about such things to a woman before and was feeling decidedly uncomfortable. For once he was at a loss for something to say. But it didn't matter. The Widow suddenly leaned against him and he automatically put his arm around her. 'Oh, Jack,' she whispered as he lay her back. 'Try and love me a little.'

He arrived home at daylight. The Kid saw him sneaking into his swag.

'So!' he mused. 'That's the way it is!'

Every evening after that, when she wasn't serving or swabbing down the counter, the Widow sat with them.

Then they found a pocket of gold. It was in a bed of blue shale that cut through the diorite country rock. There could be weeks of work digging it out.

'Why don't you and me take a holiday south, Jack,' said the Widow one day. 'Leave the gold to the Kid and Miniature, I'll shout. There's plenty of race meetings down Perth way.'

'Do you good to get out of this country for a while,' the Kid told him. 'Stop a month. We won't be going anywhere.'

The Widow had no intention of coming back or of Jack coming back. Once she got him south, she was going to hold him there. She hoped. There were people in the racing game, mates of her late second husband, still favourable towards her. They would help Jack obtain work and a trainer's licence. They would get married ...

They flew out on the next plane. Until the door finally closed on him, the Kid thought Jack was not going through with it. He looked like a roué being dragged to the altar by the power of a shotgun. The plane took off at last and the Kid and Miniature drove out to work their pocket of gold. It cut out in two weeks. They didn't prospect for any more. They had made enough money to square the account at the pub and decided to change camp.

'Long as we hang about this pub we going to get back in Bob's debt, Miniature. Nothing surer than that. Let's make a shift up to old Ted McKean's hut. He'll give us a camp till we decide what we going to do. And we'll be away from the grog.'

Ted McKean was an old-timer with a colourful past. He was a man of many parts but mostly now he was remembered as one of the early donkey teamsters. He had retired to Halls Creek several years before and taken up residence in an old abandoned hut. It was a good town for an old pensioner.

There was always someone from the stations sending in a few garden vegetables or a slab of salt beef. Also there was gold to fossick around for. Just a few ounces every month made a big difference to a man's style of living. Thirty quid could buy a lot of grog down at the Kimberley Arms. But more importantly, money got you in the door. Once you were ensconced there, there was always the chance of someone coming in and shouting a drink.

'What you done with that mate of yours? Run off with that widder woman did he?' Ted wanted to know.

'She's run off with him, Ted. But he'll be back. Next plane I reckon. The south won't suit Jack Vitnell.'

One morning they wandered down to the end of town to old Darky Rawlins' disused blacksmith's shop. He had been part of the town for as far back as anyone could remember —way back when the ridges were crawling with men working the gullies. He had joined them but arrived too late to peg payable ground so he set up a forge made out of a hollow log and reverted to his trade.

At first it was just sharpening gads and picks but as the easy gold was won the prospectors moved on and left it to the deep-lead men. There was plenty of work then for a blacksmith, with machinery on the field, and he sent south for proper blacksmith tools.

But these days the old Maori's forge had long been cold. He was now so frail he could scarcely lift the fourteen pound hammer he once swung all day, and was barely able to look after himself. The AIM sisters were continually urging him to retire to Perth.

'They not gettin' me in no old man's home,' he'd say in his squeaky trembly voice. 'Ah'm stoppin' right here. Until the box!'

Today Darky had company, one of the old-timers from Wyndham down on a visit.

'This is the young fella I was tellin' you about, Sam,' he wheezed as the Kid and Miniature strode up. 'He been up that Underworld country knocking around with old Lester. Got hisself in a bit of trouble up there. This is Sammy Lynch, Kid.'

'Know old Lester, hey?' The old chap looked pleased. 'I'd like to know where he is now. Left town three year ago and no-one's heard nothing. You the young fella got pinched with the horses, hey?'

'That's me. What you fellas hear up in Wyndham? About a gunfight and tracker getting shot?'

'Never heard that one, Kid. We heard a lot of other rubbish and we still hear it. There's even a rumour doing the rounds now that Jack Vitnell murdered a bloke over in the Territory.'

The Kid was horrified. 'Murdered who?'

'I dunno. Some fella he was giving a lift to. They reckon they had an argument and Jack pushed him out of the cab as he was driving along.'

'Oh, for Christ's sake, Sammy! 'They reckon' again. I'd like to catch up with this 'They Reckon' bloke one day, I'd give him something to talk about! Miniature here was with Jack when he picked that bloke up. Tell him about it, Miniature.'

'The bloke was so drunk, Jack wouldn't let him sit in the cab. He was a Royal Duke. You know what us Queenslanders call a Royal Duke? A bloke who gets so drunk he shits himself an' that's what this poor bugger had done. We roped him down on top of the load but somehow he struggled free and fell off. We never knew until we reached town and checked the load. Jack told the coppers and we all drove back to look for him. The poor coot was lying with his skull cracked open one side of the road. The coppers never even made it hard for Jack, they could tell what had happened.'

Sammy Lynch nodded sympathetically. 'I'm glad you told me, fellas. Jack Vitnell's a hard man, but I couldn't see him murdering anyone. It's always been the way in this country. If people stuck to the truth they'd have nothing to talk about!'

20.

Halls Creek

If you know where to look,
You can still see the place,
That caught Charlie Hall's keen eye,
The fractured rock face,
By the bed of the creek,
Where the gold lay thick in the sand,
Where he picked out the lumps and called to his mates,
Here was the Promised Land.

It was quiet without Jack, but this morning The Kimberley Kid had other things on his mind. Something was wrong. For the fourth morning he'd woken up in old Ted McKean's hut with a shocking hangover. The Kid prided himself on never feeling ill after a night's boozing. Not even a headache. But now his head was thumping. The way The Miniature Stockman was groaning, his head was thumping as well.

It could have been an off keg but they had scarcely called into the pub since coming up to camp with Ted. There had been no need. Ted made his own grog and was free with his shouts. The Kid groped for the edge of the bunk and pulled himself upright.

'It's got to be that brew of Ted's, Miniature. What you reckon he puts in it?'

'Strychnine. Now I know how a dingo feels after taking a bait.'

'I can't understand it. Mostly those old timers make a good brew. They boil raisins, sugar an' stuff an' get it fermenting and it don't taste too bad. It knocks you, but not like this. We got to watch what he puts in.'

Old Ted McKean liked company. Particularly young ringers interested in the old days. They often stopped with him. There wasn't a great choice of camp in

Halls Creek. The pub, the bed of the creek, or Ted's. Ringers seldom chose the pub. They were used to a swag on the ground and there was no reason to change because of coming to town. Besides down the creek they could come and go as they liked. Sing, argue, fight and drink, all night if they wished, without the publican or his wife complaining.

Down in the dry, tree-lined, sandy bed of Halls Creek itself, ringed around a fire gulping beer from warm bottles, drunk from alcohol and the stimulation of companions at last. Ringers in for a spell from the stations, to talk away the solitude of the cattle camps. The stockcamps. Places of wild exciting days but long lonely nights for the white head stockman alone with the blacks. And made doubly lonesome by the singing, laughing and dancing of their black workmates corroboreeing nearby. The stations of East Kimberley seldom afforded the luxury of two white stockmen.

It was an historic place this dry creek bed. But it is doubtful any of them knew or remembered — or cared. It was the site of the first gold strike in Western Australia, three years before Kalgoorlie. Now it was just a dry creek, part of the most isolated town in the West. Of the nine remaining buildings clinging to the ridge above the creek, four were constructed from mud made of crushed antbed moulded into bricks.

Late last century, thousands of hopefuls had passed through this place seeking their fortune. Nearly all found bitter disappointment. The country was too dry, too harsh, too far away. And there was too little gold. Most found just enough to pay for their tucker. Food was dear in the Kimberley. It was a long way to haul flour from Fremantle.

When the alluvial gold was won, there was still gold but in veins in the quartz blows and deep dipping beds of slate. That meant machinery. Stampers to crush the ore and release the gold. The prospectors headed off and left the field to the miners. And when all that gold was won and they left, the prospectors returned to fossick around the dry stony ridges and gullies. For pensioners it was a profitable past-time.

Ted McKean had never felt better. He was seventy-two and still strode around town and climbed the steep hills with the best. Now he sat watching the new day from his verandah. Like the other buildings, Ted's hut sat on a patch of level ground scratched from the hillside. All except Darky's. Darky's old smithy squatted on the only piece of flat ground, where the ridge dipped to a gully at the far end of town.

It was full daylight now and the rascal white cockatoo had started its screeching. Every morning as the sun came up it perched on the ridge of the pub roof and mocked the publican's wife.

'Myra! Myra! Where are those gins!'

Ted turned inside. Time for a second drink of tea and a nip. The Kid's eyes followed.

'I'm going to watch him brew up today for sure!' he vowed.

'When you come up to this country?' he asked later.

Ted's eyes twinkled. He loved this question.

'Two!' he answered proudly.

'Two?' the Kid echoed. 'You mean nineteen hundred and two?'

That was when the Kid's mother had been born.

'What was it like then?'

'Much the same as now,' old Ted smiled. 'The diggers had all gone, just a few fossickers in the hills. But the mines were still operating. The Ruby, Lady Margaret and them. The Lady Margaret was the richest mine in Kimberley but didn't hardly employ anyone. If it wasn't for the stations the town would have died.'

'The Ruby's still working, Ted. Me an' Miniature were offered a job out there.'

'Share basis?'

'Half of what we find.'

'Old Sam Wilson's been pulling that one for years.' Ted laughed. 'You wouldn't find enough gold to feed yourselves. Long as that mine's working, Sam draws sustenance money from the Government. They come up sometimes and check, that's why he likes to have someone camped out there doing a bit. Last time the mines inspector come up from Perth he copped all the prospectors boozing in the pub. Each one of 'em was drawing sustenance. He got 'em all taken off, three quid a week. That sent 'em back out to the ridges! Well, I better go fix a brew, you blokes look like you could do with a peg.'

The Kid watched him walk into the kitchen and rummage around in a dirty old sugar bag. He drew out a handful of dried apricots and threw them into a pot on the stove. Then he reached for a bottle, uncorked it and added the contents. The Kid strolled over. 'What's cooking?'

'Apricot brandy today,' the old chap grinned, adding a little water. He watched the pot come to the boil then moved it to one side to simmer.

'Be ready soon. Let's get this Miniature on his feet.'

The Kid sneaked back, lifted the pot and sniffed.

'Bloody hell!' he said.

Later he whispered the news to Miniature.

'Don't drink any more of his home brew. It's bloody metho! Boiled up, with dried apricots.'

When the old-timer later appeared with a pannikin, the Kid said, 'Not this morning, mate. Me and Miniature are going to pay Bob Smith a visit. We got enough left for a few beers. Leave your brew on the stove and come down with us.'

Old Ted was horrified.

'I'm not going anywhere without me morning nip of brandy. I'll catch you up later.'

The Kid was a kind-hearted fellow. It worried him the old timer was starting to drink such poisonous stuff.

'Don't know what we can do. Let's see if we can get Bob Smith to sell him some real brandy on the cheap.'

Bob roared laughing.

'Metho! Old Ted's been on the metho for thirty years to my knowledge. Thrives on it! Don't know why it doesn't kill him. It's finished plenty others. He drank a whole wagon load of grog once and even that didn't kill him. Ask him to tell you about it. Whatever he dies from it won't be alcohol.'

A few days later the Kid angled the conversation around to the Law. 'You ever been in court, Ted?'

'Yep, twice. Drank a wagon load of grog once and...' He paused. 'The other time I burnt a wagon.'

'What made you so thirsty to drink a whole wagon load, Ted?'

'Got bogged. For three months in the middle of a sea of mud. Caught by the Wet going out to the Fitzroy pub from Derby.'

'How many ton you have on, Ted?'

'Twelve. Wasn't more than a couple cases of whisky left when they rescued me. Lucky most of the load was beer. Hard stuff would have killed me.'

'What they do with you, Ted?'

'Charged me with stealing. But I got a lawyer up from Perth who got me off. Had to make restitution though. He was a pretty smart man, that lawyer. He almost had the pub thanking me for looking after their loading during the Wet Season. Said the easy thing to do would have been to walk off and leave it to the bush blacks.'

'Pigeon wasn't long shot in that country and everyone knew how crazy the blacks went when they got hold of grog. The lawyer said the average man wouldn't have been game to stick it alone in that country protecting his load. And it was only natural a man in that predicament would take to drink.'

'Why didn't you ride a donkey into Derby, Ted?'

'They cleared out. Had to scrounge feed. We were on a little patch of high ground in the middle of a flood. Off they swam like little motor boats. And they'll tell you donkeys can't swim. But they never went far. The whole three months they hung around a line of ridges overlooking the wagon. It was the only home they knew, that wagon.'

'Couldn't you have walked when the water went down, Ted?'

'No hope. The country around was all flooded. I would have bogged to my neck. Besides the pub at Fitzroy knew I was stranded and so did the shipping agent in Derby. They had more chance of sending out someone to me than I did of getting in to them.

'And that's what finally happened. A police patrol came out from Derby three months later when the country had dried out. We mustered up the donkeys hitched 'em up and then I turned around and headed back to Derby. The constable made me do that. Said it wasn't much use carting two cases of whisky a hundred mile to the pub. Soon as we got into town I was charged. They thought they had me cold.'

'Take you long to pay it off, Ted?'

'Took me less than a month. I won the lottery. Three thousand pounds. Squared everything up, had a month on the booze and back out on the track. But I never carted for that pub again!'

Miniature had been quietly listening to the Kid and Ted. Now he spoke.

'Couldn't you have followed the ridges and walked back to Derby that way, Ted? When the water had gone down a bit.'

The old timer's grey eyes twinkled. 'Of course I could have,' he grinned. 'But I was having too much fun!'

The Kid shot a look at Miniature. He was trying not to laugh as he said, 'Yeah, they were sure lucky they had you as their carrier, Ted. And burning the wagon? They get you on that one?'

'Judge wanted to, but the jury wouldn't convict. They knew the circumstances. I had two wagons at the time and my wife, Ella, drove the second. We never travelled together, that only got the two teams boxed, so she come along one day's travel behind — about six mile. You waste a lot of time with donkeys. They got to be rounded up of a morning and yoked up, then when you get to camp that night, un-yoked, taken on to water and feed, then hobbled out.

'But twice a week, regular, I'd walk the six mile back to Ella's wagon and camp with her. And of course we rested up together all day Sundays. So it wasn't as though I was neglecting her. Anyway this particular night I was feeling pretty lonesome and decided to walk back and see her. It was a night after I had been with her so it would be a nice surprise. Off I set, tramping along in the dark but when I got close to her fire I could see two figures standing, arms around each other. One was Ella, the other another Derby carrier.

'I got a shock, I can tell you. My first reaction was to run in swinging. Then I thought of something better. I knew he must be travelling behind Ella so I walked the six mile or so back to his wagon and found it loaded high with general station stores. Good I thought, burn all the better! There was no-one with it so I picked up all the dead wood I could find, stacked it underneath and dropped in a match.

'Up she went like a mammoth bonfire. As I walked off I could hear the dry wagon timbers crackling and exploding, then the bottles and tins started bursting. Sound travels for miles in that country and it wasn't long before I saw this teamster bloke tearin' along in the darkness. Bob his name was. As he come abreast of me, he nearly fell down in shock.

'Nice evenin' for a stroll, ain't it Bob,' I said, nice an' polite. 'Hope you have a good trip back to Derby.'

'He never answered, just kept on running. I made a detour around Ella's wagon, I couldn't see her but knew she'd be watching. There was a huge spray of sparks, flame and smoke shooting up in the sky. Two nights later I walked back and camped with her as though nothing had happened.'

The Kid looked surprised. 'I thought you would have give her a good thumping, Ted.'

The old chap sighed. 'That wouldn't have done any good, only made her worse. But I tell you one thing I did. Sold her wagon. Next time we left Derby with loading we travelled together. Now! Aren't you the young fellas said you were off to Burke's for a gallon of ale?'

George Burke, The Irish Lad, operated a general store a little further along the ridge. It was a dilapidated corrugated iron building strung together by nails and fencing wire. It used to boast a front entrance but that had long been converted to a garage for George's ancient Dodge truck. Now customers came in the back way, through George's bedroom which also doubled as an office.

There wasn't much furniture. An iron-framed wire bed which in daylight hours was always piled high with crates and boxes. And over to one side out of sight under a mess of papers and more piled boxes was a large wooden desk. To get from the bedroom into the store proper was always a struggle. Goods lay jumbled everywhere. It was as though someone had once lifted the iron roof and filled the store with cans, cartons, saddles, shirts, trousers, dresses, as well as bags of flour, sugar and crates of tea, fencing gear and coils of wire. When the whole place was just about full, it seemed as if the roof was carefully nailed back on.

Then it looked as though George had forced his way in the door and made a couple of tracks through by shovelling things out of the way. If you wanted something, George probably had it. But sometimes it was quicker to get it up by boat from Fremantle to Derby then out by truck to Halls Creek than search George's store. But George knew where the grog was. That was right under his eye at all times. No-one was going to sneak out with a bottle of rum while he was around. And he was around 24 hours a day.

There was no cold beer. George didn't believe in modern stuff like refrigeration. But his grog was cheap. Cheaper than the cold bottles down at the hotel. And there was always a spot in the shade at the back of the store to relax and enjoy a bottle or two. Mostly though it was a bottle or six. George was forced to sell grog by the gallon and his customers couldn't see any sense in just drinking a couple and then carrying the rest home. It gave a good kick too, warm beer.

Old prospector Tommy the Slave would drink nothing else. In the Dry he'd work for the Road Board driving a grader to build up a stake for the Wet. Most old timers waited till after rain to get out and prospect. And they didn't go without their evening nip. Overproof rum was the favourite to take bush. There was no sense loading up their vehicles with cases of beer when a few bottles of OP would do the same job. Besides, there was no way to keep beer cold out in the bush. A splash of rum in a pannikin topped up from the water bag made a good cool drink on a hot day.

But not for Tommy The Slave. He always carried beer, in town or out prospecting. A good place to keep it warm on the grader was under the seat. He wouldn't drink it any other way.

George Burke was busy typing a letter on his ancient typewriter when the Kid and Miniature walked in. It was the closest thing to a luxury item George had ever owned. He wrote a letter exactly as he spoke. There was no starting off, 'Dear Sir'.

'There that'll fix 'em!' he mumbled as they walked in.

'What they done to you now?' the Kid asked.

'They sent me up the same stuff as last time. And last time it was the wrong stuff. I wrote and told 'em but now they've done it again! Them fellas down south wouldn't know if they was punched or bored.'

He pulled a piece of note paper from the typewriter and handed it to the Kid. It started, 'You bastards, you done it again ...' Jumbled in with those six words were a couple of asterisks, a percentage sign, three brackets, a pound note sign and a question mark. Any time George hit a wrong key he never bothered erasing it.

'They knows what I means,' he'd say in his peculiar brogue.

A traveller for a big Perth wholesaler once told how his boss had one of George's letters framed up on his office wall.

Sometimes if George was in a particularly good mood he would pull out his ancient squeeze box and play a few tunes. He would squat on his knees and kick out his legs, one after the other, in time to the music. Then at the finish, and still pumping vigorously with his arms, flip head over heels in a somersault.

Pretty good for a man of seventy.

They were yarning with George when Bob Smith strolled up.

'Got a wire this morning from a fella after a caretaker-manager for the Wet. Either of you blokes interested? He's paying fifteen notes.'

Miniature took the job. The Kid drove him up to the airstrip at the Nine-Mile in the hotel truck.

'What you going to do, Kid?'

'Hang on for Jack. He'll be back. Can't see him putting up with the south much longer than a month — or the Widder!'

'No way! Jack's set for life! That Widder's going to get him in with the race crowd, she's loaded. We'll be reading about him one day, Jack Vitnell the famous racehorse trainer. You see if we don't!'

They didn't. Next mail day Bob sent the Kid up to meet the plane and bring back some perishables ordered from Derby.

The DC3 landed, swirling dust through the tiny corrugated iron shed that served as office and waiting-room. The door opened and out stepped Jack. He was wearing a white Panama hat, cream silk shirt and fawn trousers with 28 inch bottoms. He nodded to the Kid as though he had never been away.

'Where's the Widder, Jack?'

Jack grinned and glanced at his watch. 'Eating dinner about now I reckon and still watchin' down the road for me to come home. There's some boxes on board for the pub. Want a hand to load 'em?'

'That was the end of the conversation,' the Kid told Miniature when he ran into him later. 'He had no port, no swag, nothing. Just a wallet with six quid in it. Apparently he just walked out of the Widder's house one morning and decided he'd had enough of double harness. Bought himself a plane ticket and off.

'I took him down the pub and he said good-day to Bob Smith same as he'd said to me. Like he'd just walked up from the creek for his morning grog. Wouldn't come out prospecting again. Said he was tired of town and wanted to get back to the bush.

'We sat in the bar a couple of days drinking his six quid and what I had left, wondering where we'd go. It was December by then and bloody hot. No cattle work around. Things didn't look bright. Then Bluey O'Malley came in. He'd just bought that place up the Underworld, Elgie Cliffs, from Jimmy McCaddam and wanted a hand to put up a new drafting yard. But he couldn't pay us till after he'd turned some bullocks off the following season.

'That was okay with me and Jack. We went back with him. First up though, Jack strapped up two blankets, a swag cover and spare shirt at the store. He was also trying for a gallon of OP rum but Bluey wouldn't allow it. No grog on Elgie Cliffs. Bluey never drank, that's why he could afford to buy Jimmy's station. Ol' Jack grumbled a bit but I was glad. He was becoming a mite too fond of that old Bosun!'

21.

Elgie Cliffs

Jack was mustering with Kimberley Kid,
Far off in the lead,
When a big white bull came bursting,
And raced off at full speed,
With fine straight back and tail cocked high,
It ran with a young bull's stride,
They gave a whoop and off they charged,
To curb that scrub bull's pride!

It was April and the drafting yard was finished. It had been a light wet season and the yard builders had been able to keep working. There were four of them, Bluey and his wife's brother, Sandy Thompson and Jack Vitnell and the Kid. They took turns week about to cut timber or dig holes. No-one liked digging the post-holes, bent over a crowbar and shovel all day dripping perspiration. They preferred axe work, out in the bush amongst the trees searching for patches of good straight timber and cutting them down.

The Kid and Jack worked together, chopping and sawing the grey box and bloodwoods into ten foot lengths. Yard posts sat three foot in the ground, seven out. They set out each morning at first streak in Blue's old three-ton Dodge truck. By sun-up their axes were flashing, sinking deeply into the hard smooth timber.

After an hour's chopping that first morning Jack had called, 'How many you cut, Kid?'

'Here we go!' the Kid thought. 'Got to be best on a buckjumper, at throwing bulls, scoffing rum, fighting, now he's got to be best at cutting yard-posts!'

'Dunno,' he yelled, trying not to sound irritable. 'Never thought about it. How many you cut?'

'Eight. Keep a count and see who cuts the most!'

But the Kid never did. The work was hard enough without making it harder by trying to beat Jack Vitnell!

'Oh, hell, Jack. I keep forgetting!' the Kid would say.

'Don't worry, I'll count 'em.' And Jack did. He knew every one of his posts and every one of the Kid's.

'Jeez!' the Kid, would mutter. 'What's it matter? We're not on bloody piece work!'

But it mattered to Jack. He had to be best.

Once, the Kid remembered, in the bar at Halls Creek, Jack had been minding a drover's dog for a week.

Bob Gracey had come into the bar with his dog, noticed the dog at Jack's feet and said, 'Bet my dog can beat yours!'

The two hounds had got stuck into each other and the drover's had turned tail and fled. Jack was so furious he challenged Bob to a fight.

'Christ Jack, we're mates! Are we going to fall out over a dog?'

The Kid had promptly proposed a bull fight instead as Bob, although he had a notoriously hard head, could not fight to save himself.

'Oh, it don't matter,' Jack had said, not dodging the bullfight, but not seeking it either. 'You're right. Be silly to fight over a dog. Specially as he's not mine!'

When enough trees were felled they joined forces on the crosscut. To stop the saw jamming as the post was cut off, one side of the trunk was supported by a crowbar. The crowbar was held up by a forked stick propped under one end.

'There's a smart way and a gut-busting way for everything,' the Kid would say. 'We're doing it the smart way.'

But Jack never could get the hang of the crosscut. 'Don't push, Jack. Just pull. Every time you push it makes hard work of it.'

But Jack was so eager and keen to do more than his share he would forget and start pushing as the Kid was pulling, sometimes almost buckling the saw. The Kid gave up.

'It's just his way,' he would say. 'That's Jack. Never could tell him anything!'

Often the tree provided a ten foot rail as well as a post. It was no problem lifting the heavy timber onto the tray of the truck. The truck was driven alongside the post. The two of them then lifted one end and held it in place against the tray with a steel pin. Then they both lifted the other end and tossed it up.

When enough timber had been cut and carted to the yard site, the posts had to be morticed to hold the rails. Cutting the rail ends to fit the morticed slot was traditionally done with an adze but now they both learnt something. Bluey used an axe and was twice as quick as a man with an adze.

'I got that four inch joggle in me mind,' he would say. 'Using an adze you're flying blind. The rail's turned over the wrong way. But with an axe you can see what you're cutting the whole time.'

And he could. It was seldom he had to re-work an end. He was half their size but could work twice as hard. They had never seen anyone quite like Bluey O'Malley. Now they understood his nickname of Red Ant. A red ant could carry off lumps of meat many times larger than itself. Blue was in the same category. Jack had never been outworked before. That he was, and by a little fellow older than himself, was hard for him to accept.

Blue showed them how to use the truck for the gut-busting job of lifting the posts into the hole. He lashed two of the rails together near one end to form a vee. The post was positioned with one end over the post-hole and the vee piece laid over. Then by using the truck for power, a steel rope tied to the top of the post and the two lashed rails as a lever, Blue could easily hoist the posts up and into the holes.

'I can't believe how much we've done,' Jack said one morning. 'I thought it took about a year to build a set of yards. Here it is April and we're finished.'

It was not a big set of yards. In the centre was a small square pound. One gate led into a round yard, another led to a forcing yard and crush and the other two gates led to holding yards.

The blacks Blue had inherited when he bought the station had left on their annual walkabout, except for one old couple still in residence down at the blacks' camp.

'What for you fella never go bush with allabout?' Blue asked one morning as he handed over their breakfast — slabs of bread and beef.

'We too old for that. More better stop here, help Missus.'

'They not too old,' Blue's half-caste wife Mary smiled. 'They too cunning for all that walkin' about. They rather be here, getting good tucker. Workin' in the garden and kitchen.'

The others straggled in just as the yard was finished. They were lean from bush tucker and sore footed, eager again for bread and beef, sweet black tea and tobacco.

'Wouldn't you know it,' the Kid said. 'Bet they've been watching from the hills till we swung the last gate. They don't like this kind of work.'

'Can't blame 'em for that, mate,' Jack answered. 'I don't care for it myself. Too boring. Give me a horse anytime and a scrub bull to chase!'

Now it was the cattle season again Jack was eager for action.

'You got your yard, Blue. Me an' the Kid's going to poke off now and get a start ringin' somewhere.'

'Well, I can't pay you boys yet. Not till I can turn some bullocks off. Why not give me a hand. There's plenty of wild cattle to muster and you'll get all the scrub bulls you want. You can do me droving too, take the bullocks into Wyndham. Soon as you deliver I'll get the Meatworks to pay you out.'

First they had to muster the horses. They were not hard to find. Elgie Cliffs was rough country and the horses kept to what well grassed flat country they could find. They were easy enough to get around and block at the stony hills. They had no wish to gallop over the sharp rock and were used to being mustered. Most of them were Blue's, from his droving days. A few had belonged to the previous owner, old Jim McCaddam, and had come with the station. It was months since the Kid and Jack had been galloping on a horse.

'I'll never spend so much time away from 'em again, Kid.'

Jack grinned as they yarded a mob fresh and frisky after their long spell.

'There's plenty of colts to be broken and I bet there's a good buck in all of them. Don't think I'll bother with yard building again. I was going to sleep swinging that axe!'

'There's mobs of cattle out there to get, Jack, from what we saw today. Don't reckon old Jimmy McCaddam did much mustering the last couple of years he was here.'

'He was a good man in his day,' Blue told them later. 'But it just got too much for him galloping this rough country. When I get too old for it I'm going droving again.'

It was only a small stock-camp. Eight riders, but each man knew his job. They mustered along, branding as they went, cutting out and holding the bullocks as they came across them. As soon as they had a hundred or so they took them back into the station and handed them over to the bullock tailers, four black stockmen who tailed them on good feed during the day and yarded them in the new yard at night. It saved a lot of night-watching for the stockmen, that new yard, and helped quieten the cattle for the long trip over the ranges to the meatworks at Wyndham.

As usual the Kid and Jack rode together.

This day they were running a small mob of cows and calves into the coachers when a big white bull broke from the scrub. It was a fine animal, straight backed and fat. Away it charged in fear at these two strange figures on horseback.

The Kid was closest.

'Go get him mate,' Jack yelled, 'Your turn!'

The Kid spurred his mount and set off, Jack following. They would need to let the bull run a while to wind him. Jack hung well back. He was the backup man this time. The Kid would throw the bull, then Jack would close in, leap off his horse and help. The bull was slowing now and a thread of saliva dripped from its mouth.

'Almost time,' the Kid thought.

Then the bull disappeared over a low ridge.

On the far side of the ridge was another big white bull. It lay dozing in the mid-morning sunshine, contentedly chewing its cud. Suddenly a white bull charged over the ridge and disappeared into some scrub. The bull stopped chewing, wondering what was happening. Then a horse and rider breasted the ridge and the man jumped off and grabbed it by the tail. The bull gave a fierce snort, leapt to its feet, twisted out of the man's grasp and charged.

'Good,' the Kid had thought as he came over the ridge. 'He's lying winded. I'll soon have him tied up!' As soon as it turned on him the Kid realised it was another bull. There was no chance of pulling this monster down without a good long gallop. The Kid wheeled for a tree. There was only a skinny sapling within reach. He leapt for it as the bull rushed. But the higher he tried to climb, the lower the sapling sagged. As Jack cantered over the ridge he saw the Kid dangling from a skinny tree, a huge white bull underneath, about to sink its horns in the Kid's rump.

'Haaaa! Hey! Bull!' Jack bellowed. The bull turned its head in surprise. Another man. On a horse and charging! With a snort and toss of its proud head it was off, galloping for the scrub. The Kid let go and dropped to the ground. Jack's face was a huge grin.

'What you doing up the tree, mate? The bull's over there!'

The Kid looked up in mock surprise. 'Bull? I never saw no bull. I was up that tree looking for sugarbag.'

It was a good while before Jack let the Kid forget the episode of the white bull.

'You seem to know this country, Kid,' he said offhandedly one night around the fire.

'Know it all right! Was three year riding all this Underworld country with an old outlaw fella Lester. This here is the beginning of the Underworld.'

'Lester! You mean an old half-caste fella?'

'That's him! Where you strike him?'

'Back Seven Emu when I first came into the Territory. I spent most of a year there. That old pirate used to tell me tales every night about his outlaw days, but your name never come up. Mostly he talked of a bloke called Smokey.'

'Neither it would come up. Old Lester was pretty close that way. No-one ever spoke about a fellow outlaw to outsiders. Less the outlaw was dead. Then he might.'

The Kid thought for a while.

'So you know all about Smokey, too, Jack. You are a close one. We been knocking around a good while now and you must have known I knew Lester. Why didn't you mention him?'

'I didn't want to bring that subject up, Kid. About the Underworld. I knew you'd got into strife up here and if you wanted to tell you would. If I'd have talked about it, it could have seemed I was prying.'

The Kid placed another stick of wood on the fire.

'I don't talk about it Jack because it still hurts to remember how stupid I was. But I wasn't riding with Lester when I got pinched. Lester had retired into Wyndham by then and I had decided to give outlawing away too. But I got tangled up with an old white bloke called Joe Kimber. I didn't know Joe was into thieving at first, and when I found out, it was too late.

'All stations around here bought horses from Joe. They had to. It's bad horse poison country. Jimmy lost hundreds while he was here and that's going to beat Bluey too, if he don't look out. Wet time. That's when they die. Bluey's got to keep 'em away from the top part of his run. That's where it's bad, up there along the creeks. String a drift fence across. That's what I told him.'

'Got to be something they're eating, Kid.'

'That's a pretty shrewd guess, Jack. You hear lots of stories from worms in the stomach to something in the air. But I'm with you. It's got to be some plant that only grows in the Wet. Dry times don't hurt 'em. They can feed all over the run. But what it is, no-one knows.[1] See those ranges way yonder? That's the Cowboy Ranges. That's what the outlaws named 'em. Dunno why. Up there was where old Joe Kimber hung out. He's pensioned in Wyndham these days and he was the last of them.

'There might be an odd fella or two poking about now with shook horses but they wouldn't know the hideouts or have the contacts. Anyone can pinch horses on this open range country. But what's a man going to do with 'em? No-one going to buy from a stranger. You got to know your man if you take duffed stock off him!'

'Is that The Retreat hide-out old Lester used to talk about, where you and Joe used to hang out?'

'No! It's way north. Joe wasn't a full time duffer like ol' Smoke. He took a block up in those ranges to run cattle. But he still dealt in stolen horses. Fellas would arrive with 'em and he'd buy 'em. Change the brands and sell. He never carried out raids like old Smoke. There wasn't a station safe in the whole of the Territory when Smokey was operating!'

---

1. The plant Rattlepod was identified on Karungie Station about 1958 by the C.S.I.R.O. as being responsible for the notorious Kimberley Horse Disease (Walkabout). Cattle are immune. It flourished during the Wet season and was often the only green pick available to stock until the grass poked through.

'I was working on Karungie when I first met Joe. He sent word over with a blackfella he'd soon be mustering along his northern boundary. There was no station within a bull's roar of Karungie, so Dave Rust sent me across to attend. Old Joe was like that. Never steal from a neighbour. We got on pretty well so he asked would I take his bullocks into Wyndham with the Karungie mob. That was okay with Dave so we boxed a hundred of his in with ours.

'Joe also sent two stock boys along to give a hand. And some horses. A lot more than we needed for the trip but I never thought anything of it. But those horses never made it into Wyndham. Those two fellas dropped them off at a place we passed on the way in. But someone talked and a tracker got hold of it.

'Soon as I delivered the cattle to the Works the police questioned me about the stolen horses I'd brought in.

'What horses?' I said.

I was pretty cranky. All the years I had been duffing and the coppers never suspected. They went out to the station where the horses had been dropped, but found nothing. The station had got word and shifted 'em. But from then on I was under a cloud and you know what people are like. There's nothing to talk about so they make something up. People started talking. The next mob I brought in the police were waiting and checked every brand. Cattle and horses.

'Wasn't long after that I went to work for old Joe Kimber and he offered me a share of his block. He was getting too old to run it properly and later I was to get the option of buying him out. Only catch was it meant going back to duffing horses.

'What the heck,' I thought. 'I'm getting blamed for it now. Might as well do a bit more and when Joe gets out, I'll give it away and just run cattle.'

'That's how I got back into it. Two years later I got caught and that was that. Goodbye station, hello Fanny Bay.'

'I didn't think anyone got caught up in this country, Kid.'

'Neither they did till I come along. Sold a mare to a copper, the bloody mongrel! He knew it was shook. Bought it for his kid. Then he got a new boss. Sergeant up from the south an' he heard someone talking in the town pub one day. 'Everyone's buyin' horses off Joe Kimber these days. Even the copper's daughter rides one.'

'Wasn't long before he learnt Joe Kimber was the biggest horse duffer in the Kimberley an' I was his partner. Now that mare the girl was riding around town on was a very distinctive animal and I should never have sold it. Or bought it in the first place. It was a Kimberley creamy and we had a rule to only buy Territory horses. You ever read those stories about the western badmen, Jack? They come undone because they did something stupid. The Daltons tried to rob two banks in the one day. Cassidy and his mate shook a distinctive white mule.

'Anyway that was the stupid thing I did and I paid. They locked us both up, me and the mare. I was in the Compound and she was in the police paddock. I used to sit and watch her every day wishing to God she'd find a way through that fence. But she never did. Tell you something about that Compound, Jack. That's where you forget all about the colour business. Every man's your mate in there. From bush black to townie knob. I even wrote about it. A poem. You want to hear a bit of it?'

'A poem! I didn't know you were a poet, Kid.'

'Neither did I. It was just something that happened when I was inside.'

'Well, come on Henry Lawson,' Jack said. 'Get on with it.'

Oh, they got me in the Compound,
But let my mate on bail,
'Cause I'm the prime offender,
An' I'm not up for sale,
I'll wait here in the jail-house,
Until the next State ship,
And the travelling north-west magistrate,
Makes his scheduled trip.

There's some other fellas waiting,
Coloured boys and blacks,
And they're bringing in a murderer,
Someone saw his tracks,
And we all sit round the Boab tree,
Every man your mate,
There's no room in the Compound,
For prejudice and hate.

'Prejudice and hate, eh? That's one thing about this country, Kid, we don't hate our blacks like they do in America.'

'Only because they're no threat to us. You know any blackfellow got more than you have? Or got a better job? Who owns a house? They don't want anything and they don't have anything, that's why there's no prejudice.'

'There's half-caste's got houses.'

'Ah, there's a different story, the white blood coming out. They want to better 'em selves, ol' blackfellow don't.'

'Why should he? He's got all he wants. A full belly. Beats slogging round the ridges every morning with a spear looking for breakfast. The white man coming was the best thing ever happened to the blacks. You ever see 'em complaining about losing their land?'

'One time they were the land, Jack. But not any more. The white man's tucker buggered all that. Their land's gone and they're gone.'

'What are you talking about, *they* were the land? The country was there and they were there. The blacks and the land weren't the same thing.'

'Reckon? What did they eat, Jack?'

'Oh, hell, you know. Wallabies, goannas, fruits and flour from seeds.'

'What the wallabies eat, Jack?'

'Grass.'

'An' where the grass and seeds come from, Jack'

'What are you coming at? Out of the earth, of course.'

The Kid smiled. 'What do we eat, Jack?'

Jack started to follow the Kid's reasoning. Ha, he thought, I'm not going down that track! 'Flour and beef *that comes out of the ground.*'

'No it don't, Jack. The flour comes out of a bag. It coulda been growed anywhere. Same as the beef. A cow ain't native to this land, it's got hundreds of years of some other country bred into it. It ain't the same thing as eating a local roo. Them old people were as part of the land as the land itself. They not anymore. That's why they've lost interest in their country. It don't mean anything to them now.'

Jack gave the Kid a hard stare. 'You been thinking this sort of stuff all the time I've known you?'

'No, mate, I just got thinking it while we were talking.'

Jack gave a sigh of relief. 'Do us both a favour Kid. Stop that thinking, it don't become you. There's no need for it. Ain't you got all you want?'

'I dunno. Sometimes I feel I should be bettering myself.'

'It's that talking about the old blackfellows not wanting anything more than what they got,' the Kid was thinking. 'Me an' Jack's no different.'

'Well, don't hanker for anything better,' Jack was saying. 'I don't and there's no need for you to. I'm happy just the way I am. This country's got everything we'll ever need. But blokes can't leave you alone. They got to push you. Just because you can ride a horse better than most and are white, they want to make you head stockman. You know why I work as head stockman? Not to boss anyone around, but to work in a camp that's run properly. So I don't have to work under some useless old coot been too long in the country and prepared to take a royal root off the blackfellas. I was with Sandy Huddlestone for a while, supposed to be a good man, an' he allowed the horse tailers to run the horses from camp to camp in hobbles. Too lazy to take the hobbles off and he never said anything. How could a man put up with that? I rode off and left him to it.

'But when a boss sees you run a good camp what happens? He wants to give you an outstation to look after. Or tells you to get married and he'll work you a manager's job. I don't want any of that, looking after a station load of people, being stuck in the office and sorting out their petty little differences. If that's what they call 'getting on', I want no part of it. I want to gallop around the ridges on a good horse an' tangle with the wildest bulls I can find. Work with other stockmen, good men who know the game, men you can rely on. And find new country an' faces an' towns an' horses that ain't never been rode.'

The Kid was about to say, 'Well, that's all you'll ever do Jack,' but thought better of it. 'He don't want my advice,' the Kid muttered to himself. 'But he's got so much talent he could be anything he wanted. And the pity is he can't see it. He'll still be scrub bashing, brawling and boozing at sixty — if he lives that long!' He looked at Jack and grinned. 'Can't argue with what you say, mate. What did you think of the poem?'

'Oh, the poem! Pretty good, Kid. Take you long to write?'

'Not long an' I had plenty of time! They had me in for four months before the magistrate came up on the boat from Fremantle. He never gave me the two years for stealing that mare. He gave it to me as a pay back for what had been going on in the country for years. Later on someone told me about the First Offender's Act and that I could have got out on a bond. But I didn't know anything about those things.'

'Well, that's all behind you now, Kid. There's no-one holding it against you. You got caught doing what thousands before have done. Forget it now and get on with it. You going to try for another station?'

'They wouldn't register my brand any more. To tell you true Jack, I'm thinking of getting out of the country altogether and trying it in Queensland for a time. Anyway ... time to roll in now. I reckon we'll have enough bullocks soon to take into Wyndham and get the money out of Blue.'

22.

Droving To Wyndham

We're killing speyed cows on the floor today,
The hides are peeling off well,
We'll notch up our tally with time for a smoke,
Before the clang of the bell,
Another slumps down and rolls from the pen,
And is quickly hooked on the chain,
A slash from the Bleeder sloshing in blood,
And the Knocker-Down whacks one again.

Two weeks later they left Elgie with a mob of six hundred bullocks. Bluey stopped behind. He would spend the rest of the season breaking-in and branding.

'Soon as you deliver, wire me how many then give this here letter to the office manager of the Works. It authorises him to pay you two hundred quid each wages and five bob a head for the droving. That should be another three hundred quid you can split. It's a rough track. Take your time and don't lose any. I need 'em all!'

It was a generous payment.

'We can drink a lot of grog with that sort of money, Kid.'

'What about a droving plant. We could get a droving plant together with five hundred quid, Jack.'

'Go droving? Go to sleep! No way! Give me the stock-camp, mate. That's where the action is. I been droving, I am droving, but I ain't doing it by choice!'

'Well, I just might get a plant together with my share, Jack. Become one of those Queensland drovers. They make plenty. And it's a good life. Why a drover can even have his wife along. Can't do that in the stock-camp.'

'Wife along? Kid you're going queer all right! You need a good week on the booze. That'll chase those wife thoughts out of your head!'

I wonder, thought the Kid. Wonder if it will. I'm tired of knocking about with blokes all the time. I've hardly spoke to a woman all the time I been up here.

It was a slow trip into Wyndham. There were six of them, four with the cattle, two with the horses. Some days the country was so rough they travelled barely six miles. Single file through the ranges. Then they would find a good patch of grass and let the bullocks feed slowly along to the night-camp.

'There's no hurry,' the Kid would say. 'We want to get old Blue the best possible price. The fatter they are the heavier they kill. The heavier they kill the more he gets.'

Crossing the Pentecost Ranges Jack thought of the story Lester told him. How he and Smokey had taken the cattle from the drovers and forced them to walk into town. He told the Kid.

'Yes, Lester told me all about that. We'll be watering at that same rock-hole tomorrow. But we won't find any spinifex fairies takin' a bath. The missionaries have got hold of 'em all. There wouldn't be more than a dozen bush blacks wandering the whole of the Underworld now. Pity people can't leave them alone. If they want to come into the stations to work, let 'em. If they want to stop bush, well, that should be up to them too. But I tell you what we will find tomorrow. A feed of barra. I got Blue to stick a line in the packs. It's a top place and I've never missed yet, but it's got to be sundown. The night camp's not far away from the spot so you and the boys can put the bullocks on camp, I'll catch the fish!'

Just before sundown the following day the Kid rode off from the bullocks and headed to the river. He had Blue's heavy cord line rigged with a lure made from red rag, four shiny bottle tops and two heavy hooks.

He hung his horse to a bauhinia tree fronting the river and walked along the bank to a shallow rocky bar. The water flowed over the bar and into another pool further down. The sun had gone now and the last of the light reflected brightly from the water.

The Kid watched for a moment, then saw ripples racing across the surface.

Barramundi. Big fellas. Every evening they herded the smaller fish to these shallows and fed. He pulled off his boots, waded out a few yards and cast. He had no sooner started to pull in the line than it was almost torn from his grasp. A huge fish had taken the lure. Quickly the Kid swung around and made for the rock strewn bar. He stumbled along sliding on the stone until he had the fish safely out of the water. Then he reached down and placed a hand through its gills and lifted. Its head came level with his hat before the thick tail cleared the ground.

A six footer. He grinned. Wow! He waded out and cast again. Soon he had landed another. 'No use catching more,' he thought. 'These blokes will more than feed the six of us. All I got to do now is get 'em back to camp!'

He took out his knife and bled them but left their scales and gut intact. They would be roasted on the coals later, blackfella style, to keep the flavour.

It was almost full dark now so he took a good grip of each fish and set off dragging them along the bar towards his horse. The Kid was excited. Boy! Wait till Jack sees this lot. Then he thought of the bullocks on camp.

'If they see me riding up with this pair of monsters over me saddle they'll take off in fright. Best do a bit of a detour around 'em when I get near ... Whoa, boy! Steady old fella!'

He had reached the bauhinia tree without realising it. His horse was laying back on the reins, eyes popping in terror, all set to bolt.

'Steady, old man. They're only a couple of little fish. Nothing to be frightened about!'

He lowered his catch to the ground and unhooked the reins. The horse pulled back violently.

'How the hell am I going to get 'em on?' he wondered.

He gave the horse a good petting, talking soothingly all the time.

Then he slowly bent down and lifted one of the fish.

The horse jerked backwards again, snorting in fear.

'I know what I'll do,' the Kid thought. 'Stick 'em up the tree.'

He led the animal across to a nearby bloodwood and tethered it. Then he walked back and hoisted the two fish up into a fork of the bauhinia, about five foot from the ground.

He mounted the horse and urged it forward. It took a dozen steps then propped. The Kid patted its neck and tapped gently with his spurs. It still refused to move. The Kid spurred harder. The horse danced sideways.

'Hell,' thought the Kid. 'I'll never get back to camp.'

He doubled the reins and whipped the horse under the belly.

'Get up!' he yelled. The horse dropped its head and started bucking.

The Kid knew he was beaten.

'Okay, mate,' he said. 'Let's head for camp. I'll have to come back with a pack-horse.'

He only went a few yards when he saw a shadow looming ahead. It was Jack.

'Where's all the fish?' he yelled.

'Up the bloody tree! I can't get me horse near 'em!'

He led Jack towards the bauhinia. Jack was riding a quiet old night-horse, well used to the strange ways of men. The horse wasn't happy about this, but it allowed Jack to ride to the tree, hoist up a fish and lay the fish over its withers. Now the

Kid's horse, with a good deal of patting and coaxing, allowed itself to be ridden up to the tree. The Kid quickly grabbed the second barramundi and lowered it over the pommel of his saddle.

'Just as well I come along, Kid. Otherwise we wouldn't have got a feed tonight. I reckon those fish would have gone rotten in the tree before you got 'em back to camp!'

They double watched the cattle while the fish were cooking. Cattle could be just as silly as horses over a strange smell. Jack said it was the best feed of fish he'd had ever. But the Kid got no thanks. He got ribbed for the rest of the trip and for a good while after over the fishing episode.

'Couldn't even bring a couple of little fish back to camp without calling for help!'

The Kid took it as usual. He had to. 'That's one of the disadvantages of riding with someone like Jack,' he thought wryly. 'Somehow or other, he always comes out on top!'

A week later they were in Wyndham, delivering the cattle to the Meatworks' head-stockman. 'So that's what happened to you,' the Kid said when he saw who it was. 'Sacked?' It was the policeman father of the girl he had sold the stolen mare to.

'No! Resigned! One step ahead of the axe! And never been better off. Now when I work overtime I get paid. Good to see you back in the saddle, Kid. I heard you was out. Sorry I had to finger you in court, but I had no choice. It was either that or go in with you and I couldn't see any sense in that.'

'I understood that. How they treating you?'

'To my face, good. Behind my back, who knows? Well, we getter give these fellas a count.'

They were four short. 'Could have been worse, Jack,' the Kid said as they rode off and left the Meatworks' stockmen to yard the cattle. 'The way we had to string 'em through the ranges we could have lost a hundred.'

Jack grinned. 'I did once. But delivered a full mob. You not the only one done a bit of duffing, Kid!'

They rode through the Meatworks and under the huge race that led from the holding yards to the three stories high Killing Floor.

'That's where Blue's bullocks will be walking tomorrow, Jack. Up that race to meet the hammer.'

Jack had never been in a Meatworks before. 'Why they kill 'em up there on the top floor?'

'For convenience. Saves lugging the bits and pieces around. They kill 'em up top, strip the hides off and drop the hides down a chute to the ground floor. Fellas down there salt and bundle 'em up to send away on the boat. All the bones and offal get tipped down a chute to the second floor. They got big pots there and they boil 'em all up. The freezer's three storey high and the boning rooms are spread over a couple of floors. It's a big place and over a thousand work there.'

'I might try it one day, Kid. They get good money?'

'Six times what we make but we'll never get a job there. All them fellas come from down south. Some from as far as Melbourne. Been comin' up to Wyndham for years. They never employ locals. It's a closed shop, that Meatworks. Fella leaves, there's ten slaughts down south with their name down to get his spot.'

'What about your copper mate? He got a start.'

'Well if that's all you want to do, yard up cattle other drovers bring in, you can get a job. But there's no money in that. You're better off out on a station. Least you're away from the grog!'

They rode down to the office, presented Blue's letter and collected their money. In cash.

'Be a good place to rob, Jack, if you could get away somewhere. Everyone's paid cash here. They must have a hundred thousand quid in that safe paydays.'

Then they rode out the gate and along the gravel causeway that led over the salt marsh.

'That's the town,' the Kid said. 'That little mob of buildings squeezed between the range and the water. The water's the Cambridge Gulf and the mountain's called the Bastion. And that's why Wyndham's one of the stickiest places out. The heat radiates out of the rocks and forms clouds of steam with the water. Don't know why anyone wants to live here!'

It was scarcely bigger than Halls Creek. There were a dozen or so tin shacks that were mostly Chinese stores and a few corrugated iron Government buildings. The pub made every other building look insignificant. It was a grand two-storey affair, a relic of the gold rush days. They rode past the Police Station and wire Compound and pulled up in an alley opposite the pub.

'This is as far as me an' Jack go,' the Kid told Blue's four black stockboys. 'You fellas better keep moving out to the Three-Mile. If that policeman finds you in town after sundown he going to lock you up.'

The Kid and Jack unstrapped their swags from the packhorses and swung them on their shoulders. Blue's boys never moved.

'Hell,' Jack said. 'I know what you fellas want!'

He reached into his shirt pocket and fished out a five pound note. The boss horsetailer took it and smiled. He was responsible for taking the plant back to Elgie. The Kid grinned and dug into his pocket.

'You know how much money that is?'

The horsetailer held it up, turned it over and grinned. 'He proper money that one. Got Captain Cooky. Jumbuck too. Might be five pound, eh?'

'He five pound all right. Two of them are five pound. You fella can buy plenty tobacco with that lot. Don't let that Chinaman cheat you!'

Blue's stockboys got the horses together and rode off grinning. The Kid and Jack headed across the main street to the pub. The inside of the bar was crowded with meatworkers.

The Kid ordered two beers.

'That'll be three bob, mate.'

'Three bob! Hell! That's about what we get for droving one bullock a hundred mile. Reckon I know who's got the better job.'

Jack shouted and they settled on to stools to enjoy their first grog since Halls Creek the previous year.

A big hard looking meatworker strolled over.

'What cattle you blokes bring in?'

'Elgie.'

'Well, I hope they skin better than what we killed today. These aren't bullocks you got up here, they're bloody mongrel goats.'

Jack looked at the meatworker and didn't like what he saw — a leering know-it-all face and the pale skin of a man who had never known life out in the open.

'Nothing wrong with the cattle up here mate. Must be the way you use a knife.'

Another meatworker touched the Kid's arm.

'Tell your mate not to get mixed up with that Rocky Spargy. He's got a record long as a gumboot and can fight too.' He gave a friendly grin. 'Bring him over with us and have a game of darts.'

But it was too late.

'You'd be just the bloke to know,' he heard Jack say.

Rocky stood with a puzzled frown, gazing down at the grinning face.

'Know about what?'

'Goats. You being one yourself.'

'So!' Rocky sneered. 'That's the way you want it! You going to be sorry mate if you don't take that back. You know who I am?'

'I know what you look like, mate. A bloody, know-all townie!'

The meatworker made a lunge but there was no-one on Jack's stool. He had twisted sideways, stepped forward and swung a tremendous right hand against the meatworker's head. Rocky was knocked sideways and crashed against the bar. There was blood on his cheek but if he was hurt it never showed on his face.

'Aha!' he snarled. 'What we got here? A fighting man! Come outside, fighting man and see how you go against a man who takes 'em on two at a time!'

The Kid winced. Jack would be giving away about two stone and this fellow was tough. The same friendly meatworker was whispering in his ear. 'Your mate's got a ton of guts but he's in for a hiding. That mongrel's got too much weight over him and will be too good. He used to be an Army champion.'

Jack swaggered across to the Kid, tugging at his shirt pocket.

'Here, mate, mind me roll.'

As he handed it across he pulled out a note and held it up for the crowd to see.

'This is what I'm backing myself for. Twenty quid. How about you, sport? Game to risk the same?'

It was the Jack of old, the showman. In front of the audience at the Buckjump Show.

Rocky smirked.

'Risk it? I'm risking nothing! It's wearing my name. Here Charlie,' he called to the barman. 'You hold it. That's forty quid you'll be handing me in a minute when I've fixed this fella.'

The whole of the bar followed outside. They made a circle around the single street light at the side of the hotel as the contestants stripped off their shirts. The Kid shot a look at the Police Station on the opposite corner. The sergeant was standing in the shadow of his verandah watching.

'At least he'll stop the boot,' the Kid thought. 'This fella's too big for Jack and if he gets him down, look out! I'll need a hand to stop him sinking that slipper.'

Rocky was a head taller, heavier and had a longer reach. It hardly seemed a fair contest. He walked straight in stabbing with his left, probing for an opening. Jack moved warily around then suddenly stepped forward and smashed a hard right hand to the side of his opponents jaw. But in an instant Rocky replied with a vicious left to Jack's face. Jack forced a grin.

'That the best you can hit, Powdy-Puff?'

Backwards and forwards they battled with first one, then the other landing punches. But it seemed to the Kid and the crowd, it was only a matter of time before the heavier punching of the meatworker would wear Jack down.

Suddenly Rocky drove a right cross through Jack's guard. It smacked hard against his face again and spun him sideways.

The crowd gave a long drawn out, 'Ahhh!'

But straight away Jack retaliated. He charged back in and landed a heavy right on his opponent's nose. Blood gushed everywhere. Rocky's nose was twisted on his cheek.

'Set the drinks up, Charlie,' Jack yelled, as though the barman was placidly waiting behind his counter instead of standing on the steps gaping at the fight. 'Get that forty quid on the bar,' he yelled. 'I've got this bloke on the skids!'

That was the turning point of the fight. Rocky needed only to continue fighting and keep landing his heavier punches to win. Jack's face was red from the blows he had taken and he was starting to stagger. But the fierce wallop on his nose and the confidence and bravado of his smaller opponent so unnerved Rocky Spargy, that he allowed himself to be knocked out.

'That was the best I've seen you fight, Jack,' the Kid told him later as they helped drink the meatworker's twenty pound. 'I thought he had you for a while. He looked too big and too strong.'

Jack downed a beer and looked the Kid straight in the eye.

'Kid, I was done like a goanna on the coals! I only had another three hits left in me. By the jeebers he could whack! But that's something I learnt early in life. Never let the enemy know when you're hurt. Sometimes that's the only way you can get up and win!'

That was the last the Kid saw of Jack for a while. Everybody wanted to buy him a drink or take him somewhere. Up to the meatworks for a meal or a session's boozing on the verandah. Down to the jetty to the big overseas ship loading beef for the UK — to meet the skipper, look over the bridge and try out the tucker in the officers' mess. To the Six Mile Hotel to check out the barmaids. To someone's house or camp for a party ...

The Kid mooched around on his own. He yarned with the Chinese storekeepers about the old days. He spent one day climbing the steep slope of the Bastion Mountain until stopped by the red walls of rock at the very top. He took his own tour of the meatworks. And drank little. 'There's no future in this life,' he told himself. 'I'm thirty and all I've got is me swag and a roll of notes getting thinner by the day. There's got to be something better than this. If I don't get out of the country now, I never will.'

The sixth morning after the fight the Kid woke to find Jack had returned. He was lying on his swag on a wire bunk next to the Kid on the pub verandah.

'Where you been hiding, Kid? Been having a good time? Hey! You got a bottle handy, Kid? By the ghost I'm crook!'

'I got no grog but I'll get you a drink of tea from the kitchen. I'm a mite sick of all this boozing, Jack. What are you going to do? Stop in town or go back bush?'

'I'm not going bush while I got a quid in my pocket. It's no use out there. I'm going to buy some new clobber today and drink the rest. What you reckon?'

'I dunno, Jack. I took a walk down the jetty yesterday. A state ship's unloading. They got to call into Darwin. I was thinking I might go with them and have that spell east I was talking about.'

'That's a good idea, mate. I had a break away last year, down south. Do you good. I'll be round here somewhere when you get back. Or over in the Territory. But look out those women don't get a hold of you like that Widder got me!'

The next morning Jack was missing again. Someone said he was out the Six-Mile where a mob of drovers were celebrating. The Kid settled his account with the publican, swung his swag over his shoulder and headed for the boat. The crew were hauling in the springers as he arrived, all set to sail.

'You coming with us, matey?' someone yelled.

The Kid nodded and threw his swag over the rail. He jumped aboard and made his way aft. Soon the jetty, town and finally the meatworks slid out of sight. Only the top of the Bastion Mountain remained. Then it too disappeared at a bend of the channel.

'Slipped me hobbles!' he whispered. 'Slipped 'em at last. If I see you again, Wyndham, it'll mean I'm awful hard-up!'

Betty Walden, 1959. First white woman to settle in the North Kimberley Underworld. With Mavis Lacey and the author.

The author points to the remains of the "Fatal Fence", Kununurra. 1990.

Bill Yeomans supervising erection of headstone on Jack's grave, 1989.

"The Best of Us All"
Jack's grave at Kelley's Knob. (Kununurra)

23.

The Last Camp

Did you shudder, last time, old comrade,
You camped by Kelly's Knob,
Did you see a ghostly spectre,
As you rode your sleeping mob,
Did you hear old bones pass rattling,
The scuff of a dragging boot,
And yet if you did, old comrade,
I doubt you'd have cared a hoot!

Big Bob McLachlan was worried. Here it was a week or so to the new cattle season and he was still short of a horsebreaker. A good one at any rate. There were a few around, but none that he would bother sending out to Jimmy Burns at Birrindudu. Otherwise it would be another wasted plane ticket. You had to be a good man to break in horses for old Jimmy.

Bob was Pastoral Inspector for the Vesteys Cattle Company. Vesteys held more country in the north of Australia than there was land in the whole of Europe. One time labour had never been a problem. Year in year out the same names appeared on the stations books. Men got that way they wouldn't, or couldn't, work anywhere else except the remote stations of the north. Then suddenly — progress.

Main Roads had started it, Bob reflected, coming north and offering double station wages to anyone prepared to learn to drive a road grader or any of the other machines they used to construct or maintain roads. And they provided better tucker and accommodation plus paid overtime. Ringers were smart people. It hadn't taken long for them to start leaving the stations and join Main Roads. It was quite a problem.

Bob sighed. He closed his office door and walked out into the heat of the late Darwin afternoon. A State Ship had just berthed at the Jetty. He would stroll down and have a yarn and drink with the officers. Bob knew everyone worth knowing in the north, including the State Ships' crews.

He was nearing the wharf when he saw the familiar figure and gait of a stockman, swag up, wobbling on high heels towards him. Bob wondered if he would know him and whether this would be the horsebreaker he was looking for.

Suddenly he grinned. Just his luck. As good a man as he could hope for.

'Kid!' he called happily. 'What the hell are you doing in town?'

The Kimberley Kid was pleased to see the familiar face. He had just spent a lonely three days on board a ship where he had been the only passenger. The seamen had been some company but he had little in common with them. He hadn't understood their talk nor they his.

'Doing?' he replied. 'Nothing much. Just come up on the boat from Wyndham for a bit of a look around.'

He wasn't prepared to admit to a man like Bob McLachlan he was really on his way to take a holiday down south. The Kid was too much a northerner to admit needing a spell away from it.

'Thought you would have seen enough of Darwin, Kid,' Bob was saying with a smile.

The Kid almost flared, then saw that the big man was only letting him know that he knew. The words had been said easily and were meant to be taken lightly. The Kid smiled back.

'I only saw the inside of Fanny Bay last time I was here, Bob. This time I'm going to take a look around the outside before I head back to Wyndham.'

Bob chuckled.

'Where you planning to put in next season?'

The Kid shrugged his shoulders.

'Nowhere in particular. Something will come up I guess.'

'Hell,' the Kid was thinking. 'What am I saying? I'm getting out of the country, aren't I? Catching the bus tomorrow that goes to Mount Isa so I can get the train to the coast and find myself a wife and settle down. Why don't I tell him?'

Bob McLachlan rubbed his hands.

'How would you like to work for me, Kid? As Vesteys' top horsebreaker? You can start right away now, down at Birrindudu, with old Jimmy Burns. You know Jimmy don't you?'

'Sure do. One of the real old timers. Him and me get on real well.'

'Good, that's settled. Two quid a colt and keep.'

The Kid was getting in deeper. There was still time to say that he was heading down south for a short holiday but somehow he could not get the words out.

Instead, as a final hope that it may get him out of the situation, he said, 'I got a partner now, Bob. Jack Vitnell. Back in Wyndham. I'd want to be cutting him in.'

Bob's smile got broader.

'He's a pretty smart man, that Vitnell, from what I've heard. We've never had him working for us before. That would be just great, Kid. Just great.'

'One more try,' the Kid thought, and if that doesn't work, well ...

'Jack's pretty keen on me and him going up to that Underworld country, Bob, and starting a station. We'll need to talk it over.'

Bob wasn't sure why, but he felt his man was trying to wriggle away. He would have to get tough.

'This Vitnell got any money, Kid? It takes a lot to start up a cattle station. You got a plant of horses? Gear? A team of blacks lined up?'

The Kid looked at his boots and cursed under his breath. These bosses were too damn smart! He knows we got nothing. We're a pair of flamin' no hopers, me an' Jack. We got no horses. No men, not even a block of country! He thought of all the money they had earned at Elgie. Half of his was gone and by the way Jack was ya-hooing around Wyndham, his would soon be finished. He frowned. Maybe this time. Birrindudu. Maybe they'd get a stake there and hang on to it long enough to start out on their own. He looked up at big Bob and took a deep breath.

'We ain't set to start out on our own just yet, Bob. We'll take the job. I can speak for Jack.'

The Kid returned to Wyndham on a State Ship. The skipper hadn't intended calling in to Wyndham on his way back to Fremantle but Bob McLachlan was a good mate. He also wielded a lot of power around the North. Carrying Vesteys' station stores had just about kept State Ships from going broke many times over the years.

Jack Vitnell had been having such a good time he had scarcely missed his mate. The Kid found him out at the Six Mile Hotel surrounded by a boisterous crowd of ringers.

'Hey, Kid! Where you been? Somebody said you'd run out on me. How you holding? Got a quid?'

Jack was broke and had been borrowing money for the last couple of days. He was more than ready to leave town. The Kid squared his partner's debts and ordered a taxi to the aerodrome. Jack was three parts under the weather.

'Where we going, Kid?' he slurred. 'Got a good place lined up?'

'We're flying out to Birrindudu, down the desert. They got the best horses you ever seen there, Jack. Buck like crazy. You an' me's got a contract to break in for Vesteys until there's not a colt left. We won't be seeing town for a while.'

They finished the colts at Birrindudu and received a wire from Bob McLachlan to move on to Gordon Downs. From Gordon Downs they caught the DC3 further south to Sturt Creek.

'Hell, Kid,' Jack complained. 'At this rate we going to be breaking in for Vesteys for the rest of our lives.'

It wasn't that long, but it was to be nearer ten years than five. From time to time, the Kid and Jack would split up. One would decide to take a head stockman's job, the other to go droving. Or head off with a contract musterer or fly off to a race meeting. But most seasons they would get back together for a while, breaking in Vestey horses.

Wherever they went the worst horses were brought out, known buckjumpers, rogues that lesser men feared to ride. And always there were men keen to see them beaten.

'Makes me feel like one of those old time western gunslingers,' Jack grouched to the Kid. 'Everybody waiting to see us gunned down. We haven't been to a station yet where they haven't had either some outlaw horse lined up or some yahoo ringer ready to try and give us a thumping.'

They were in the kitchen after supper one night on Helen Springs listening to the cook's radio. A new country and western singer was introduced.

'Hey, Jack!' the Kid called. 'Remember that jackaroo on Wave Hill last year? The one with the hill-billy guitar? Sounds like he's made it. They got him on next. Have a listen.'

They were stunned to hear him sing:

They're breaking in for Vesteys,
Wave Hill to the Ord,
Two quid a head and tucker,
And Queenslander's Award,
Vitnell rides the rough ones,
Ol' Kid takes a turn,
And all the ringers asking,
'Where them fellas learn?'

Horses to be handled,
Outlaws everyone,
Stockhorses mean and sour,
That the stockmen shun,
The Kid grabs a bridle,
Vitnell lugs the gear,
And all the stockboys whispering,
Top hand ringers here.

Jack's eyes were shining.

'Well, what about that! Hell! Now I'm sorry I called him a loose-pizzled new chum jackaroo!'

Wet times found them in town with other local ringers, paid off until the next cattle season. Katherine, Pine Creek, Daly Waters, Alice Springs, but not Wyndham. They didn't return there until what was to be the last Wet of their partnership.

That year they finished the season breaking horses on Carlton Station in the East Kimberley.

'Looks like another Wet in Wyndham, Kid. That's the nearest town. Be like old times again.'

But Wyndham had changed. It was no longer a cattle and meatworkers town. The Government was preparing to dam the Ord River. The town was filling up with construction workers and already contractors were busy building quarters for the workers at what was going to be a new town, Kununurra, fifty miles down river at Kelly's Knob.

'Hell! That's right on the stock route. What's going to happen to the drovers?' they asked the publican at the town hotel.

'What drovers? Droving's finished boys. The Main Roads blokes are out there now pushing through the bitumen. Once that reaches town there won't be any drovers. Only truck drivers driving trucks. Road trains they call 'em.'

There was an old three ton Thames Trader truck for sale up at the Meatworks. The Kid and Jack walked up to take a look. The cab was somewhat battered and the timber tray was just holding together but the engine ticked over first crank. With a truck they would be independent. They paid sixty pounds for the Thames and drove it away.

'Let's head out to this place they're building at Kelly's Knob,' the Kid suggested. 'We might get a job there. Better than hanging around town.'

The new town of Kununurra was just starting to take shape. There were several Government offices, two large mess buildings, and six newly built weatherboard houses. The farmers, when they arrived later, were going to live in town and would drive out daily to work their ground.

On the way, a few miles from the town site, the Kid and Jack passed a line of star picket fencing. There were no strainer posts and the wire had not been run.

'What do those mongrels think they're doing,' Jack growled. 'They're blocking off the stock route.'

'That's right, mate. Any cattle coming in this season have to go around that fence. Any drover camped near it who loses his mob in a rush is going to have a terrible smash. That fence will cut 'em to pieces.'

The Kid sighed.

'No good fighting it Jack, that's the future we're looking at.' He added, after a pause, 'We might as well be part of it. There's nobody working on that fence, maybe they're looking for men. Let's look the contractor up when we get to town.'

The fencing contractor welcomed them. 'Thirty quid a week, tucker, and Sunday's off. Ten hours a day.'

'Wages!' snorted Jack. 'Hell, I thought we'd be on contract.'

'Can't do it mate. I'm not allowed to sublet.'

The boys turned to go.

The contractor thought a moment, impressed by the look of the applicants and called them back. He could tell they were locals. He was having trouble keeping men on the job and was way behind schedule. The weather was hot and steamy, the flies thick, the work hard. The fence line was no place for workers from the south.

'Tell you what I'll do, fellas. If you work like I reckon you're going to work, I'll make it forty a week. The tucker's good. You'll eat up in the Wages Mess.' He grinned. He was an old fencer himself. 'No johnny cakes and salt beef here. Proper food.'

They took the job. Forty pounds a week was a fortune and the work no harder than they had been used to.

'Ten hours a day!' Jack snorted. 'That means we can knock off at four. What we going to do with ourselves?'

The Kid and Jack were allocated two rooms in the men's quarters. They took one look and walked out. The rooms were tiny, hot and stuffy. They sampled the tucker at the Mess. It was good but opened too late to suit the way they would be working. Up in the dark and a daylight start. It was the only way to work in that heat. They decided to camp.

They drove into Wyndham, loaded up with stores, and borrowed a tent and a heavy steel forty-four gallon water drum.

'What are we going to do?' the Kid asked. 'Make it a dry camp or take out some grog?'

Jack thought for a moment. Normally bush camps were dry. There was an old saying. 'Don't drink when you're working and don't work when you're drinking.' But this was going to be different. Two blokes stuck out in the bush on their own, with no blacks or other whites around for company, was a good way to fall out.

'Reckon we'll take out some rum, Kid. Do us the world of good.'

It was a bad decision. Perhaps in his heart the Kid knew it. If they could confine their drinking to a few nips each night, all would be well. But could they? On past form it would be unlikely. The stations were dry for that very reason. Like most other northern bushmen they had learnt only one way to drink. Hard and fast until there was nothing left. They pulled into Vagg's gallon licence store and loaded on a case of Bosun overproof rum.

'Only a dozen,' Arthur Vagg chided with a grin. 'What are you blokes going to drink next week?'

They grinned back.

'You got a second case?'

As it turned out, there had been no need to take out liquor. A wet canteen had been provided on site at Kununurra for the workers. It opened every afternoon at five and closed at eight. There was only one type of drink. Beer. Sold by the jug only. It didn't take long to down a jug of icy cold beer after toiling out in the sun all day. And it didn't take long to get drunk. But there were no fights. Every man among them was too tired for fighting.

'What are we going to do now,' the Kid wanted to know, at four o'clock in the afternoon on their first day's work. 'Knock off or keep going?'

'Can't see any sense in keeping going. We're only on wages. Let's slip into the mess and get a decent feed into us.'

They cranked up the truck and headed in towards the town site. It was four miles from their fencing camp.

'Look at all those blokes,' the Kid cried as they drove up. 'Scoffing grog. It's a wet canteen!'

That first night, they ate cold salt beef and stale bread back at their campsite. The canteen did not wait for boozers, it closed at six sharp. They soon learnt to visit it first.

Saturday night was picture night — providing it wasn't raining. As soon as it was dark, the seats were dragged out from the canteen and set up in rows facing a large portable screen. Everyone including the police sergeant attended. There were even some women present. Civilisation was coming fast to the Kimberley.

'Might as well stay on for the flicks,' Jack grinned. 'It might be John Wayne showing off his barroom brawl style. Might get a few pointers, Kid. There's no work tomorrow anyway. Sundays off, what a life!'

They sat towards the back and the show started. The Kid complained he could not see.

'Take your hat off, mate,' he called to a tall construction worker sitting bolt upright a few rows in front. There was no response. The Kid frowned and wriggled on his seat, trying to get more than just a glimpse of the screen.

'Hey, mate!' he suddenly yelled. 'Take your flaming hat off. All I can see is your big boofhead.'

A few heads turned, frowning at the noise. The hat remained unperturbed, on the large head. Jack started to laugh.

'You want to change places, mate? I'm taller than you.'

The Kid was getting angry.

'I'm not changing places with nobody,' he snarled. 'Hey! You with the hat on. If you don't take it off, I'll knock it off.'

The hat man did not move. The Kid suddenly jumped out of his seat, lunged forward, grabbed the offending hat and threw it to the rear. Its owner immediately leapt from his chair, wheeled around and charged the Kid. The Kid was jammed between two seats and was unable to sidestep. He fell over, bringing his attacker on top of him. Locked together, they grappled, snarled and struck at each other sending chairs and people flying.

The film was forgotten. Here was some real life action. The workers cheered, the staff men grinned, the women looked on uncertainly. Finally the police sergeant broke it up.

The Kid glared at him, his blood up.

'What's it got to do with you?'

'I'll show you what it's got to do with me, fella.'

He grabbed the Kid in an arm hold and marched him over to the lock-up. The hat man helped straighten the chairs and resumed his seat. This time he held his hat on his knee.

Next day the Kid was fined ten pounds and barred from the canteen. Now instead of driving to the canteen in the evening for their supper and a few jugs of beer, the fencers sat in camp and cooked for themselves.

The Kid opened up one of the cases of rum and took out a bottle.

'No-one's stopping me drinking,' he fumed.

'I can understand how you feel, Kid,' said Jack, grinning as he grabbed a pannikin. 'It will take more than a copper to stop us, hey!'

It suited Jack, he had been missing his rum. They decided to spell a while, the fence could wait and the contractor could pay them off if he didn't like it. But the contractor wasn't around to know. He had flown down to Perth to see his family. The Kid and Jack took six days to drink the first dozen bottles of overproof. It was a hot, dry camp.

'This is the last bottle, Jack,' the Kid croaked one morning. 'We going to start work tomorrow?'

'Why didn't you tell me it was the last yesterday? How in hell can I work tomorrow? Look at me, I'm sick as a mangy dog and about as underfed. I got to wean meself off this stuff. Open the other case.'

It was then the destructive boozing started. Until then they had been happy. Yarning, joking, talking of the station they were going to own one day. The final week of the bender they became morose. Now everything around them seemed changed for the worse. The old ways were going fast and there was no room for them in the future.

They cursed the road trains, the dam, the construction workers from the south, the farmers. They even cursed themselves for working on a fence that was helping to build the dam that would soon flood Argyle.

Argyle, first cattle station in the Kimberley, original home of the Duracks, where scores of ringers had ridden. Soon it would lie under a hundred feet of water. A new town full of strangers was springing up on the old Kelly's Knob night camp. There would be no more watching of cattle, waiting for the first streaks of dawn, ready to set off on the final leg of the journey into the meatworks. Not around Kelly's Knob any more. Not around anywhere soon.

Day and night merged. They drank whenever they were awake and passed out whenever their senses collapsed. Neither thought of cooking a feed. A day came when Jack woke with a raging thirst and found the waterbag empty. He staggered to the truck and tapped the water drum. The hollow ring was a mocking sound that hot windy afternoon. Jack cursed and fell down again on his swag. He reached for the rum bottle, at least that was not empty. The fiery brew taken neat on an empty stomach made him retch. Vaguely Jack saw clots of blood. The Kid lay on his back, oblivious to the situation.

'Get up, mate,' Jack called. 'We're out of water.'

The Kid opened his eyes, muttered something, and went back to sleep. Jack crawled across to where the Kid lay and prodded him in the stomach with the neck of an empty rum bottle.

'Mate,' he called weakly, 'We gotta clear out. There's no water left.'

The Kid woke again and this time managed to lurch to his feet.

'What are you saying? No water?'

He stumbled across to the truck, then turned to his mate.

'You're right. There's nothing in the drum and nothing in camp. Geez I'm dry, but I ain't touching any more rum. That's a quick way to perish, drinking straight OP. Come on, jump in the truck. We gotta head into Kununurra.'

Jack glared.

'I ain't going back there, ever, not with that lot tearin' the guts out of our country. We can't get a drink there anyway, we're barred. Let's get into Wyndham.'

He staggered to his feet and fell over.

'Christ I'm crook. I can't make it Kid. You'll have to go yourself. Fill up the water drum at the Six and fetch back some tucker and another gallon of grog from Vagg's. But don't get on it. If you do I'll be crow bait by the time you get back.'

The Kid looked where Jack lay huddled on his swag.

'Sure you can hang on, mate? Geez you look bad. You better come with me. You gonna die if I leave you here.'

'I'm going to die if I get in that gut shaking truck. I'll be right, just get back fast as you can.'

The Kid managed to crank the motor. He was feeling the effects of the two weeks bender but not as badly as his mate. He drove off and called a final warning.

'Don't touch that bottle, Jack, no matter how thirsty you get. Water is what you need, not rum. That will kill you quicker than anything, straight OP without water. I'll be back.'

The Kid had seen a few men die on the rum and heard of dozens. He didn't understand exactly why, but he knew a bender on the rum was a dangerous thing.

'Christ, we were stupid,' he thought. 'We must have been on it a fortnight. In the sun mostly and not eating.'

The Kid was almost shocked sober. He was ending up the same way as a lot of others he had seen.

'This is it,' he muttered as he crashed the gears and headed for the main road, 'If I don't get out of the country after this, I'll never get out.'

Jack lay quietly on his swag after the truck left, wishing he could pass out. His mouth was sand dry and his gut felt on fire. In the distance he thought he could hear the gurgle of water. It was the Ord. Rain had fallen upstream and the river had risen and had begun to wash over Bandicoot Bar, a cattle crossing and soon to be the new dam site, less than a mile away across country. He tried to sit up and fell back. His hand brushed the half full rum bottle. He picked it up. The face of the woolly headed Bosun, the trade mark on the label, leered at him. Jack scowled back.

'You're not getting me yet, old man.'

He placed the bottle to his mouth and gulped. Then he slipped into a fitful sleep.

It was after dark by the time the Kid got started and the Six Mile Hotel was closed when he reached it some hours later. It had been a slow trip. He had stopped the truck several times to clear his head and stop from passing out. Now he eased out of the cab and staggered across to a tap by the hotel verandah. He drank deeply, then filled the water drum. He thought of how Jack had looked as he drove off and almost turned the truck around.

'Hell,' he thought. 'If I do, and arrive without any tucker and a bottle to get him on his feet he'll die anyway. Another hour won't hurt. I better get in to Vagg's.'

He drove back to the road and headed into Wyndham, six miles further on.

The main street of the town was in darkness, with only the single street lamp outside the pub casting a little light. The stores and pub had closed but Vagg's store showed a gleam of light inside. The Kid pounded on the side door just as the police sergeant was completing his rounds. He saw the Kid and yelled at him.

'What the hell do you think you're doing?'

The Kid wheeled around, stumbled and fell. That drink of water at the Six Mile was making him feel worse.

'Nothing,' he answered weakly. 'Just trying to knock Arthur up.'

The sergeant glared. He was new to the north and did not recognise the Kid.

'You're drunk, that's what you are. You're spending the night inside.'

The Kid stared at him, anger on his face.

'Like hell I'm drunk. I'm crook, that's all. I gotta get back to camp. I got a mate out bush going to die if I don't get back with some water.'

The sergeant looked at the grubby figure clutching at the store verandah post. The Kid hadn't washed for days and stank of liquor. The sergeant sneered.

'That's a new one! Haven't heard that before.' He grabbed the Kid's arm. 'Come on.'

He was a big man and towered over the Kid. The Kid tried again.

'Sarge, I'm not trying to put one over. I got a mate out there in the bush. We been on a bender for weeks. He's crook, real crook. I gotta get back with some water to him tonight otherwise he's going to perish.'

The sergeant laughed nastily.

'You got a mate you're anxious to get back to all right. A bottle of rum.' he twisted the Kid's arm up the middle of his back. 'Come on,' he snarled. 'Move it!'

In the cell the Kid hollered until he was hoarse.

'The coppers are killing me mate. Help! The coppers are killing me mate.'

The few that heard took no notice. Just another drunk in chokey acting up. Finally the Kid sank to the floor of the cell exhausted. It was daylight when he woke.

'Help!' he screamed again. 'The coppers are killing me mate.'

In the cold light of morning, it didn't sound so much like just another drunk. The sergeant walked down the police yard to the cell block.

'Are you still drunk?' he snapped at the Kid.

'I'm not drunk now and I wasn't drunk last night. Like I already told a dozen times, my mates stuck out in the scrub without any water. If he's dead when I get back out there, it will be your fault.'

The sergeant became a little concerned. Maybe this fellow was telling the truth. He roused up his senior constable.

'There's a bloke in the cells, Andy. Take him out to his camp and see what he's on about.'

Andy ate a leisurely breakfast, fuelled up his Landrover, unlocked the Kid's cell and sat him in the front seat. It was nearly midday before they arrived at the camp.

At first glance the Kid thought Jack was asleep. But as he leapt from the Landrover he saw the blowflies. They were crawling in and out of Jack's open mouth.

The Kid then knew they were too late. The old Bosun had won.

The Legend had met his match.

24.

The Kid Returns

You may see them shuffling slowly round town,
And think they're just drunken blacks,
But I rode with those fellows, you may think as pests,
Along the wild cattle tracks,
And some were the best ringers I ever knew,
At throwing or roping a steer,
The rough stony ridges, the pot holed flats,
They galloped without any fear,
And some of them know me and walk up and talk,
And nip me for two or three quid,
I'm not yet forgotten by that old brigade,
They remember the Kimberley Kid.

It was August and a cold south wind was blowing in Halls Creek. Two old timers sat in the bar of the town's only hotel and watched the Saturday night crowd.

'Look at that lot,' one snorted. 'Ringers! Can you believe it? Wearin' baseball caps.'

'An' sandshoes,' his mate answered. 'How they going to kick a horse along with them?'

The two old timers eyed the noisy bunch of boozing black stockmen with disgust. At a table behind them, a young woman of about twenty nudged her father. 'I know, Marjorie,' he whispered, grinning. 'I heard 'em. Pretty hard for old blokes like that to understand. They belong to a past era.'

'Your era, Dad,' she whispered back. 'Do you know them?'

This was what The Kid had been dreading since his return to the Kimberley, that he would meet up with someone who would talk about his past in front of his wife and daughter. The two old timers were well known to the Kid from his Halls Creek days. He shook his head and was about to suggest it was time to return to camp when his daughter stopped him with a shake of her hand. 'Listen to them, Dad!'

'— an' just as well he is dead! Ol' Jack Vitnell couldn't have put up with these blokes. He woulda put the cleaners through the lot of 'em.'

'Where you first strike Jack? Here in Halls Crik?'

'No, the Pine Creek Pub. Back in me drovin' days. I had never seen such a handsome face on a man.' The old timer launched into his story about Jack Vitnell ...

'Who's that young fella?' I asked the barman.

'Jack Vitnell,' the barman says. 'A real rip snorter. And you're going to see him in action soon, that big ugly looking ringer over there has been eyeing him off all night.'

Wasn't long after Jack bought a couple of bottles and started to walk to the door. The ringer followed, grabbed Jack by the arms and shook him.

'Oh!' says Jack, turning around. 'So that's what you're after!'

He handed his bottles to the barman.

'Mind these a moment mate.' And walked out the door.

Outside, he stripped off his shirt.

'Get yours off,' he sang out as the ringer joined him. Soon as the ringer had his shirt over his head, Jack raced over and tied him up in it. Wrapped it a few times around the ringer's head and left him standing helpless. Ol' Jack never hit him, just stood laughing as the fella bellowed out beneath his shirt.

Finally the ringer got it off and looked around. Jack was nowhere to be seen.

'Over here!' a voice yelled.

The ringer turned.

Bang! A fist flattened him. It was Jack, big grin all over his face.

'You going to have a drink, mate, or do you want some more?'

The ringer chose the drink, he wasn't after another whack. Ol' Jack could hit like a steam hammer.

The other old timer chuckled at his mate's story.

'He could fight, all right. So could that Kimberley Kid.'

'Why you reckon the Kid and Jack never clashed? Everyone was waiting for it.'

'On account they was good mates that's why and also I'll tell you something. Never see two top blokes clashing. They got too much respect for each other. Less they get drunk or fall out over a woman or something. Then they will. And look out! Someone always finish up hurt bad then! But normally they won't clash.'

'Like two old rogue bullocks sloping off together.'

'Same as you and me, old timer!'

'Oh, Dad, wasn't that wonderful!' Marjorie exclaimed, as the two old men finished their drinks and headed for the door. 'Hearing somebody else talk about Jack Vitnell. Why didn't you say something? Surely you must have known them.'

'No idea who they were,' the Kimberley Kid lied. 'They were years older than me anyway. They must have been knocking around the Territory when I was out this way. There was heaps of blokes you never met.'

'Did you know that Kimberley Kid they were talking about, Dad? I don't think I ever heard you speak of him.'

'Think I may have heard the name,' the Kid said evasively. Then to change the subject he said, 'Did I ever tell you about that time with Jack in Alice Springs?' The Kid began to reminisce about the old days ...

Towns are like people, I guess. Sometimes you take to them, sometimes you don't. A town might be no more than a couple of scattered tin humpies amongst the scrub or a few weatherboard shacks stuck out on a dust yellow plain — but it can still make you feel welcome. Or it could be a place like Alice Springs, well laid out, by the banks of a big wide river, set before magnificent ranges changing colour by the hour, but make you feel lost.

I didn't take to The Alice and never went back after that trip with Jack. It was a lot different to what I'd been used to, I just wasn't comfortable there. I'd never felt that way before, perhaps I was just too far out of my territory. I know fellas who couldn't stand Halls Creek but to me it was home.

We split up for a time after all the breaking in we did for Vesteys and I didn't see him for about a year when we both hit Katherine at the same time. It was one of the few times I struck Jack flush with cash. Mostly it was the other way about. He'd just finished a droving trip and insisted I went with him to The Alice. He'd heard that Gill Brothers' Buckjump Show was due and that they were claiming the man hadn't been born who could ride their feature horse, the Guyra Ghost.

Jack wouldn't stop down the Todd where ringers mostly camped when in town, but booked us into a room at the Stuart Arms Hotel. When Jack had a quid he lived high and anyone with him lived high. You would never think money was hard earned the way Jack got rid of it. Saving was something he never thought about. If he was broke he'd soon get more. Something always turned up, particularly when you had a name like Jack Vitnell. There wasn't a man in the country wouldn't have fell over themselves to offer him a job.

The second day in Alice we sat on a seat in front of the Stuart Arms under a big peppercorn known as The Tree of Knowledge. Half a dozen locals joined us and we had just got talking when a neat blue painted truck pulled up. It had '*Lucky Al*' sign-written on the door and belonged to Al McDonald, a prospector from Tennant Creek, who had found a swag of gold over the years. He was about forty-five, big, brawny and inclined to boast about his luck. He had once been middleweight boxing champion of New Zealand so it wasn't any surprise when he and Jack took to each other. I mean got on well, not into holts.

'I chased a bit of gold around Halls Creek couple of years ago,' Jack told him. 'You been over to that west?'

'Not since I got a lift there about 1935, Jack. I walked into the pub and there was half a dozen old time prospectors lounging around sipping rum.

'Where they find the gold around this place?' I asked.

'Why,' one of them says, walking over with a big wicked grin on his wrinkled old face. 'There's gold right outside this front door, down that crik there, just waiting to be found.'

'So down I went, to that dry old Halls Creek, with a shovel and a dish and tramped back and forth to that little rock dam they got there. But I never found gold. And they knew I wasn't going to find any. It was mid winter, too dry to be looking for gold in that country. They were waiting for the Wet, those old fellas, for when the rain come. That was the time to be out with the dish, with the creek running and the water swirling and scouring the bottom and washing away the banks. But by that time I was over at Tennant and that's where I found gold. Pounds of it, but I was lucky. Met up with an old Kiwi fellow who knew all about me. Could tell me every fight I'd had and what round I'd won in. He showed me how to find gold — but I worked for it. I was the one done all the digging.'

Al was keen to take me and Jack prospecting out to some promising country he'd heard of way west of Alice Springs but Jack wasn't interested. He'd had enough of prospecting and was keen to get back ringing — a bit more scrub bull and horse action. I sat and listened for a while, couldn't edge a word in, so decided to check out the Alice Springs Hotel further down town. It was a big new brick place that most of the bushies hadn't taken to yet. They preferred the atmosphere of the ramshackle Stuart Arms.

I walked into the bar and blow me if I didn't hear a couple of blokes talking about Jack and saying what a good fighter he was. There were half a dozen half-caste blokes drinking nearby and one of them, a big, tough-looking coot, walked over.

'Vitnell!' he said to them with a snarl. 'All I hear is Vitnell these days. By the Christ I'll give him Vitnell if he pokes his head into this town while I'm here.'

'Who's that?' I asked, when he walked off.

'Terry Tiger. Knock you down as soon as look at you. He can go, too, no-one around this town can hold him. He's boss over all those yella fellas, they do what Terry Tiger says. Used to be a station man but he's too heavy for horse work now and follows yard building. They reckon he tosses posts on his truck it takes two other men to lift. I wouldn't like to be Vitnell if Tiger starts on him, reckon Vitnell wouldn't stand a chance.'

'You ever see Jack Vitnell fight?'

'Never met the man. We heard he beat Laurie Troy but Tiger beat Troy too, bashed him something terrible and he'd bash that Vitnell too, I reckon, if he ever come across him.'

This Terry Tiger must be pretty hot stuff, I thought. One minute those fellas were saying what a great fighter Jack was, next how he would go down to Terry Tiger. I finished my beer and went back up to the Stuart Arms. The blue truck had gone and the seat under the Tree of Knowledge was empty. Jack and a few other ringers were in the bar, telling of horses ridden, bulls thrown, dry stages travelled, blokes they'd met, blokes they hadn't met, all the stuff ringers talk about in town. I don't know that we ever talked about women. Jack spotted me soon as I walked in.

'Where you been mate? Ducking out on your shout?'

'No, I been up the Alice Springs listening to a bloke tell how he's going to give you a bashing if you come into town while he's around.'

Now there were a couple of ways a man could handle that. He could say, 'Well, I'll be here if he comes looking for me' and just carry on, or ignore it and make sure he never went near the Alice Springs Hotel or even, maybe, finish his drink and suddenly find something to do that took him out of town. But Jack, being Jack, said, 'Is that so. Well, come down and point him out.' So down we all trooped, about eight of us, to the other pub.

I ordered and we stood at the big square bar sipping our drinks and looking around. It was a Saturday and there was a fair crowd lounging about, mostly whites, but down one end of the bar, by themselves, were the half dozen half-castes. They were a tough, surly looking bunch, allowed to drink by virtue of their Citizenship Rights dog tickets. They looked across to where we were drinking and started to laugh and whisper amongst themselves.

'Bloody white shit-ringers,' one of them suddenly said, in a voice loud enough for us to hear.

We talked amongst ourselves for a while, ignoring them, then suddenly Jack turned and asked, 'Which is him? That big hoon in the middle?' I nodded and without any hesitation he put his glass on the counter, walked over and planted himself in front of Terry Tiger.

'My name's Jack Vitnell. I hear you been hoping I'd come to town.'

'Oh, you're him, are you?' Tiger snarled. 'Yeah, I've been waiting for you to turn up. And any other white bastards that thinks they can fight.'

With that he slammed his glass on the bar. But before either of them had time to swing a punch there was a yell from the publican.

'Hold it! Down the Todd if yez want to fight. I won't have any of it here. Any man throws a punch in my pub gets a busted head.'

He lifted up a pair of heavy wire cutters and waved them in the air.

'Come on, then,' Jack snapped to Tiger. 'Down the river.'

Everyone piled out of the bar, Jack with us, Terry Tiger with his mob, and headed down the road to the Todd. Jack was quite unconcerned, talking and joking as though he was off to a picnic race meeting instead of heading to a contest with a big tough eager to tear him apart.

The river was mostly dry so we climbed down the bank to a level sandy spot and the two of them stripped off. Terry Tiger was a big muscley coot all right, taller and heavier than Jack but sporting a flabby beer gut. Jack didn't have an ounce of spare flesh on him and I knew he was rock hard. Tiger didn't waste time. He rushed straight in and swung a right that would have flattened a bullock. Jack was just a blur. He twisted to one side, then crashed a left fist deep into Tiger's gut. It was the same move, minus the punch, I'd seen him do a hundred times, toying with a charging bull. There was only one more hit in it. A right under the chin from Jack that lifted the gasping half-caste a foot in the air and dropped him senseless.

Two lightning hits and it was all over. Terry Tiger didn't land a punch. Two of his mates pulled him to a sitting position while we crowded around and congratulated Jack. Jack was getting his shirt back on when we heard Tiger say, 'Come on you blokes. Someone else have a crack at him. Don't leave it all to me.'

Jack had his shirt back off in a flash.

'Yes!' he yelled. 'Why not? There's plenty for all. Come on, I'll fight the lot of you, one after the other.'

A tough-looking half-caste almost as big as Tiger was next to strip his shirt. He stood with fists raised in the boxer's stance waiting for Jack to come in. Suddenly Jack lunged forward, crashed a left and a right straight through his guard and dropped him to the sand. Number three walked across and shaped up, there was a flurry of fists, a few grunts and curses, then down he went next to his two mates. Jack must have been at his very best then, about twenty-six years old and as fit as a stone-bred scrub bull.

He had sent three hard men spinning, now he turned ready for the fourth and last. But this man was little more than a boy and decided he'd seen enough. He tried to edge away through the crowd.

'Where are you going?' Jack bellowed, full of fire now and ready for more.

Someone pushed the young half-caste forward. He looked at Jack, went to speak, but no words came out. Finally he stood sullenly, staring at his boots.

'Are you one of Terry Tiger's mates?' Jack demanded.

'He's my brother,' he whispered. Then he looked up at Jack with a pleading look. 'I'm only seventeen, mate. I never came down here to fight you.'

'If you're old enough to drink in a pub and give cheek you're old enough to take the consequences,' Jack answered, moving closer.

Suddenly though, he appeared to change his mind. He stooped down, picked up his hat where it had fallen, stuck it on his head and called out, 'Go on then, hop it if you don't want to fight, but don't get in my way while I'm in town.'

Then he turned to the crowd.

'Well, who's shouting?'

Jack was magnificent, the idol of every man there. If he'd said, 'Come on, let's walk to Darwin,' I reckon we would have followed. Back we went to the Stuart Arms and Jack didn't buy a drink for the rest of that afternoon or night. Soon as his glass was empty there were two full ones waiting. He pulled me to one side at one stage and whispered, 'Don't let on to any of these fellas I'm in town to ride that Guyra Ghost, because if you do and Gill finds out who I am, he's going to find a way to bar me for sure.'

'Because you rode for Thorpe?'

'No, because I rode Thorpe's Swanee, that's why. Those showmen all get together and talk and one thing that gets to them is having their feature horse ridden. They're not easy come by, good buckers. Most of what you see around the stations are only pig-rooters. You know how many horses there's been that's never been ridden? None. Or how many riders never been throwed? None. If you listen to some old girl talking about her Grandfather and how he was a great rider and was never thrown you can bet one thing. Old Granddad never got on a horse good enough to throw him.

'I couldn't count the times I've been upended. You got to take a fall sometimes to ride a good horse. That's why those showmen never let you have a second try. They frightened you going to ride it second time round. Takes a lot of hunting to locate a dinkum feature horse but from what I've heard of that Guyra Ghost I reckon I can take him. He bucks same way as that Swanee and I rode that horse before I turned fifteen.' That was the only time I heard Jack mention Swanee. Everybody in the country knew he'd rode it but he never spoke about those things.

A few days later Gill Brothers' Buckjump Show arrived in town and set up out at the racecourse. People came in from the stations from miles around to attend. The Guyra Ghost was star bill, an ordinary looking grey horse bred around Guyra in New South Wales, that had the reputation of throwing every rider who had tried within three seconds. To get a ride, you stuck your hand up and sung out when Jack Gill called for volunteers. Some nights no-one would want to try and then one of the show riders would give an exhibition on it but always being careful to step off after a few bucks. Gills' didn't even want their own men riding the horse. It had to be seen as being un-rideable.

I don't know how Jack felt being back inside a show tent again — where he'd started his working life. I could never quite understand why he'd left it. To me it was the most exciting life of all. But I suppose it just lost its challenge to Jack. He always needed to be doing something different, going somewhere new, attempting something no-one else was game to try. Night after night riding the same buckjumpers, twirling the same ropes, springing on and off the same horses as they cantered around the ring ... Yes, suppose I could understand.

But to the average ringer knocking about the stations, they were gods those riders in the buckjump shows. Men who rode as well as the average men dreamed of riding. Doing things nightly they would never be good enough to do. Being applauded by the crowd, strutting the streets of towns with kids chasing after them. The envious glances of lesser men. It was a far cry from the loneliness and isolation of the stockcamps.

The night Jack and I attended, the tent was packed, as it had been the previous two nights. Jack reckoned by waiting until the last night there would be more chance of getting a ride. There was sometimes a rush of ringers wanting to try the feature horse — until they saw how good he buck and how quick he downed their mates. No-one liked being a loser in front of a crowd.

We found seats right next to the chute. That way Jack would be on the horse quick. We sat through an hour of the show before Jack Gill stepped into centre ring and announced the feature ride was next. Soon as he called for a rider from the audience, Jack sung out, 'I'll test him,' and then climbed up the side of the chute. He was on the Ghost before Gill had asked him his name and where he came from.

'Jack Vitnell, from under me hat,' he called. 'Come on! Let him out.'

If Gill did remember Jack as the youngster who had rode Swanee, it was too late for him to do anything. At the very least he would have made sure that it was he himself who held the flank rope. But it had happened too quickly and that was left to Wally Woods. Wally was one of Australia's great professional rough riders who would soon be only the second man to ride the outlaw, Curio, eight years unridden. His brother, Alan, would be the first.

If Jack Gill had held the flank rope he would have tried to flip Jack off the horse, an old trick played on anyone who looked like riding their feature horse. Lance Skuthorpe used to boast to his men, 'I can unseat any man in the country.'

As it was, Wally just held one end of the rope as he was supposed to, tight around the horse's flanks and standing back about twenty paces. There was a buzz of excited chatter around the tent then out of the chute charged the Ghost.

Snorting and squealing and spinning around,
Crashing like thunder thumping the ground,
Twisting and whirling and rolling his eyes,
Climbing and raging and reaching the skies ...

as that song written later told. Except it wasn't the sky but the ceiling of the tent. It was a lot easier for Jack, mounting a bad horse in a chute. Dropping into the saddle from the top rail, getting his boots properly into the irons and set before the horse sprung into action. Most of his rough riding was done out in the open, swing on best way you can, as the horse is already bucking. That's why he seldom bothered with the stirrups, it was twice as quick to leap on — if you were smart enough! A lot of times, too, at those bush rodeos he'd be three parts drunk from a session in the beer tent before they brought the star attraction out.

Like the time he got upended at a Brunette Downs race meeting. There was a journalist out from England attending that year and soon afterwards the London Times published an article captioned, 'Buckjump Champion Meets His Match!' There was no mention that Jack had been in the race-course beer tent all day. He flew straight onto the horse and came straight off, over its head. I done ten pound cold because I reckoned there was no way it could have beat him. It didn't either, but the grog did.

Jack wore his Wave Hill spurs that night on the Guyra Ghost. He would have felt naked without them. He had them on as he walked in the tent, back to front, over his boots so as not to draw attention to them. Only a very good rider will deliberately wear spurs on a buckjumper, but if fellas only realised, it helps you get a grip. Yeah! And makes the horse lift higher too! Jack was at his very best that night. The Ghost lifted him out of the saddle once, and the crowd all give an, 'Ah!' and someone yelled out, 'He's got him!' but I knew he would get back in the saddle. The man hasn't been born who doesn't shift a bit when a horse is tearing itself inside-out like that.

Jack wasn't in a hurry to get off neither, he was enjoying it, in front of a crowd again. Wally Woods let go of the flank rope soon as about twelve ten seconds were up but Jack kept spurring. I thought Jack Gill was going to burst, he was getting so red.

'Git hold of that horse, damn yez,' he was screaming. 'Get him off it!'

Big Gordon Beetham, a bull riding and dog champion working for Gills' grabbed it. When things had settled down and Jack had collected the ten pound, I heard Wally Woods say, 'That was the best ride I've seen in my life, and I've seen a few!'

We didn't linger and left soon afterwards, ahead of the crowd. It was dark by then and when we got outside the tent, we nearly walked into a woman riding a horse.

'Do a bit of riding, hey lady?' Jack sung out, cheeky as ever.

She wheeled the horse around and stared at us.

'Yes, I do. Do you?'

'Oh, now and then,' Jack replied with a grin.

'Now and then!' I said. 'He's just rode Gill's Guyra Ghost!'

'What's that?' she asked. 'A horse?'

'About the best buckjumper in the whole of Australia,' I replied.

Jack was looking annoyed. 'That's a good looking chestnut you're on,' he said, changing the subject. 'You got any more like him at home?'

'I got a big high stepping black needs a workout. You want to try him tomorrow?'

That's how it started, but it would have finished there and then if it had been left to Jack. He was too busy boozing and yarning and sky-larking around to worry about a woman. But sure enough, next day she was down at the Stuart Arms, riding the same chestnut and leading a smart looking black gelding. She was looking pretty good too. In daylight I could see she was a bit older than Jack, about thirty-five, with long reddish hair, and a neat figure that showed up well in her white frilly blouse and brown jodhpurs. A mob of us was sitting on the seat under the Tree of Knowledge. Soon as Jack saw her, he jumped up and walked across. They talked a bit and I heard her laugh, then he sprang on the black and off they went. That was the last we saw him at the Stuart Arms for nearly a week, but he was seen, riding with her a few times, along the Todd. We were in the bar boozing one afternoon when the door banged open and in he walked. Everyone turned and stared. He saw me and came straight over.

'What have you done with your lady friend?' I asked with a smile.

'She's feeding the horses,' he said, giving me a blank look. 'Whose shout?'

He downed his drink, ordered another round and started talking to the barman.

'Hey!' I said. 'Aren't you going to tell me about it? Where have you been?'

'Oh, just stopping at her place and doing a bit of riding. She's mad on horses. Had a husband once, that run off. You ready to leave town yet?'

He wouldn't talk about her. Seems as though a week with a woman was as much as he could stand. I never referred to her again until later, when we were back out bush. He'd been getting letters and photos which he would glance at and throw in the fire. I knew it must have been her because no-one had ever written to him before. I didn't comment but one day I got a letter as well.

'That woman's wrote to me now Jack. Want's to know if you've got leprosy.'

'That so,' he answered. 'Might be a good idea to write back and say I have.'

But I didn't. I carried her letter around for a good while and finally chucked it away too. There was nothing I could do to help her — or him.

When the Kid finished speaking, Marjorie gave him a sad look.

'He was a hard man, Dad, but you're not. It's a wonder you ever mated up. What place was that, where the woman sent the letters?'

The Kid glanced at his watch. 'I'll tell you tomorrow, along the track. We better get back to camp or your mother will think we're on the grog.'

25.

Kununurra

Twenty years have passed since that fateful day,
Tourists and buses go that way,
The cattle are gone, horse plants sold,
And farms and farmers have taken hold,
And though I'm sad at his early end,
I'm somehow glad that he doesn't spend,
His days like me watching town-bred blacks,
And road trains roar down the cattle tracks.

Father and daughter headed down the dark street towards the caravan park.

'Here's Mum now. Thought she might start looking for us.'

The Kid's wife looked at them anxiously. 'I was just starting to get worried. Find anyone you knew?'

'No, Mum. But we heard two old timers talking about Jack Vitnell.' She looked around at the starry night. 'Oh, isn't it exciting! Being up in Dad's Kimberley at last!'

She looked at her mother. 'Are we going to Kununurra tomorrow?'

The Kid's wife shrugged. 'That's up to Dad, but I think so.'

It was only a few hours' drive to Kununurra. The Kid could not believe the road.

'Look at it! A highway. It used to take a full two days to drive from Halls Creek to Wyndham — and that was in the Dry. Wet time the road was closed for four months.'

There weren't many familiar landmarks. The Kid felt betrayed.

'Hell!' he cried, as they zoomed over a concrete bridge. 'That was the Bow River. We're not going anywhere near the station. There used to be three crossings of the Bow, each one a challenge. The Big Bow, wide and deep, The Sandy Bow, a mess of fine clogging sand, and the main crossing where the station was, Butler's Bow. Remember me talking about the big Boab with the life-size carvings of two bare knuckle fighters shaping up? That was at the Butler's Bow crossing, not far from the station. Some old teamster must have done that, caught by the Wet.'

They drove on.

'Ironical, ain't it. Now we got good vehicles, cars that could charge over a steep hill at fifty mile an hour, there's no hills left. The dozers have hacked 'em all down to nothing.'

He pointed.

'Now look at it. A strip of lifeless black bitumen and not a drover, stockcamp, or carrier in sight.'

The Kid was becoming agitated. Marjorie decided to divert him. She turned to her mother and mouthed, 'He's getting all cranky. I'm going to get him to talk about the old days.'

'Tell us about that place where Jack got the letters, Dad.'

'Oh, yeah. I forgot.'

The Kid resumed his story about Jack ...

That place Jack and I were working on when he got those letters from the Alice Springs woman was Eva Downs, out of Newcastle Waters. Not that we left The Alice to go there, we were heading for Darwin which Jack wanted to take a look at, but it didn't work out that way. All because of a horse. Some blokes are suckers for women, Jack was that way over horses. He could never resist a ride on a known rogue. We settled our account at the Stuart Arms, bought two tickets on the Darwin bus and set off. There were only five passengers for what was to be a three day trip. First night out camp at Tennant Creek, the second Daly Waters and third Darwin. No-one travelled at night those days.

On board was a good looking sort of about twenty and every time we pulled up that first day for a break, she would look at Jack and try and catch his eye. He just ignored her. She wouldn't look at me and damn me if that night the bus driver didn't finish up having a few drinks with her. Hell, we should have cut him out, he was busy driving and we had the whole day to get on to her, but no, Jack had had his fill of women so we spent the day yarning and gazing out the window at the country.

About dinner time next day we pulled up at Newcastle Waters for a feed and who should be sitting on the front steps looking pretty drunk but big, red, bushy-bearded Doug Scobie. He had just come through the Murranji scrub with a mob of Victoria River bullocks and was spelling for a few days before taking them on to Dajarra. His men were tailing the cattle and his horses were let go in the police paddock where his horsetailer was handling a colt.

'What are you doing sitting by yourself like a mongrel cur,' Jack hollered as we climbed down from the bus. 'You fly-blown or something?'

Well! That was the last time that young lady made sheep's eyes at him. When she saw us walk over and shake the big, rough-looking drunk by the hand she stuck her head in the air and went off to dinner with the bus driver. We followed Doug Scobie to a hut where several other drovers were on the booze and caught up on a bit of local news. Newcastle was right on the stock route and there was always drovers hanging about. We weren't there long before Scobie's horsetailer, Tommy Kahl, who I knew to be a good ringer, came in looking pretty distressed. He walked straight up to Doug.

'I can't do anything with that horse, Doug, he's no bloody good.'

Doug glared at him a moment then snapped, 'What do you mean he's no good? He's a good horse, I broke him meself. He just wants a bit of work.'

'Well, he might be a good horse but I can't handle him. He's got me beat.'

'What do mean he's got you beat? Did he throw you?'

'No, I haven't got on him yet. I can't get close enough to get a saddle on.'

This horse of Doug's had played up during the trip and thrown every one who had tried to mount it, including Doug himself. Doug had told Tommy Kahl to run it into the police yard when they reached Newcastle and give it a ride in hobbles to work the sting out of it, then to take it for a gallop. There wouldn't have been many horses that Tommy couldn't handle but this was a bad one he had come up against and had him bluffed. Doug got pretty cranky when Tommy said he couldn't handle it.

'Hell,' he snorted. 'I thought you was a ringer! I'll show you how to get a saddle on him. All he needs is to learn who's boss. Come on you blokes,' he said to me and Jack. 'Finish your drinks and come up to the yard.'

Just as we walked out the door, the bus driver and the good sort appeared.

'Where do you blokes think you're going?' he snapped. 'I'm pulling out of here in two minutes and if you're not on the bus you'll stay behind.'

'You can bloody well pull out,' said Jack, 'But chuck our swags off before you do. We've had enough of you and your jerky gear changes.'

Jack didn't wait around to see if they were thrown off, they were only two bundles of canvas and blankets far as he was concerned. Hell! There was a bad horse to be rode and Jack had an idea he was going to be the man to ride it. One of the drovers had a truck outside and he ran the four of us over to the yard. I could see Scobie was pretty drunk by now and on the way across tried to get him to let

Jack get in with the horse but he wouldn't hear of it. Soon as we pulled up out he jumped and grabbed a bridle off a rail.

'Look at him!' he bellowed, pointing to the horse. 'Does he look like an outlaw? I bred him, broke him, and now by Ghost I'll ride him,' and with that he slipped through the rails and into the yard. The horse swivelled its eyes towards him and flattened its ears but didn't move. If ever I saw a horse about to attack it was this one, a rough looking roman-nosed bay with a black mule stripe running down its shoulder. Over its head was a rope halter with a long head-rope attached and around its front feet a strong set of greenhide hobbles. Scobie strode towards it, full of bravado, but as he got close, the bay reared up on its hind legs. For an instant Scobie gazed upwards, too shocked or drunk to move, then the horse crashed down, the chain tethering its feet looping around Scobie's neck. He fell head first into the dirt and lay prone with the bay standing triumphantly over him.

Jack was through the rails and into the yard in an instant. He grabbed the horse by the neck and squeezed its jugular till its eyes near popped. I wasn't far behind and quickly unhooked one of the hobble straps and got Scobie's neck clear of the chain. He didn't move. Tommy Kahl and the driver of the truck jumped into the yard and pulled him out of the way and slapped his face until he came to.

'Get this halter off and slip a bridle on the mongrel, mate,' Jack snapped. 'But don't pull that other hobble strap off. I want the chain to swing and I want the mongrel to feel it swinging. He wants to play games I'll give him a good one.'

Jack was going to let the chain dangle from one of the bay's fetlocks so that it would bash against its legs if it tried to rear again. Soon as I had it saddled, Jack let go of its neck and sprang on. It was groggy from the throttling and lurched to and fro for a moment, then Jack hooked it up the guts with his spurs and it bounded into the air all set to buck but stopped when the chain started lashing.

Scobie was on his feet now with blood pouring from a deep gash on his forehead.

'Get into the mongrel, Jack,' he yelled. 'Make him take it.'

Jack looked across at me and sung out, 'Open the gate and slip up behind and we'll give him a run to town.'

'Here,' Scobie called, as I was about to leap on. 'Stick it into the bastard with this,' and held out a short bull whip.

So off we went, at not much more than a trot with the horse trying to drop its head and buck but thinking better of it with the chain swinging free, Jack in the saddle, spurring and yack-aing, me sitting on its rump, waving the whip and clinging to Jack's shirt. By the time we reached the station the drovers had all left the hut and were lined up on the road watching. Once we reached the road Jack took the whip and told me to get down and pull the hobble and chain off. Then he lashed the bay from one side to the other with the whip and didn't it perform then!

It was a high bucker with a good twist and as it dropped down it would dip a shoulder low to the ground, and Jack's boot and stirrup iron on that side of the horse would scrape along the stones, shooting up sparks. Then it would bound up again, come down low and dip its other shoulder so Jack's other boot and iron would grate. Each time the sparks flew the drovers lining the road all gave a shout and the more they shouted and applauded the more Jack lashed the horse and made it buck. The truck had arrived from the yard by now with Scobie standing up on the tray, blood still streaming from his head, one hand holding on and the other bashing the top of the steel cabin.

'Follow that horse,' he yelled to the driver. 'Chase the mongrel.'

Soon as Jack saw the truck, he wheeled the bay around and galloped the bucking horse alongside, cracking the whip and grinning up at Scobie.

'That's the style, Jack. Give it to the hoo-er. Make him know who's boss!'

By the time they finished galloping it up and down the road the horse was a lather of sweat and could scarcely get into a trot. Then Jack leapt off and shouted out for a pair of hobbles. He bent down and hobbled the horse and sung out for Scobie.

'Come and take these hobbles off him Doug. I'll bet he won't rear up and strike you this time.'

It stood blowing and snorting while Scobie unfastened the loops. Then he jumped on and spurred it back to the yard.

'Jeez, I'd like to have that man out on Eva Downs with us!' a voice sung out as Scobie disappeared across the flat. It was Peter Murray, the manager of Eva Downs, in to pick up some mail and he was indicating Jack. So that's how we come to work there. The bus, of course, had long gone by now, but our swags were by the side of the road. Not that it mattered to Jack if they weren't. He would have just bought another. I never knew a man who had as few possessions or who cared as little for what he did have. A change of clothes, towel, shaving gear and maybe a coat was all I ever knew him to own. Yet enough money passed through his hands for him to to buy whatever he wanted.

One year he won the Sandford Cup at the Victoria River Races, riding at thirteen stone in an ordinary stock saddle, against some of the best hoops in the north. When he was presented with the trophy, a big, polished, engraved timber clock, he turned around and gave it to the same Doug Scobie.

'Here Doug, you take the bloody thing, its no use to me. It's too big to take out on watch.'

Doug was different to most and always made a trek home at the end of every cattle season and saw his mother so Jack knew it would finish up on a mantlepiece and be appreciated.

We got out to Eva Downs to find Cammy Cleary running the camp. There weren't many horses had ever thrown Cammy. The Marrabel rodeo committee wrote to him once during the time Curio was un-ridden and invited him to come down to their next rodeo for a try but he never wrote back. He wasn't that sort of a person. If Jack had got an invite he would have gone. But I doubt he would have rode it. He could fight drunk, but not ride drunk, and the few times he rode at rodeos he was always half shot.

Cammy wouldn't have been any good in rodeo, anyhow. Jack could ride that way, sitting up straight, right arm held out shoulder high, but not Cammy. He had his own style. Laying back on a horse while it was bucking, grabbing it by the flank to make it climb higher, leaning back twisting its tail, or forward nipping its neck — he was all over a horse. No-one else rode that way — he was a freak rider if ever there was one.

He wasn't better than Jack, but he was as good, and that's saying something. But he didn't go hunting up rogue horses like Jack. He was a quiet, shy man and would only get on an outlaw if he was asked — and then only if there wasn't a crowd about. Unless he was drunk, then he would lose his reserve — and still be able to ride it. They were a pair, those two, a cut above everyone else in the country but totally different in style.

Cammy was one of old 'Camooweal' Tom Cleary's sons. Cammy told us once of the time the Native Affairs people came to Lake Nash to take all the coloured kids away and send them off to the missions. His mother, a half-caste woman, took all her children out into the desert and hid there with them until the whites had gone. That's how come Cammy grew up in the stock camp and learnt to ride before he could walk. But he could read and write. When Bill Perks gave the butcher's shop away one time in Camooweal, Cammy took it over for a couple of years, as a change off ringing. He ran it well, too, and did his own book work, so someone must have taught him.

Cammy was one of the few head-stockman Jack ever worked under. He was about fifteen years older and had Jack's full respect. There wasn't too many around who had that, even in that country of good men. Peter Murray was a good bloke and got on well with Jack but he finished up having to sack him. We had put most of the season in and were cutting out bullocks for the last mob to be turned off. Johnny Darcey had come out from Camooweal to take delivery and he and his men were on the camp with us, giving a hand. Cammy and Jack did most of the cutting out until Peter Murray drove up. We had one of his top camp horses with us so Cammy sung out and told one of the boys to catch it and bring it across.

Those station managers like to get out of the office and back on a camp horse occasionally and Peter was no exception. He had a blackboy with him, Jingle, a loud mouthed know-all sort of a coot, who acted as gate opener, guide and tyre-changer. Because he was the boss's boy, Jingle had good deal of influence over the other blacks and when the horsetailer brought Peter's horse over he told the horsetailer to saddle him a good horse too. He never rode into the mob of course, to cut out — Cammy and Jack would have quickly hunted him if he'd tried — but he stopped on the face and tried to show his form there.

When Peter rode into the mob, Cammy rode out and held the cut to allow Peter plenty of space. Jingle, being Peter's boy, should have rode the face of the mob where Peter Murray was cutting out and help push Peter's bullocks towards the cut, but he sat his horse opposite to where Jack was cutting out. It didn't take long to work out why. Every time Jack cut a beast out, Jingle would turn it back into the mob. He must have thought this would show Jack up and make Peter Murray look the better man. I couldn't believe anyone could be so stupid, obviously he had no idea what sort of a man he was dealing with.

The first time he did it Jack just cursed him and hunted the beast out again. The second time he raced over to where Jingle was sitting his horse with a stupid grin and told him to get the hell out of the way. But the third time Jingle turned Jack's bullock back into the mob Jack set his horse at him full gallop. Jingle saw him coming, spurred his horse, and headed for the scrub. But he had no hope of dodging Jack. Jack's blood was up and he was unstoppable. He raced up alongside Jingle as though he was a bullock he was going to bulldog. Then he leapt from the saddle, grabbed Jingle around the neck and crashed him to the ground. The horses kept galloping.

'I'll give you turn my beast back,' Jack bellowed, sitting astride Jingle, raking him with his spurs. 'You'll never be able to work the face of a camp again when I've finished with you.'

Peter Murray had seen what was happening and galloped over.

'Oh, for God's sake, don't kill him, Jack,' he pleaded. 'We'll be in more bloody trouble than the world if you do. Get off him. I think he's bad hurt.'

Jingle could have been lying there with a busted neck for all Jack cared. He was livid with rage. He walked away from Peter Murray and sung out to the horsetailer to fetch his horse. Then he rode back to the cattle and started drafting again. Peter brought the Jeep across and drove Jingle back to camp. I rode across to help. One side of Jingle's face was torn and bleeding and he was moaning and holding one arm. Peter felt around his body and determined he had a broken collar bone and what seemed to be a couple of cracked ribs.

'I'll have to get him back to the station. What happened to make Jack do that?'

'Oh jeez,' he said when I told him. 'Fancy trying that on Jack. Didn't anyone tell him who he was?'

He was back next morning looking pretty miserable.

'I had to get a plane out to take that Jingle to hospital, Jack. He told the sister how it happened and she said he's got to report it to the Native Affairs when she gets him into Katherine. You know what that means. They'll have the coppers out here like a shot, you'll get charged with assault and I could lose my license to work blacks. Christ, I don't know what the country's coming to when they can do that. Time I got out of it I reckon. So I told the sister not to waste her time reporting it because I'd finish you up. There's a mail plane calling in at Anthony's Lagoon tomorrow on it's way to Darwin, I'll drive you over and you can get on it.'

'That's okay,' said Jack. 'I was heading for Darwin anyway. I want to get back over to that west.'

It didn't worry Jack. He knew this wasn't Victoria River or the Kimberley where you could still get away with things like that. There wasn't a man amongst us either, white or black, who didn't applaud what he'd done and would have done the same if he'd had the ability and guts. Peter Murray turned to me.

'What are you doing? Stopping on or going with your mate?'

Now I was getting on pretty well in the camp with Cammy and didn't want to up and leave. Some headstockmen run a sloppy camp but Cammy run a good camp. Every man pulled his weight, knew his job and had plenty of good horses to ride. Besides, I didn't want to go into Darwin at that time of the year. I wanted to see the season out so that when I did go to town, it wouldn't be such a long wait, boozing, till the next cattle season. At the same time, though, I didn't want to pull out on Jack. So I stood there a second or two, looking at my boots, wondering how to answer. But Jack answered for me. We'd knocked around long enough together for him to know what I was thinking.

'It's nothing to do with him, Peter. He'll be stopping on.'

'No, I won't,' I finally said. 'We come here together, we leave together,' and walked across and rolled my swag and tossed it in the jeep. Jack did the same. Two weeks later we were back in Kimberley.

The Kid and his wife and daughter were now close to Kununurra and the country changed to farmland with irrigation channels sweeping away at right angles to the road. Now and again they could glimpse the red roofs of farm buildings tucked in amongst the yellow of crops. The Kid looked with distaste at the miles of greenery. Far to the west was the blue of the Durack Ranges, leading in towards Wyndham.

They booked in at a caravan park by the river in Kununurra, set up their tents and strolled around the town. The Kid looked at the neatly laid out streets, car park and big shopping centre. There was nothing standing that he remembered. He made a face.

'This town's got about as much colour as a pound of goat's butter! Come on, let's go find old Jack's last camp.'

They parked outside the cemetery gates. It was a pleasant enough setting, well grassed with scattered gum trees. They didn't have to look far. The grave was close to the gate. It had a fresh looking concrete border and headstone with a shiny brass plaque with neat black letters which stated:

Beneath This Mound of Yellow Clay,
The Remains of Old Jack Vitnell Lay,
A Ringer, None Better, and Few as Good,
The Best of Us All
R.I.P.
JACK VITNELL
1930 — 1964 *B.Y.*

The Kid looked surprised.

'That grave don't look so old. Seems it was only put up a few months ago. Don't tell me he lay here all this time without anything to say who he was.'

'You were with him when he died, Dad. Didn't you fix it all up before you left Wyndham?'

The Kid shook his head.

'You can't put headstones on right away, love. Got to wait for the earth to settle. Soon as we buried Jack, I cleared out. If I hadn't gone then I would never have left.' He looked at her and grinned. 'And if I hadn't got away you wouldn't have been born. But I left some money with a bloke to put up a headstone later on. Looks like he didn't do it.'

Marjorie looked shocked.

'Dad! That's terrible. I can't believe it!'

The Kid grinned.

'You'd believe it if you knew some of the rascals me an' Jack knocked about with. Not that the bloke concerned didn't mean to put up the headstone. I'd say he certainly meant to. But I reckon the old Bosun tapped him on the shoulder one day and reminded him he was thirsty.'

'The old Bosun?'

'Bosun rum. He was a mighty popular character around here one time, the old woolly headed Bosun and his mate Captain Kettle.' He thought for a moment. 'Yeah! The Bosun. The only man to ever beat Jack Vitnell. Reckon that was written in the script years before, about the time young Jack sunk his first pannikin of overproof rum to show what a tough guy he was.'

They stood in silence for a while.

Finally the Kid said, 'He was so full of life and now he's just a bundle of bones down there. It's still as hard to believe as the day I found him.'

'What do you suppose that B Y is?' the Kid's wife asked, pointing to the headstone.

'Dunno. Unless it's the initials of the bloke that put the plaque there. Suppose he wrote the text. *The Best Of Us All*. Us! He must have been a ringer too.'

'You were his mate Dad, don't you know?'

'I didn't know all about Jack, only about the times me an' him were together. He knocked around with plenty of others. There's so many stories could be told!'

They sat quietly for a while.

The breeze stirred the gum leaves and the Kid's daughter said softly, 'Why don't you tell those stories, Dad? Write about him. He won't be just a heap of forgotten bones then. Bring him back to life. Then everyone will know what a fine man he was.'

He looked at her strangely for a moment. 'Do you think I could?'

'I'm sure so. Give it a go, Dad. Mum and I will help you.'

'Well, there's something you should know. Jack was no knight in shining armour. He got up to a lot of mad things in town and a lot of people wouldn't have very good memories of him. Only us ringers, who knew him out in the bush, knew the real Jack Vitnell and even then he had plenty of bad points.'

'So did Ned Kelly, Dad, and look at all the books that have been written about him. People don't want to read about little goody-two-shoes characters. They aren't interesting. They want to read about characters who did things they weren't game to do or didn't have the ability to do. A knight in tarnished armour! That's what you could call the book.'

The Kid's wife smiled and said, 'Let's go into Wyndham now and see if there's anyone there who can tell you about this grave. If you can find out who Mister B Y is, maybe you can look him up one day. He's sure to be able to tell you a lot about Jack's early life.' She smiled. 'And that's where you'll have to start your book.'

The Kid stood up.

'Maybe I could,' he thought. 'Maybe I just could! I wrote some poetry once.'

He walked slowly towards the road, his wife and daughter followed.

They stood for a moment by the cemetery gate and looked back at Jack's grave.

The Kid opened the gate.

'I'm sure I liked this country better the way it was,' he sighed, as they walked through the gate and headed down the dull, grey street to town.

The Author, Geoff Allen
Photo courtesy of Martin Brannan

About the Author

Geoff Allen left school at 15 and for the next twenty years roamed the outback of Australia.

He worked at all kinds of bush work, but preferred horsebreaking and ringing. 1950 found him in the Kimberley at a time a man was measured by how well he rode a buckjumper, threw a scrub bull and handled himself in a fist-fight. 'Who is the best rough-rider around?' Geoff asked. 'Jack Vitnell!' came the reply. And the best scrub bull thrower? 'Jack Vitnell!' 'The best fighter?' Again Jack's name came up. This must be one hell of a man, Geoff said to himself.

Over the next ten years Geoff was to see a lot more of Jack Vitnell and in all the tough situations Geoff saw him in, Jack was never found wanting. 'Jack used to do things we wished we were game enough or had the ability, to do,' Geoff says. 'He was utterly fearless and never took a backward step in his life — against man or beast. He was no knight in shining armour — a knight in tarnished armour might describe him better — his wild exploits were legendary, but to the ringers who rode with him out in the scrub, he was simply the best of us all.'

When Geoff took his family back to the Kimberley for a holiday thirty years later he was surprised to find that Jack was virtually forgotten. The ringers of old were no more. A new generation had grown up with road trains to shift the cattle and helicopters to do the mustering. Geoff visited the graves of many of his old contemporaries in the cemeteries of Derby, Halls Creek and Wyndham — most of them lying in nameless plots without a headstone. But it was when Geoff sat on the concrete plinth surrounding Jack Vitnell's grave in Kununurra, that he decided to do something about it. To bring them back to life by writing about them. At first Geoff wrote ballads and was soon being published by the *North Queensland Register*. When Geoff's book *Ballads of the Kimberley* came out, *The Register* had the following to say:

... the man who rode stirrup to stirrup with blacks in the Kimberley Underworld, who spurred after cleanskins on the soaring limestone escarpments and who bedded down at night on canvas under countless empty skies, has produced a book that tells it like it was. His verse taps deep into the rich vein of drama, humour and pathos which is outback life ...

After winning many major prizes — including gold, silver and bronze medals in the Diamond Shears Henry Lawson Poetry Competition — Geoff branched into a successful career writing short stories. Now Geoff has taken a further step and produced a book that brings The Top End and Kimberley vividly to life. Not only stories of Jack Vitnell and his contemporaries whom Geoff knew so well, but tales of an earlier time about the poddy dodgers of the North Kimberley Underworld, where Geoff battled for three unsuccessful years to form a station.